1,000,000 Books

are available to read at

www.ForgottenBooks.com

Read online
Download PDF
Purchase in print

ISBN 978-1-5276-7090-7
PIBN 10879747

This book is a reproduction of an important historical work. Forgotten Books uses state-of-the-art technology to digitally reconstruct the work, preserving the original format whilst repairing imperfections present in the aged copy. In rare cases, an imperfection in the original, such as a blemish or missing page, may be replicated in our edition. We do, however, repair the vast majority of imperfections successfully; any imperfections that remain are intentionally left to preserve the state of such historical works.

Forgotten Books is a registered trademark of FB &c Ltd.
Copyright © 2018 FB &c Ltd.
FB &c Ltd, Dalton House, 60 Windsor Avenue, London, SW19 2RR.
Company number 08720141. Registered in England and Wales.

For support please visit www.forgottenbooks.com

1 MONTH OF FREE READING

at
www.ForgottenBooks.com

By purchasing this book you are eligible for one month membership to ForgottenBooks.com, giving you unlimited access to our entire collection of over 1,000,000 titles via our web site and mobile apps.

To claim your free month visit:
www.forgottenbooks.com/free879747

* Offer is valid for 45 days from date of purchase. Terms and conditions apply.

English
Français
Deutsche
Italiano
Español
Português

www.forgottenbooks.com

Mythology Photography **Fiction**
Fishing Christianity **Art** Cooking
Essays Buddhism Freemasonry
Medicine **Biology** Music **Ancient Egypt** Evolution Carpentry Physics
Dance Geology **Mathematics** Fitness
Shakespeare **Folklore** Yoga Marketing
Confidence Immortality Biographies
Poetry **Psychology** Witchcraft
Electronics Chemistry History **Law**
Accounting **Philosophy** Anthropology
Alchemy Drama Quantum Mechanics
Atheism Sexual Health **Ancient History**
Entrepreneurship Languages Sport
Paleontology Needlework Islam
Metaphysics Investment Archaeology
Parenting Statistics Criminology
Motivational

PRACTICAL SERMONS,

IN TWO VOLUMES:

BY THE LATE

Rev. JOSEPH MILNER, A. M.

MASTER OF THE GRAMMAR SCHOOL, AND
AFTERWARDS VICAR OF THE HOLY TRINITY CHURCH
IN KINGSTON-UPON-HULL.

TO WHICH IS PREFIXED,

AN ACCOUNT OF THE LIFE AND CHARACTER
OF THE AUTHOR,

BY THE

REV^D ISAAC MILNER, D.D. F.R.S.

DEAN OF CARLISLE,
AND PRESIDENT OF QUEEN'S COLLEGE, CAMBRIDGE.

VOL. II.

FOURTH EDITION.

London:

Printed by Luke Hansard & Sons,
FOR T. CADELL AND W. DAVIES, IN THE STRAND

PRACTICAL SERMONS.

IN TWO VOLUMES.

BY THE LATE

REV. JOSEPH MILNER, M.A.
MASTER OF THE GRAMMAR SCHOOL AND
LECTURER ALSO OF THE CHURCH OF HOLY TRINITY CHURCH
IN KINGSTON-UPON-HULL.

TO WHICH IS PREFIXED,

AN ACCOUNT OF THE LIFE AND CHARACTER
OF THE AUTHOR,

BY ISAAC MILNER, D.D. F.R.S.
DEAN OF CARLISLE,
AND PRESIDENT OF QUEEN'S COLLEGE, CAMBRIDGE.

VOL. I.

FOURTH EDITION.

Boston:
Printed by Little Brown & Co.
FOR J. OSGOOD AND J. DAVIS, 34 LINE STREET.

PREFACE.

THIS Second volume of Sermons, selected from the manuscripts of the late Rev. JOSEPH MILNER, by the original Editor of the First, is offered to the Public with an earnest wish that it may prove equally useful and acceptable. The literary fame of the excellent Author has been less consulted in the selection than the edification of the Christian Reader. In all his ministrations, Mr. Milner was known to have had this object solely at heart, even to the utter contempt of every ornament of style, and display of learning. He thought with the Apostle, whom he so much admired, that to affect "wisdom of words" was to make "the cross of Christ of none effect;" and that "to the poor the Gospel is preached," is a circumstance which ought to characterize the labours of the servant as well as those of his Divine Master. This "plainness of speech," though it may diminish the value of these Sermons, in the eyes of critics and mere readers of taste, will add to their value with humble persons, who in the simplicity and godly sincerity of their hearts are seeking instruction.

In turning over the MS. Sermons of his departed Friend, in order to make a proper selection, the Editor had two objects constantly in view. The one was to give a just and fair specimen of the Author's ordinary MANNER, or style of preaching. This indeed was so far accomplished in the First Volume, that many of those who had enjoyed the benefit of

Mr. Milner's personal ministry, were heard to say, that while they were perusing some of the Sermons contained in it, they seemed to be hearing the voice of the Author speaking to them from the pulpit. But having attended more to this point, in preparing the present Volume for the press, the Editor hopes he has now succeeded still better, and that the peculiar cast of instruction which distinguished the Pulpit Compositions of Mr. Milner, is so well preserved in these Sermons, as to give them an increased interest with his surviving friends and hearers.

But the other object which he has had in view is of far more importance; and this was to select such Sermons for publication, as in the opinion of the Author himself, were he now alive, would be best adapted to the spiritual condition, and the "existing circumstances" of his audience. Now the Editor certainly knows, that during the latter years of Mr. Milner's life, his mind was deeply affected on account of the religious declensions and divisions which he saw taking place in the town of Hull. He thought he perceived a proud, worldly spirit, and the excessive love of gain, eating out the love of Christ, of his cause and people, in many who had once seemed to walk humbly with their God, to be zealous for the truth as it is in Jesus, and to provoke one another to love and to good works. He beheld with grief the awful progress of gross wickedness and vice, of lewdness and impiety, in that place. These evils he ascribed to its rapid increase in commerce, in wealth, in population, in buildings and in luxury. Against this subversion of religious principle and practice he failed not to lift up a warning voice; and had he lived to see how widely the mischief has been extended within the last ten or twelve years, he would have cried aloud, and not spared to tell the people their transgressions and sins. But his honest heart grieves no more, sighs no more on account of the abominations of the age. This righteous man has, happily for himself, been taken "from the evil to come." He is gone to that place "where the wicked cease from troubling, and where the weary be at rest." He is spared the anguish and sorrow, felt by his surviving friends, at the sad effects of commercial prosperity on the one hand, and of the check which it has received from desolating and corrupting judgments on the other.

The tongue, indeed, which was ever ready to rebuke and exhort with all long-suffering and doctrine, lies silent in the grave; but, though dead, he yet speaketh in these Sermons. He calls to the numerous Flock, once committed to his charge, to repent and do their first works. Many of these Discourses are exactly suited to their case, and even more applicable to the present circumstances of his Parish, than they were at the time when they were preached. The Sermon, with which the Volume concludes, composed and delivered not long before his decease, may be considered as his dying testimony to this great truth, that "to be carnally minded is death, but to be spiritually minded is life and peace."

W. R.

York, November 1st, 1808.

CONTENTS:

OF THE

SECOND VOL. OF SERMONS.

SERMON I.

THE GAIN OF THE WHOLE WORLD NO COMPENSATION FOR THE LOSS OF THE SOUL.

Mark viii. 36, 37. *For what shall it profit a man, if he shall gain the whole world, and lose his own soul? Or what shall a man give in exchange for his soul?* page 1

SERMON II.

THE GAIN OF THE WHOLE WORLD NO COMPENSATION FOR THE LOSS OF THE SOUL.

Mark viii. 36, 37. *For what shall it profit a man, if he shall gain the whole world, and lose his own soul? Or what shall a man give in exchange for his soul?* - p. 15

SERMON III.

THE INESTIMABLE VALUE OF FAITH IN THE RIGHTEOUSNESS OF GOD AND OUR SAVIOUR JESUS CHRIST.

2 Pet. i. 1. *Simon Peter, a servant and an apostle of Jesus Christ, to them that have obtained like precious faith with us, through the righteousness of God, and our Saviour Jesus Christ* - - - - p. 28

SERMON IV.

PARDON AND PEACE OBTAINED BY FAITH.

Nahum i. 7. *The Lord is good, a strong hold in the day of trouble; and he knoweth them that trust in him.*
p. 43

SERMON V.

THE SINFUL LUSTS OF THE FLESH OVERCOME BY FAITH.

2 Pet. i. 4. *Whereby are given unto us exceeding great and precious promises; that by these ye might be partakers of the divine nature, having escaped the corruption that is in the world through lust.* - - p. 55

SERMON VI.

THE WORLD OVERCOME BY FAITH.

1 John v. 4. *Whatsoever is born of God, overcometh the world: and this is the victory that overcometh the world, even our faith.* - - - - - - p. 69

SERMON VII.

THE DEVIL OVERCOME BY FAITH.

Rom. xvi. 20. *And the God of peace shall bruise Satan under your feet shortly.* - - - - p. 82

SERMON VIII.

TE SELF-DECEIVER SHOWN TO HIMSELF.

Prov. xxx. 12. *There is a generation that are pure in their own eyes, and yet is not washed from their filthiness.* - - - - - - - p. 94

CONTENTS.

SERMON IX.

THE DIFFERENT MANNER IN WHICH THE RIGHTEOUS AND THE WICKED DIE.

Prov. xiv. 32. *The wicked is driven away in his wickedness: but the righteous hath hope in his death.* - p. 108

SERMON X.

ST. PAUL'S DETERMINATION TO KNOW NOTHING ELSE, SAVE JESUS CHRIST, AND HIM CRUCIFIED.

1 Cor. ii. 2. *For I determined not to know any thing among you, save Jesus Christ and him crucified.* p. 120

SERMON XI.

THE DIFFERENCE BETWEEN A CARNAL AND SPIRITUAL KNOWLEDGE OF CHRIST.

2 Cor. v. 16. *Wherefore, henceforth know we no man after the flesh: yea, though we have known Christ after the flesh, yet now henceforth know we him no more.* p. 133

SERMON XII.

THE CONVERSION OF ST. MATTHEW.

Luke v. 27—33. *After these things he went forth, and saw a publican named Levi, sitting at the receipt of custom: and he said unto him, Follow me. And he left all, rose up, and followed him. And Levi made him a great feast in his own house: and there was a great company of publicans, and of others that sat down with* them. *But their scribes and pharisees murmured against his disciples, saying, Why do ye eat and drink with publicans and sinners? And Jesus answering, said unto them, They that are whole, need not a physician; but they that are sick. I came not to call the righteous, but sinners to repentance.* - - - p. 149

SERMON XIII.

THE HAPPY EFFECTS OF FEARING ALWAY, AND THE DANGER OF PRESUMPTION.

Prov. xxviii. 14. *Happy is the man that feareth alway: but he that hardeneth his heart, shall fall into mischief.*
p. 162

SERMON XIV.

THE FOOLISHNESS OF MAN PERVERTETH HIS WAY, AND HIS HEART FRETTETH AGAINST THE LORD.

Prov. xix. 3. *The foolishness of man perverteth his way: and his heart fretteth against the Lord.* - p. 176

SERMON XV.

THE FOLLY OF ATTEMPTING TO MAKE THAT STRAIGHT WHICH GOD HAS MADE CROOKED.

Eccles. vii. 13. *Consider the work of God: for who can make that straight, which he hath made crooked?* p. 189

SERMON XVI.

THE SCRIPTURE DOCTRINE OF DIVINE AND HUMAN AGENCY IN THE WORK OF OUR SALVATION.

Philip. ii. 12, 13. *Work out your own salvation with fear and trembling: for it is God which worketh in you, both to will and to do of his good pleasure.* - p. 203

SERMON XVII.

THE SEAL OF GOD'S FOUNDATION, OR PRIVILEGE AND DUTY CLEARLY STATED.

2 Tim. ii. 19. *Nevertheless, the foundation of God standeth sure, having this seal, The Lord knoweth them that are his. And, Let every one that nameth the name of Christ depart from iniquity.* - - - p. 217

SERMON XVIII.

AN AFFECTIONATE ADMONITION TO SEAMEN.

Acts xxvii. 20. *And when neither sun nor stars in many days appeared, and no small tempest lay on us, all hope that we should be saved was then taken away.* - p. 233

SERMON XIX.

PARABLE OF THE RICH MAN AND LAZARUS, CONSIDERED.

Luke xvi. 22, 23. *And it came to pass, that the beggar died, and was carried by the angels into Abraham's bosom. The rich man also died, and was buried: and in hell he lifted up his eyes, being in torments, and seeth Abraham afar off, and Lazarus in his bosom.* - p. 246

SERMON XX.

DUTY OF DRAWING NIGH TO GOD, AND RESISTING THE DEVIL.

James iv. 7, 8. *Resist the devil and he will flee from you draw nigh to God, and he will draw nigh to you.*
p. 259

SERMON XXI.

A PRICE IN THE HAND OF A FOOL TO GET WISDOM.

Prov. xi. 16. *Wherefore is there a price in the hand of a fool to get wisdom, seeing he hath no heart to it?*
p. 273

SERMON XXII.

THE TEMPORAL ADVANTAGES OF GODLINESS.

1 Tim. iv. 8. *Godliness is profitable unto all things, having promise of the life that now is, and of that which is to come* - - - - - p. 284

SERMON XXIII.

THE USE AND ABUSE OF HEARING SERMONS.

1 Cor. iii. 5, 6, 7. *Who then is Paul, and who is Apollos, but ministers by whom ye believed, even as the Lord gave to every man? I have planted, Apollos watered; but God gave the increase. So then, neither is he that planteth any thing, neither he that watereth; but God that giveth the increase.* - - - - p. 297

SERMON XXIV.

PARABLE OF THE RICH MAN, WHOSE GROUND BROUGHT FORTH PLENTIFULLY, CONSIDERED.

Luke xii. 16—21. *And he spake a parable unto them, saying, The ground of a certain rich man brought forth plentifully: And he thought within himself, saying, What shall I do, because I have no room where to bestow my fruits? And he said, This will I do: I will pull down my barns, and build greater; and there will I bestow all my fruits and my goods. And I will say to my soul, Soul, thou hast much goods laid up for many*

SERMON XXXI.

IMPORTUNITY IN PRAYER.

Luke xviii. 1. *And he spake a parable unto them to this end, that men ought always to pray, and not to faint.*

p. 411

SERMON XXXII.

CHRISTIANS IN DANGER OF LOSING THOSE THINGS WHICH THEY HAVE WROUGHT, AND NOT RECEIVING A FULL REWARD.

2 John 8. *Look to yourselves, that we lose not those things which we have wrought, but that we receive a full reward.*

p. 426

SERMON XXXIII.

TO BE HEAVENLY-MINDED, A NECESSARY PREPARATION FOR FUTURE HAPPINESS.

2 Cor. iv. 16, 17, 18. *For which cause we faint not; but though our outward man perish, yet the inward man is renewed day by day. For our light affliction, which is but for a moment, worketh for us a far more exceeding and eternal weight of glory; while we look not at the things which are seen, but at the things which are not seen: for the things which are seen are temporal; but the things which are not seen are eternal.* - p. 439

SERMON I.

THE GAIN OF THE WHOLE WORLD, NO COMPENSATION FOR THE LOSS OF THE SOUL.

Mark viii. 36, 37.

For what shall it profit a man, if he shall gain the whole world, and lose his own soul? Or what shall a man give in exchange for his soul?

IF any consideration can overcome that profane and careless indifference, with which many are now accustomed—to *hear* shall I say—or to *seem* to hear the great doctrines of the Scriptures; it is that view of their infinite importance, which the sentence of the text exhibits. We are alive after trifles " light as air," which however important they may now seem to us, will presently leave us naked and destitute, and in a few years, at most, will be of no use or consequence to us; and oh! how do we slight the consideration of eternity, though all our bliss depends upon it!

This proneness to slight eternity, this excessive attachment to the things of time, is a certain proof, that man is in a fallen state by nature. In arithmetic we know, full well, the difference between seventy and millions, and though no man has an adequate idea of eternity, yet the negative idea itself, that it never, never shall have an end—this of itself causes us clearly to understand, that there is no sort of comparison to be made between the largest number, that ever was actually reckoned, and eternity: imagination is lost in conceiving of its extent; and all time, and all the events of time, appear as nothing in comparison. How is it, then, that men can spend weeks, and months, and years, with the main stream of their thoughts running after this world, and hardly allow themselves in any serious thought after the eternal state!

In worldly things, we think it wise to spend time beforehand, in preparing for any new scenes we may have to enter on. A seven years apprenticeship is not thought too long to prepare a youth for a trade, which he may never live to enter on, and in which, perhaps, he may never have any profit or success. Oh! surely, all is wrong with us by nature; the most holy of God's people must be sensible of it, if they carefully look into themselves. It is so far from being natural to us to weigh eternity in any practical sense, that it is very difficult to be brought to any deep and serious thought of it at all. Set apart some time for the business—how slowly move our thoughts! how like a fable or a dream appears the revelation of Scripture! Confirmed, though it be, with miracles and prophecies, and every internal mark of truth, yet how little is it believed to be true! How little are we affected with ideas of the fulness of joy and pleasures at God's right hand for evermore! and the lake of hell, that burneth with fire and brimstone for ever—how little does it move us!

These things show the human mind to be depraved. In the things of eternity we have lost the powers of arithmetic. He knew this well, who prayed, " So teach us to number our days, that we may apply our hearts unto wisdom." This prayer is answered in converting and quickening grace. Perhaps men might seek more for this grace, were they more seriously impressed with ideas of eternity, or, which is much the same, the worth of the soul. When our Lord asks " What shall it shall profit a man, if he shall gain the whole world, and lose his own soul?" we should, to understand the force of the question, balance the account, by considering what it is to *lose* the soul, and what it is to gain all we could wish in the world.

Let me beg your earnest attention. The subject is alarming, I own. But will HELL be charmed away by our ceasing to think of it? There is an impudent profaneness in the times, which will not allow men to think that hell has any existence; but to say that it is ETERNAL, this they will not endure: they think it unjust. I know none more likely to obtain the heaviest punishment there than such fearless reasoners, who show themselves so unmeasurably arrogant as to set up *their* reasoning against God's word. Are you judges of the quantity of evil there is in sin? No man can say it. You cannot then judge of the propriety of the degree of punishing it. It is surely above reason, and revelation alone must determine.

Let me beg of you then, brethren, to attend to what far more concerns us—to weigh the case stated in the text. Bring it home, each man, each woman

—and O! Spirit of Christ be with us; and quicken, and illumine our dull, dark souls, while we consider —1st, what it is to lose the soul in hell, and—2d, what is the emptiness of the gain of all the world: whence we may—3d, apply to the conscience the infinitely weighty question of the text.

1st. What it is to lose the soul in hell.—Did you ever consider what this loss is? Did you ever set aside any portion of time in your life to weigh it? Conceive the greatest and most terrible losses that humanity knows, in this vale of tears and sorrow; suppose, with Job, you lost all your substance; all your children, and dearest friends; and was then, with Job, smitten with sore boils from head to foot; and, with Job, afterwards cruelly insulted and treated as an hypocrite by those from whom you ought to receive comfort. Nay, conceive also the most terrible pains and tortures of the body, worse than even Popish barbarity ever invented, and the bare mention of which would affright and affect many of my audience. All these evils are nothing at all compared with the loss of the soul in hell. Do not talk of any harsh representation of things. It is true, as sure as the Scripture itself is true; and if you will not bear the idea of hell beforehand, how ill will you be prepared to bear the real hell itself hereafter?

Consider: the way to hell is broad, and many there be which walk therein. What reason have you to suppose that you shall not be of the number? But "I hope." Yes! these deluding hopes! They are the uncharitable preachers. They damn the souls of men. You who will not endure with patience a minister to represent to you the horrors of hell, with a charitable view to induce you to flee from the wrath to come, have a black evidence in your souls, if you knew how to read it, that you are travelling the broad road thither. You have no business with HOPE, remaining as you are. You ought to be alarmed; rouzed; quickened; made to know, and feel yourselves on the brink of hell itself. There is but a step between you and death; and oh! that you would consider it to good purpose.

Suppose this night your souls were required of you! You would be among the " spirits in prison," that St. Peter speaks of, "reserved to the judgment of the great day." Scripture says little of what would be your condition during the interval between death and the judgment of the last day; and as little of the state of the righteous during the same interval. "The spirits of just men made perfect" must be, no doubt, in a happy state; and yours must be in a very dismal, dreadful state, expecting, I should apprehend, the coming of the Judge, with terror, at the last day. Were there no other consideration to make such a condition terrible, this would surely suffice. But I say little here, because Scripture says little.

Pass we on to a field, in which Scripture gives more dreadful light, and renders visible the images of woe, when the Lord Jesus with " his mighty angels, in flaming fire, shall take vengeance on them that know not God, and obey not the gospel of our Lord Jesus Christ, who shall be punished with everlasting destruction from the presence of the Lord, and from the glory of his power." Can you bear the sight of the Judge? " Behold! he cometh with clouds, and every eye shall see him, and they also which pierced him, and all kindreds of the earth shall wail because of him." Yes, your astonished heart may probably cry, "This is he whose doctrines I neglected; whose people and ways I hated; how severe, how grand, how awful his looks! Alas! I hated instruction: I crucified him afresh, and put him to an open shame. O mountains, fall on me, O rocks, cover me from the wrath of the Lamb! For the great day of his wrath is come, and how shall I be able to stand!" And when you have heard the words, " Depart, ye cursed, into everlasting fire, prepared for the devil and his angels:" Oh! what horror in the sound; what a morning of the resurrection-day must it be to you, to be first awakened by the voice of " the arch-angel and the trump of God," " Arise, ye dead, and come to judgment!" The sentence of the Judge must complete your horror. Were I to pretend to describe particularly what follows after, my folly would be evident. I shall keep, therefore, to those general ideas which Scripture gives. A few considerations seem to occur in this matter.

1. The lost soul, after sentence is passed, and hell has shut him up, may then understand fully what is meant by being deprived for ever of communion with God, and all hope of his favour. His loving kindness is better than life itself. When " HE lets his breath go forth, his creatures are made, and he renews the face of the earth." He gladdens universal nature. How pleasant is it even here, to taste that he is gracious by believing! When the Psalmist says, " there be many that say, Who

will shew us any good?" He adds, "Lord, lift thou up the light of thy countenance upon us.". This is *his*, and it is the true idea of happiness.

It is pleasant to enjoy the light of the sun, and many worldly comforts, and conveniences; but a still more joyful and pleasant thing it is, in enjoying them, to be thankful to the Universal Lord, "whose tender mercies are over all his works." It is best of all to enjoy the light of his countenance in our souls, and know his pardoning love, and feast on his grace in Jesus. But how dreadful to have lost all hope of these things; to be shut out from all prospect of happiness, and banished, in comfortless despair, from God! This must, of itself, be hell, were there no positive punishment besides. To dwell in God, is to be happy; to be for ever disjoined from him, must be misery. There can be no bliss without him, in the nature of things. It is for want of this union with God, that the wicked are in this world " like the troubled sea, when it cannot rest, whose waters cast up mire and dirt: there is no peace to the wicked."

Hence, wicked men are miserable here, and know not often why. They roam from object to object, and use rounds of pleasure and business to kill time and thought. They indulge here also their vices, and this world has in it many refreshments, notwithstanding its many miseries. But remember, in hell these refreshments will be lost. It is written, " they have no rest day nor night*." To be shut up in hell is to be void of God, and condemned to a restless state, with no relief from amuse-

* Rev. xiv. 11.

ments or refreshments, no prospect of deliverance for ever.

Nor is it possible for them to be happy, were they taken up into heaven. The joys of heaven are holy, and would be to them intolerable. Wicked men here hate holy conversation. They confess it makes them dull and melancholy. How much more would heaven be offensive to them!

If men considered this more, they might feel the need of being made new creatures in Christ here. The conversion we preach would appear necessary to them. Be sure, if here you love not heavenly things, you will not love them hereafter. Then "he that is filthy, let him be filthy still," as it is written*. The change must be here, not there. How vainly do men talk of God's mercy, without considering that misery is in the very nature of sin, and that, if here they be not changed, all hopes of happiness must be vain. And how miserable may we conceive the damned will be through the force and violence of their sins. How miserable and tormenting is pride, and carnal lust, and impatience! Every sin has hell in it. Those who lie, then, in hell, in all this filthiness of flesh and spirit unsubdued, and in the company of none but human souls and evil spirits of the same character, what misery must they feel: what woe, we may suppose, must they inflict upon one another! Thus to be deprived of God must, in its consequence, bring hell and its horrors, indeed!

2. But though the misery of the damned may be thus shewn to arise from the nature of things, yet

* Rev. xxii. 11.

I do not mean to exclude the idea of positive punishment. God is the Governor of the World; as such he has a right to punish as well as to reward. It is not for me, or indeed for any one, to say what is the nature of the fire in which they will be tormented. Whatever it be, it is the fire of God's wrath; "the breath of the Lord, like a stream of brimstone doth kindle it." " If any man worship the beast, the same shall drink of the wine of the wrath of God, which is poured out, without mixture, into the cup of his indignation, and he shall be tormented with fire and brimstone in the presence of the holy angels, and in the presence of the Lamb, and the smoke of their torment ascendeth up for ever and ever, and they have no rest day nor night." Agreeable to this is the sentence of the Judge, " depart, ye cursed, into everlasting fire." The beast and the false prophet, in *Rev.* xix, are said to be " cast alive into a lake of fire burning with brimstone;" and the devil himself, at length, " that deceived them, was cast into the lake of fire and brimstone, where the beast and the false prophet are, and shall be tormented day and night for ever[*]." And lest we should imagine that sinners of an inferior magnitude may escape, we are told that will be the doom of all who are not in Christ. For it is added, " whosoever was not found written in the book of life, was cast into the lake of fire." In *Rev.* xxi, we have a list of the characters of the condemned. Let my audience attend, and look within and ask what their own characters are. " The fearful, (by which I apprehend is meant those who fear man more

[*] Rev. xx. 10.

than God) the fearful and unbelieving, and the abominable, and murderers, and whoremongers, and sorcerers, and idolaters, and all liars, shall have their part in the lake which burneth with fire and brimstone, which is the second death." What images of pain and horror are these! I do not pretend to be able to describe the precise nature of these torments! God keep us from an experimental knowledge of them, by an experimental knowledge of his grace here! but surely, here are ideas of real torture and positive pain inexpressible! and men, in our times, need to have these awful scriptures set forth; for the pride of self-conceit, and the profaneness of infidelity, render it difficult indeed for them to feel that there is any thing in sin so bitter and dreadful, as to issue in punishment like this!

3. The idea of being in an unpitied state, and destitute of every alleviating consideration, must sharpen exceedingly the horrors of hell! "To him that is afflicted, pity should be shewn of his friend;" but who will pity in hell? We may conceive the damned more likely to aggravate each others woes, by accusations and invectives, than to soften them by the exercise of mutual compassion. It does not appear that even Jesus himself (and who can tell the extent of his grace and compassion?) will exercise, in practice at least, any pity toward them. We have seen how "they shall be tormented in the PRESENCE OF THE LAMB!" To me this circumstance gives a keen idea of the anguish of hell. What! the pitiful and meek Lamb of God, who always went about doing good, and healing the oppressed; who even died for his enemies, and

prayed for his murderers—HE see poor souls tormented for ever, and yet afford them no relief—What! is his nature changed? Oh no! He may as soon cease to be, as cease to be gracious and merciful, slow to anger, and of infinite loving-kindness. SIN, SIN, has that infinite evil in it, which renders it fit for the glory of God, and the support of his government, that thus it should be.

Men who reason against it ought to be sure that they are judges of the case; which it were folly, past the power of description, in any mortal to pretend to. But this boldness of reasoning against God's word, in things beyond our depth, I take to be the mark of pride in its essence, and one of the most horrible sins of our land. "Not a drop of water to cool the tongue," represents in a well-known parable, the punishment of the damned. To have no relief, no alleviation, no soothing of pity: to have sinned away the loving-kindness of him who is infinite goodness itself, is a most dreadful state!

Nor will the damned have any comfort from within. No: "there the worm dieth not." They would not come to Jesus for life when they might. "God will be clear when he is judged:" "to me every knee should bow:" "the lofty looks of man shall be humbled, and the haughtiness of man bowed down, and the Lord alone shall be exalted." Lay these scriptures together, and they will teach the ungodly that however they may brag of their goodness, and reason against God, saying, "wherein have we wearied him;" however they may exclaim against the idea of hell torments as inconsistent with the idea of God's mercy; in the world to come, all such thoughts will cease. Their consciences will then proclaim them to be what they are, and they will not be able, however dreadfully they suffer in eternity, to say their punishment is too great. Oh! to suffer thus, and have no friend from within or from without, and look around and see only devils and damned spirits, as miserable as themselves—This is hell indeed!

4. The consideration of the value of the blood of Christ must give a strong idea of the horror of hell. Jesus delivered us from the wrath to come. Let us behold the sinner, now in hell, deprived of communion with God; positively tormented in the lake of fire and brimstone, without any relief, or mitigating circumstance; yet knowing that Jesus had died for him, through whom he might have been saved, if, while the breath was in his nostrils, he had really come to him. Suppose him to reflect what infinite dignity and goodness there is in Christ, and thence conclude what a dreadful thing a state of sin is, and what a happy thing a state of holiness is, since to redeem from sin to holiness required such precious blood and such bitter sufferings as he underwent. Yet for the sinner to have thrown all away; to have refused his remedy, and set at nought such an amazing effort of divine power, wisdom, and goodness, as this of Christ's redemption—conceive, if you can, how bitter the thought must be—and if you cannot but think that this will probably be a most aggravating circumstance in hell, certainly none in the world are more likely to experience it than we are who have such means, and yet love darkness rather than light. Oh! then turn

to him who gave himself a ransom for all, while time remains, and "kiss the Son" and delay not, from this day, to seek him with the whole heart.

We have considered the horrors of hell—1st, in the view of the soul's total want of God—2d, of its positive punishments—3d, of its friendless state, and—4th, of its having sinned away the most precious of all remedies. But the most killing circumstance remains to be considered.

This misery is ETERNAL. It would alleviate the sense of woe, if the man could think, after suffering as many years as there are blades of grass, and sands on the sea shore, and stars in the firmament added together, he might then come from the place of torment. But the torment, after all, STILL TO BEGIN! Who can tell, indeed, what it is to "dwell in everlasting burning!" Shall we be told, that such and such great names are of another opinion, and deem hell torments not to be eternal! Will their reasonings help out of hell those who once find themselves there? What is the way to settle this matter? Surely mere reasoning on the mercy of God, set in opposition to his other perfections, must be an impious boldness. Do men consider that the justice and purity of God is as infinite as his mercy? and especially that Reason must be here an impudent caviller, taking upon her what is vastly unbecoming? For the Scripture revelation of the eternity of future torments is so plain, and so void of, even any thing like, hints to the contrary, that I suppose were it not for this imagined contrariety to reason, men would never have pretended to bring any thing from Scripture against the doctrine.

Let several chapters towards the end of Revelations, and particularly the solemn declaration in the last chapter, " he which is filthy, let him be filthy still, and he that is righteous, let him be righteous still," be well considered. This representation takes away all idea of any change after this life taking place in the state, or on the hearts of men, and the eternal punishment of the wicked will appear as true and real as the happiness of the righteous. Read the latter part of the ninth chapter of St. Mark's Gospel. Three times our Lord says, " Where their worm dieth not, and the fire is not quenched." Read his account of the last judgment—" These shall go away into everlasting punishment, and the righteous into life eternal." On this scriptural ground I rest the matter. May we all here, be in fear for ourselves, and flee from the wrath to come.

SERMON II.

THE GAIN OF THE WHOLE WORLD, NO COMPENSATION FOR THE LOSS OF THE SOUL.

Mark viii. 36, 37.

For what shall it profit a man, if he shall gain the whole world, and lose his own soul? Or what shall a man give in exchange for his soul?

To balance the account fairly, a man should, as I observed, weigh on the one hand what it is to lose the soul, and on the other what it is to gain the whole world. The first has been attempted; and though the description of the ruin of the soul in hell has been faint indeed, and much disproportioned to the subject, yet enough has been said to show it dreadful beyond all powers of description, and a loss not to be repaired by any advantages which the world can give. Let us now observe a little,

What it is to " gain the whole world."—Suppose, then, the god of this world, the devil, to take you up, as he did our Lord, into an exceeding high mountain, and to show you " all the kingdoms of the world, and the glory of them," and to say, what he had the power to make good, " all this will I give thee, if thou wilt fall down and worship me."

—He has the power of deceiving the nations, and he engages them to worship him in effect, when their hearts are overcome with the love of this world.— Let the gain of the whole world, I say, pass in review, and what is there in it all, that should move the affections of men? Solomon has long since pronounced the whole to be " vanity and vexation of spirit." And who had more wisdom, more riches, more power of commanding all sorts of pleasures than Solomon? Yet he was well nigh brought to despair; nay, he " hated life" itself. The reason is, the world has not in its best state of things any real happiness to give; the immortal soul famishes amidst its richest abundance, and finds no suitable sustenance and support.

Let young persons, whose hearts are easily smitten with the gay appearances of pleasure, before they have had any experience of the world, be assured that the world has nothing but emptiness, nothing to fill the soul. Let them ask any who have lived fifty or sixty years, if they ever found any substantial happiness in it, and even those who have been the most prosperous, and who have moved in the most easy spheres of life, will own, if at all honest to their own feelings, will own, the world has disappointed them: it never gave them that, in enjoyment, which it promised, in expectation; even though every thing succeeded to their wish. Let a man dictate the terms to Satan, in this case, and ask a long life, health, beauty, agreeable friends, riches, honours, pleasures, and knowledge. Let him stipulate for whatever his very heart could wish, and he would experience the whole to be vanity and vexation of spirit. For every temporal blessing that can be desired to make life happy and honourable was Solomon's, for a long season, though not from Satan, but from God.

There is an uneasy void in the heart, which is not filled up by all that the world can give. " Open thy mouth wide, and I will fill it," says God. Yes, in the knowledge of him is life and joy. This is the true happiness of man; the kingdom of God within; which is righteousness, peace, and joy in the Holy Ghost, and which even much affliction does not take away. " There be many that say, who will show us any good? Lord, lift thou up the light of thy countenance upon us." There is " gladness in the heart, more than when their corn, and wine, and oil increased."

Let young persons be persuaded to attend to this. God's favour and Holy Spirit can give them real bliss, even with all worldly things against them. But the most prosperous and the most pleasurable of worldly things will not give them it, if they be void of God within. And as our Lord has decided the case, " Ye cannot serve God and mammon," one of the two masters must be uppermost; and if mammon, they cannot be happy. Let them seek for the wisdom of God to determine them aright. For whatever experience a man has of this world's vanity, unless he has a taste of what is better, he will still follow it. And though in following the world, and giving it your heart, instead of God, you do not directly fall down before the devil, and worship him, yet surely you do worship him in effect. You serve his kingdom: he is " the spirit that worketh in the children of disobedience," and he works by alluring men's hearts after the world instead of God. So that you ought to know, that if the world draw you after it with any of its vanities, you are serving the devil with all your hearts, and are going along the broad way to the lake of fire and brimstone. Nothing but God's own Spirit can set you right in your choice: in his light only can you see light: pray therefore that you may be enabled to form a proper estimate.

Can riches feed the immortal spirit? Do not we see the more men have of them, the more greedy they are after filthy lucre? Suppose the wealth of all the Indies your own; all the jewels and all the shining ore of the whole earth, what would you do? You would satisfy the demands of nature. So you might if you were a day-labourer. You could only make Solomon's experiments of pleasures, wine, buildings, servants, musical instruments, and all kinds of delights of the sons of men; and when you looked on all, you would find all vanity. The health of the soul is holiness, conformity to God.—This your wealth would be so far from promoting, that it would hinder it exceedingly. Pride, arrogance, ill tempers, and troublesome imaginations, grow upon men, as they grow in wealth, while their hearts are strangers to God. For "the prosperity of fools destroys them," and renders them a curse to themselves, and a burden to all around them.

What can carnal pleasure do for any man? Who knows not that its end is bitterness and woe? Take your fill of pleasure; withhold nothing from you, that your eyes lust after, and then tell us the result. Let the votaries of pleasure, in this house, confess from their feelings, that happiness is yet a stranger to their breasts. And if riches and pleasures be thus unsatisfactory, when enjoyed, how empty must they appear, when it is considered that man is subject continually to disappointment. And this is the misery of worldly advantages; that though when obtained they never satisfy the soul; yet disappointment is sure to sting the minds of men, and render them exceeding miserable.

But besides the thousand thousand losses, cares, and mortifications to which all worldly situations are liable, Death, that king of terrors, will soon strip the proudest men of all their greatness. Over hill and dale, over land and sea, their steady eye may pursue the gaudy butterfly of pomp and grandeur. Yet, behold! in the midst of their pursuits, Death, with silent hand, precipitates them into the gulph of eternity. Admit you were master of the whole world; yet we must not admit you are master of your existence here for one hour. And does not this embitter to the man of this world all his greatness! Must he not now and then reflect with anguish, " very shortly, how soon I know not, I must leave all these darling objects of pleasure!"

What has an end, cannot satisfy the immortal spirit. At God's " right hand, is the fulness of joy and pleasures for evermore," and there only. So that let a natural man be asked what he would have, and from the vast variety of the world's goods let him select what is the dearest to his soul—he is miserable still: possession cannot bless him:

the least disappointment can torment him, and death will soon deprive him of all.

Honour and praise seem, however, to many, more noble objects of pursuit. The ancient Greek and Roman heroes, so much admired by the bad taste of a bad world, in the scripture's eye are the slaves of pride, rank, diabolical pride. Look at them all, and surely misery marks them for her own, amidst their greatest successes and their highest honours, which they so much coveted in the temple of fame. Alexander conquers the world, and dies in a fit of drunkenness. Cæsar enslaves his country, and just after he has waded through oceans of blood, to the summit of his greatness, he falls in the senate-house. The pride of Cato swells with the idea of patriotism. He basely sinks under calamity. Too weak to endure the will of God, and too haughty to submit to it, he rushes out of life in self-murder. Hannibal, after a life of war and constant fatigue, and fleeing from place to place for means to gratify ambition and revenge, dies by poison. To come nearer our own times, Oliver Cromwell, after a thousand stratagems and arts of policy, no sooner sees himself in possession of his ill-gotten power, than he is harassed with endless fears and terrors for his own life. Within a very few years this much-envied, and highly-prosperous man, the terror of Europe, yet constantly terrified himself, lest some conspiracy should rob him of life, dies the prey of disease, and his family sink into their former obscurity.

If it be asked, of what use is all this to us? It may be answered, of more, it may be, than many apprehend. It is a minister's business to warn the people of all the dangers that threaten them. This empty bubble honour, connected with the idea of the love of liberty, is working, I fear, at present, some dire evils in the land. I do not wonder if men, void of the fear of God, and flattered with high ideas of honour and liberty, are easily seduced to countenance these factious meetings, which are now conducted with such heat in the kingdom. Let christians, however, be wise, and remember their principles, which are not to be of this world. I am endeavouring to show, according to my text, that really there is nothing in this world, even if a man could gain all he could wish, worthy our affections, and that therefore the whole vehemence of our affections ought to be directed for the care of the soul. On this account, as well as others, real christians are always called on in scripture " to submit to the powers that be;" " to fear the Lord and the king, and meddle not with them that are given to change." Ye who reverence God's word, obey it, and prove by your conduct that you believe the gain of the whole world to be mere emptiness. If you do believe it really and heartily, you will not be drawn by the flattering sounds of liberty, patriotism, honour, or any such like bubble, to join a multitude to do evil.

Attend to the signs of the times : what do these threaten ? What are the evils which factious meetings pretend to remedy, compared with those which they tend to bring on ? Should a civil war, in God's wrath for our sins, rage in a year or two's time among us, I am persuaded well-intentioned people will not then, with comfort, reflect that they helped to forward it. No man will be seduced to act warmly in these scenes of political strife and contention, but from that very love of the world, which it is the business of the care of the soul to destroy. To be quiet, peaceable, loyal, and submissive to the powers that be, is God's rule; nor can I conceive that any other rule can be given, to prevent the people of God from becoming like the people of the world. Brethren, beware: pray to God very seriously for his direction, pray to be prepared for the events which may be hastening, and help your country by praying to him who stills the noise of the waves, and the madness of the people. As a minister of the Prince of Peace, and in obedience to the Almighty's direction—" put them in mind to obey magistrates"—I have done my duty here in exhorting you to follow what makes for peace and legal subjection. I now return from this digression, if it may be so called. By this time the vanity of this world's gain has been shown in the present discourse, as the worth of the soul and the infinite evil of the loss of it were shown in the last, I proceed therefore, in application, to illustrate the force of the question in the text.

Let Satan place before you the charms of all this world; its profits; its pleasures; its honours, in the most tempting point of view; let his serpentine subtilty hide the sting of sin as much as he pleases, and solicit your natural senses ever so powerfully; yet that they are all vanity and vexation of spirit, and at best will, within a few years, leave a man naked and destitute, and send him a breathless corpse into the silent tomb; this is the voice of truth and universal experience. Now for the sake of such empty goods to lose the soul in hell, and be consigned to a place of endless torment, and hopeless separation from the living God, whose loving kindness is the life and joy of all creation—who can say what folly this is! Who could believe any man to act so absurdly, did not experience witness that thousands so act; that the many do thus ruin themselves by running in the broad road to destruction! Not one in this house, then, but will own that such an exchange is madness in the extreme, and that for any man to lose his soul for the greatest of earthly advantages, is folly in its essence.

There is a farther deceit in this business. The spirit that worketh in the children of disobedience suggests, " What need of such precise strictness?". May not we follow the world in some degree, and give our hearts to it, in some measure, and yet from a merciful God expect pardon and salvation, if we keep clear of gross crimes, and attend some religious duties at certain seasons!" Ah! brethren, who was it that said, " ye cannot serve God and mammon?" and, inspired by his Spirit, does not one of his disciples say, " whosoever will be the friend of the world, is the enemy of God?" Does not another say, " if any man love the world, the love of the Father is not in him?" And does not another say, " be not conformed to this world," and give us his own pattern, that he " gladly suffers the loss of all things, and counts them but dung, that he may win Christ?" Thus Christ himself; thus James, John, and Paul his servants, with one voice declare. A man cannot place his heart on this world, and on God together. The objects are inconsistent with one another. As easily may a man travel northward and southward at the same moment. Do not mistake. It is one christian duty among others, "not to be slothful in business," and for every man to "provide for his own house." But the heart, the heart must be only for God; he is a jealous God; he will have the whole heart, or none of it. He alone must be our portion. We must sit loose to every thing else; be ready to part with any thing; with all things, when he calls. We must not make out our happiness from any thing, but from himself.

Now you who talk thus of dividing between God and the world, are evidently living for this world only. Were it not for a pang of conscience now and then, and for slavish fear, religion would not be at all attended to by you. When you comfort your minds with prospects of pleasure, confess it is not from the thought of a reconciled God in Christ, and the prospect of a blessed resurrection to eternal life, but from gain or pleasures, or something or other of a worldly kind. The reason why you feel not the impossibility of serving God and mammon together, is because you are at ease as to your soul. Its worth you never felt. Satan keeps you asleep in sin, with a view to ruin you for ever, and you talk of the easiness of being religious, with the same spirit as any man, who never made trial of any trade or art, talks how easy it is. He is aware of no difficulty, because he knows nothing of the subject.

Awake, awake to careful thought, and be alarmed; for all the horrors of hell, that have been described, belong to you, in your present state; and the vain world you seek, with all your heart, is vanity indeed. To you let our Lord's question in the text ring a loud alarm. Conscience! do thine office in these men; let them not sleep the sleep of the second death, in Satan's chains. Oh! may the good spirit of God show you what you are, and make you feel the force of the question.

For after men are awakened indeed, and begin in earnest to ask "what they must do to be saved," and obtain some light, and put some things which they know in practice, they feel in real experience, what, in former carelessness of thought, they could not understand; that, indeed, there is no such thing as serving God and mammon. They see the world to lie in wickedness, and the glory and service of God, and the beauty of holiness to be quite contrary to it. Then the opposition between the two interests, that of God's kingdom and of Satan's kingdom, becomes palpably evident; and they find that " in them dwells no good thing." They have a lazy, lustful, blind, proud, rebellious nature, that needs to be mortified and brought down universally, or there is no living to God at all. But besides the strife and conflict, from the evil nature, which all have in common, according to men's different tempers and situations and temptations, they find, in many particular things, the effects of this conflict, which shake their inmost souls, and cause a civil war within.

Feel you not thus, O seeking souls! " Oh! this and that lust, how strong do I find it! How does it overcome me again and again! This fear of the world, what a snare does it bring to me! These tempers, how bitter and obstinate! This pride, how stubborn! This love of the world, how bewitching!" None of you who feel with power these things, are thinking that you can be saved, while these lusts and these sins remain unmortified, and you continue at your ease. No, you have not so learned from the Spirit of Christ. Thank God, your eyes are thus far opened. This is more than the easy, careless souls have learnt, to whom I first addressed myself. Be hence encouraged, however, to press on for victory, lest your latter end be worse than the first.

But mind the manner in which you are to press on for victory; for in the little that remains of this discourse, I shall carry you forward to complete everlasting victory; I mean so far as man can do it in word. And may the Holy Ghost do it with power for you and for me.

You should be led, then, and if led by the Spirit of God, you *will* be led to bring the worth of the soul, and the worth of the world, each into opposite scales of the balance. And you will weigh them in the balance of God, that is, of truth. The soul will infinitely outweigh. To escape hell; eternal, remediless, pitiless hell, in the company of the Devil and his angels; to gain heaven, the fullness of joy, the likeness of God, and fellowship with Jesus Christ:—This will be your simple, infinitely weighty object. The world, its gains, pleasures, friendships, honours, all together, will kick the beam, light as air; as a shadow; as nothing. The most alluring lusts will lose their hold. You are called to give up, what? a nothing; that which is not worth keeping; what it is infinitely better to lose than to hold, whenever God pleases. You are called on to receive freely happiness itself. You will know, that the end of the love of the world is the second death in the lake of fire: you will see that the love of the world deserves the lake of fire; nay, that you deserve it for what is past already; how much more for the continuance of such a state of sin for the time to come.

Does this conviction come hardly to you! Indeed it does; but, oh! Christ, thou canst do it, and the spiritual view of thee crucified and made a curse for us, shows it invincibly. Then pride receives its death wound: man fell by pride, and he must rise again by humility. Saved by grace alone you now feel you must be, if at all; and you will now hear Jesus inviting you so to be saved, and telling you he shed his blood, that you might live. You believe and are pardoned, sanctified and live new creatures. But how is this brought about? You find you must part with all, even your righteousness, for Christ. You have no strength for this. Into Christ's arms you fall as the clay, and there lie. He raises you by faith. He tells you his victory is yours. "These things have I spoken unto you, that in me ye might have peace. In the world ye shall have tribulation; but be of good cheer: I have overcome the world."

SERMON III.

THE INESTIMABLE VALUE OF FAITH IN THE RIGHTEOUSNESS OF GOD AND OUR SAVIOUR JESUS CHRIST.

2 Peter, i. 1.

Simon Peter, a servant and an apostle of Jesus Christ, to them that have obtained like precious faith with us, through the righteousness of God, and our Saviour Jesus Christ.

THIS Epistle was written to christians, with a view to confirm them in the faith, and to build them up in the truth as it is in Jesus. The foundation of their character is set forth in this verse, and it is very descriptive of a christian spirit. He is a true christian, who, like those to whom St. Peter writes, has obtained the same precious faith which the apostles had, (for in this there is not the least difference between an apostle and the meanest real believer) the same precious faith, I say, in "the righteousness of God and our Saviour Jesus Christ."

I am aware that the text in our translation is rendered, "faith *through* the righteousness;" but the Greek is εν *in* the righteousness; and as no doubt can be made of this, I shall constantly prefer this rendering, though it is certain that both renderings will run up into the same meaning. If our translation has in this, and a very few other places, deviated a little from the original, the consequences are of no importance. The translation is, in general, as faithful, I apprehend, as can be expected from human infirmity; and blessed be God! "the righteousness of God and our Saviour," received by "precious faith," is a truth conveyed through the scriptures, and is, together with all its connections and consequences, too well established, to be at all affected by verbal criticisms on Greek particles.

A chrristian then, according to St. Peter, is one who has " obtained precious faith in the righteousness of our Saviour Jesus Christ." What a christian then was, he is now. " Jesus Christ is the same yesterday, to-day, and for ever." The Saviour is the same, and a true faith in him is still the same. There will arise then three distinct questions, which will require to be distinctly handled. I will briefly speak to each.

1st. What is the righteousness of God and our Saviour here spoken of. 2d. What it is to have precious faith in it. 3d. Whence this precious faith is to be obtained. Nothing will need to be explained but these three things, in order to take in all that was meant by the apostle when he tells us, that a christian is one who has obtained precious faith in the righteousness of God and our Saviour Jesus Christ.

1st. The righteousness here meant deserves to be called the righteousness of God, because he who performed it for believers is God, and was manifest in the flesh. In the gospel the righteousness of God is revealed from faith to faith, saith the apostle. All men are by nature under the covenant of works, which requires perfect obedience. By guilt, both original and actual, every soul of man is cut off from any pretension to the divine favour on the footing of this covenant, whose terms Moses thus describes: "The man which doeth those things shall live by them." There is but another covenant by which guilty men can live, and that is the covenant of grace; and "if by grace, then it is no more of works, otherwise grace is no more grace. But if it be of works, then it is no more grace, otherwise work is no more work*." So that upon the whole there is no place found for a middle covenant; a way of acceptance made up of man's doings, and Christ's put together. Be they blended as they will, the word of God allows no such ways, and all whom death finds thus depending, will be tried according to the covenant of works, and by it will be condemned.

Every man of this congregation, whenever death seizes him, will be tried either by the covenant of works, which requires perfect obedience, and for want of that obedience be sentenced to perish; or else by the covenant of grace, which will declare him pardoned, and eternally accepted of God. This all-important benefit of the covenant of grace results from the righteousness which it *gives* the believer, and not from any works of righteousness that he has done. For "blessed is the man to whom God imputeth righteousness without works." But it is a righteousness perfectly adequate to the demands of the law, being the righteousness of Jesus, who "is the end of the law for righteousness to every

* Rom. xi. 6.

one that believeth." Whatever the law requires or threatens; whatever it orders or inflicts; the believer depends upon Jesus alone to fulfil its demands, and to save him from its curse. He dares not undertake one jot of the matter; any more since his conversion than before. If he allows himself in hope from his own doings, he changes his plea for life; "he is of the works of the law, and is under a curse." But while he trusts in the Saviour as surety to his servant for good, HE, the surety of the better covenant, will never fail him. "The mountains may depart and the hills be removed, but my kindness shall not depart from thee, nor shall the covenant of my peace be removed; saith the Lord that hath mercy on thee." In brief, then, both a deliverance from the curse, and a right and title to life eternal, is granted to the believer through what the Lord Jesus did and suffered in the days of his flesh, beginning with his incarnation, and ending with his resurrection; and all this becomes the believer's own by imputation.

Enough has been said to show what is meant by "the righteousness of God and our Saviour." Should any think this strange, and very different from what man would naturally imagine, it may be granted, without affecting the credibility of the gospel report. We may well suppose the way of acceptance before God would be widely different from what man would naturally imagine. "For as the heavens are higher than the earth, so are my ways higher than your ways, and my thoughts than your thoughts." The fifth chapter of the Epistle to the Romans explains to you whose this righteousness is. The tenth chapter explains the doctrine of the two covenants, and in these two chapters all I have said may be found in as express words as you can well desire. Let us hear the apostle himself, in the third chapter of his Epistle to the Philippians, express his own dependance for salvation. Though touching the righteousness which is in the law, he had been blameless, he suffered the loss of all things, and counted them but dung, that he might win Christ, and be found in him, " not having mine own righteousness, which is of the law, but that which is through the faith of Christ, the righteousness which is of God by faith."

The next question is, " What is that precious faith by which a man makes this righteousness his own?" We have seen that if men ever be accounted righteous in God's view, it must be by a righteousness not their own. The righteousness of Christ must be pleaded before God, and by this alone can they be accepted at last. But still the question recurs, how shall we obtain it? To the distressed, burdened, repenting sinner, who would gladly possess this righteousness, and who cannot rest without the assured knowledge of it, to such an one, I say, (those who are otherwise minded will not regard it) a very ample direction is given by the same apostle. " Say not in thine heart, who shall ascend into heaven, that is to bring down Christ, or who shall descend into the deep, that is to bring up Christ again from the dead." Give not way to such distrustful thoughts: there needs not any thing new to be done by Christ for you: He has come down from heaven; he has gone through the work of performing a righteousness for you, finished by his resurrection.

" The word is nigh thee even in thy mouth and in thy heart; that is the word of faith which we preach. That if thou shalt confess with thy mouth the Lord Jesus, and shalt believe in thine heart that God hath raised him from the dead, thou shalt be saved. For with the heart man believeth unto righteousness; and with the mouth confession is made unto salvation. For the Scripture saith, whosoever believeth in him shall not be ashamed*."

This is the answer to our second question, " what is this precious faith?" You see it is the receiving of this gift of righteousness in Christ. " They which receive abundance of grace and the gift of righteousness." Faith itself no more will justify a man than works. It justifies only as it receives Christ's justifying righteousness. Well then may it be called PRECIOUS. It is the closing act of the soul, by which she receives Christ, becomes one with him, and partakes of all his saving benefits, besides this of his righteousness. For he who has one benefit of redemption, has them all in right and title. Inestimably great as all this salvation of the gospel is; wonderfully joyful as its tidings are, which we preach to you, Jesus can do no mighty works where unbelief prevails. According to men's faith, so it is unto them. BELIEVE, that is, receive Christ heartily, (men will not do so till they see and feel themselves perfectly helpless and miserable without him) and Christ with his righteousness and eternal life, is yours.

If I need say any thing more to show the preciousness of faith, (its nature has been shown)

* Rom. x. 8—11.

I would carry myself and you to a sick-bed, a dying hour. What is the comfort of the dying saint, think you? Is it a life well spent here? Ah! no: this is nothing to build on. St. Paul has called his well spent life dung in this view. So it is. Observe the remarkable passage at the close of 1 *Cor.* 15, " the sting of death is sin, and the strength of sin is the law; but thanks be to God, which giveth us the victory through our Lord Jesus Christ." In this faith a Christian has been taught to be stedfast and immovable, and hence to abound in the work of the Lord, knowing that his labour shall not be in vain in the Lord. The fruits of faith in good works will be rewarded in eternity, according to their quantity. But they would be of no avail in taking away the sting of death. That which makes death terrible is sin; and that which makes sin terrible is the law, condemning it. But he thanks God who has given him the victory through Jesus's righteousness. He has satisfied the law. Hence sin is taken away, as to any power of condemning him, for that is the meaning of the passage. By this alone the sting of death is drawn. Oh! happy soul, that dies thus in Christ. " Let me die the death of the righteous, and let my last end be like his."

When men come to a death-bed, they may see that that faith is precious which thus takes hold of a precious Christ, and enables a believer to leave the world, and go to the Father, in his name. But, ah! what right have those to expect the Christian's comfort in death, who in life have despised that which disarms death of its sting? Justly is it said that they have no right to expect to die like the righteous, who will not lead his life, and his life is altogether a life of faith in Christ.

3d. It remains to consider " whence this faith is to be obtained." For the apostle speaks to them who have obtained this ".precious faith in the righteousness of our Saviour." It is not derived from men: for " there is none that understandeth, there is none that seeketh after God," by nature. It is obtained from above, being the gift of the Holy Ghost; for the natural man discerneth not the things of the Spirit of God; to him they are foolishness. Hear how the apostle prays for this gift of faith in behalf of the Ephesians: " Peace be to the brethren, and love with faith from God the Father and the Lord Jesus Christ." " To you it is given," says the apostle, speaking to the Philippians, " in the behalf of Christ to believe on him." If any would hear our Lord himself speak on the subject, they may hear him, *John* vi. " No man can come to me, except the Father, which hath sent me, draw him." To the unbelieving Jews he says, " ye believe not, because ye are not of my sheep: my sheep hear my voice, and I know them, and they follow me." Then after giving them precious faith in their Redeemer, he takes care, in his glorious faithfulness, to ensure to them all the happy consequences. " And I give unto them eternal life, and they shall never perish, neither shall any pluck them out of my hand."

Thus have I, my brethren, briefly and plainly considered, according to the Scriptures, (and if this will be of any weight with men, according to the articles and homilies of the Church of England) the three questions implied in the text. I have set forth to you what that righteousness is by which alone a man is entitled to expect eternal life. And by all Scripture it appears to be, not any thing done in a man, or by a man at all, but the righteousness of Christ received as a free gift, by a guilty fallen sinner, without the least mixture of dependance on his own works, even the very best of them.—2d. What this faith is which receives this righteousness, and is deservedly called PRECIOUS. Our Reformers found it so. By it, as the instrument of receiving and enjoying a precious Christ, they emerged out of Popery, and transmitted to us the doctrines of the gospel, for which they glorified God in the fires.— 3d. Whence this precious faith is to be obtained, and it appears to be the gift of the Holy Spirit alone.

I trust there are some souls before me, who know these things to be true in experience. You were made restless and uneasy in your consciences. You became more and more sensible of your wretched, undone, perishing condition. You found your very natures depraved, and notwithstanding all the pains you took to work out a righteousness to appease your consciences, you could not.—Perfection you saw was what the law required, and the more enlarged your understandings were concerning the extent and strictness of the law, the farther distant from perfection you found yourselves. Gladly did you hear of Jesus Christ, " the end of the law for righteousness to every one that believeth." You then found that to be delivered from wrath, and to enjoy eternal life, you needed precious faith; and when you strove to believe in Christ, you found you had not a heart for it. Then, at last, you learnt that faith was the gift of God, and that you never really had been believers in Christianity. You prayed heartily for the Holy Spirit, which our Saviour taught you to ask; and in God's time you believed, rejoicing in the Lord. HE became your glory and boast. " Blessed are ye who know the joyful sound: ye shall walk in the light of God's countenance: your delight shall be daily in his name, and in his righteousness shall you make your boast: for he *is* the glory of your strength, and in his loving-kindness he shall lift up your horns. The Lord is your defence, the Holy One of Israel is your King."

So rich a subject as this, the very fundamental of our Christianity, and without which the gospel is a mere name, deserves our most serious consideration; and I am persuaded would be more regarded than it is, if men would think more deeply of death and judgment, of sin, and the holiness of God. But while men have a slight view of sin, and think that a merciful God will readily pardon their enormities, which they please to call frailties, they go on contented with a round of external duties, which they make their righteousness. All this time their hearts are wedded to the pomps and vanities of this wicked world; so that there is a certain previous view of things which every man must have, before he will heartily relish, much less comfortably experience, the gospel-truths I have set forth.

A man ought to know, that sin deserves death eternal. He ought to be affected in some worthy manner with the view of the infinite majesty and greatness of God. He ought to be practically convinced, that God's ways and thoughts are so much above ours, as to make it no sort of presumptive proof against a doctrine's being true, that it contains in it things hard of digestion to us. He ought to give over making so audaciously free with the mercy of God, as too many do; and to open his eyes, and behold in the world many dreadful symptoms of his divine wrath against sin, displayed even in the present scene of things. And if he considers how severely sin is often punished in this world, in long, awful, and horrible inflictions, he may justly suspect that there is something in sin not so slight as he apprehended. A good and gracious God, "whose mercy is over all his works," would not punish it so severely as he does, even here, if it were not an infinite evil.

He will find reason then to ask seriously, when he views himself a sinner, and makes any observation on the greatness and number of his sins, "What must I do to be saved?" If he looks abroad into the world, notwithstanding the flattering view of it which too many writers have given, he will find that matter of fact proves it as a wicked and a miserable world, in a state of war and enmity against God. Yet it is utterly inconceivable that such a vain, wicked, miserable world could have originally been formed in the state it now is in: it must have been thus degraded, by the just punishment of God for sin, in consequence of the fall of Adam.

Reflections of this kind (says the late judicious Bishop Butler) are not without their terrors to serious persons, the most free from enthusiasm, and of the greatest strength of mind: but it is fit things be stated, and considered as they really are. There is in the present age a certain fearlessness with regard to what may be hereafter under the government of God, which makes it quite necessary that men be reminded, and, if possible, made to *feel*, that there is no sort of ground for being thus presumptuous. For may it not be said of any person, upon his being born into the world, that he may behave so as to be of no service in it, but by being made an example of the terrible effects of vice and folly? And is there any pretence of reason, for people to think themselves secure, and talk as if they had certain proof, that, let them act as licentiously as they will, there can be nothing analogous to this, with regard to a future and more general interest, under the providence and government of the same God?— What other use is to be made of these striking observations of this very judicious author, and of many more such awful observations as may be made, than that to escape hell, and to obtain heaven, deserves to be thought of most intensely by us all!

Surely it is not enough for a man to say, we must do our best, and then God's mercies may be hoped for. This is a wretched plan of religion. Here are no distinct resting-places for the weary soul; no decisive instruction for a bewildered mind; no guidance and comfort for a burdened conscience. I am persuaded, that none but careless people, however decent they may be in outward conduct, can rest in such views as these. They whose minds have been previously exercised with careful thought, and who have obtained a just sight of human corruption and wickedness, as well as of the Divine greatness and purity, will never rest in a general notion of a Saviour, and call *that* Christian faith. For is it not plain, that immense numbers, who profess this general notion, are as unhappy in sin, and as enslaved in corruption, as deists, or those who avowedly disregard Christianity altogether? But the faith of the gospel is the instrument of all sanctification, which I have not considered in this discourse, as well as of justification, which I have been considering. It is called a PRECIOUS thing in my text, and exceeding great things indeed are said in Scripture to be the effect of it—nothing less than the being born again, the total change of a man's state before God, and the bringing him into happiness out of misery. Now may not I appeal to too many, that they know of no such effects of their faith? May not too many justly say, certainly I have not the right Christianity, because I know no good it has done me?

My brethren, a general notion of Christ is not that which the Scripture calls faith in Christ, neither will it be of any more service to a sinner than a general notion of a physician will be to a sick man. The people who were bitten by serpents in the wilderness were not cured by A GENERAL NOTION of the brazen serpent which Moses made. There was a particular looking at the object required of each wounded man, and then the good effect ensued. Thus are we to obtain the healing of our souls. For " as Moses lifted up the serpent in the wilderness, even so must the son of man be lifted up, that whosoever believeth in him should not perish, but have eternal life."

This, then, is the advantage to be derived from those awful, affecting, and if you please *melancholy*, but true views of our sin and misery, which I have said are necessary to make a man relish true Christianity. They lower a man's pride, and cure him of all hope from his own works. They show a man the inefficacy of all general notions of religion, and of Christian faith. They prepare a man to receive the real gospel. I have no doubt but every person who is seriously affected with the actual state of human nature, will receive the righteousness of Christ as the very thing that is calculated to relieve his soul. Despised it may and will be by too many; but they are only the careless, the proud, the deluded votaries of this world, who have no abiding conviction of the value of eternity and their need of a Saviour.

I may ask such, did you ever feel and deeply consider the need that you, in particular, have of a Saviour? Were your hearts ever humbled and affected with the thought of your deserving hell? Did sin ever appear to you in such a light, your own sins in particular, as to make you see the propriety; adore the wisdom; be humbled before the holiness; and admire the goodness of that way of God, by which he sent his Son to redeem us? Then, in the view of his righteousness, and the utter want of any in yourself, did you, as in the case of those bitten by serpents, did you receive this gift of righteousness? Did you make it your own by faith? This is Christianity indeed, taken out of the dead line of general notions, and applied to particular use. You may well call this faith PRECIOUS, you obtained it from above. By it you rest in Christ your Redeemer. You are completely recovered, in title and by divine promise, as we have seen, and will in fact be more and more recovered, from the evil and ruin of the fall. Eternal life awaits you in the world to come, and joy unmixed, uninterrupted in your God for ever and ever. You can say a good word for Christ, as the physician of a sick soul, by experience.—But if you are void of these things, you are yet under the condemning covenant of works, the gift of righteousness in Christ, by which alone a man can obtain eternal life, is not yours, and if death seize you thus, judgment without mercy will overtake you.

I have delivered the gospel doctrine and application of it. To those who have received it, I would say, rejoice alway in the Lord, and live up to your privileges—To those who have not, I say, " repent ye and believe the gospel."—But after men have thus believed, have they nothing to do? Ah! yes: much. If they be spared to live any time on earth, very much. I have described only the door, the entrance of Christianity, in this discourse. If you will hear, I will endeavour, as God shall help me, to go on with a course of Sermons on the progress of religion. At present, be this observed. Let not men over drive either themselves or others. Are you clearly instructed in the fundamental doctrine of the righteousness of Christ, and precious faith in that as all your justification, for ever, before God? If you be steadily placed on this foundation, go on and build, and you shall grow up an holy temple to the Lord. If not, do what you will besides, you build castles in the air; for " other foundation can no man lay, than that is laid, which is Jesus Christ."

SERMON IV.

PARDON AND PEACE OBTAINED BY FAITH.

Nahum i. 7.

The Lord is good, a strong hold in the day of trouble; and he knoweth them that trust in him.

This beautiful description of the grace and goodness of the Lord, and the way in which he exercises it, interrupts the horror of the vengeful scenes of Nineveh's desolation. It is like the refreshing influence of some momentary beams of the sun on a cloudy tempestuous day. Such a gleam gladdens the face of nature, and bears her a comfortable witness, amidst the gloom, that the Lord has not forsaken her, and that by the power of the sun, even when its sensible light is withdrawn, he still preserves her from hopeless darkness, and gives an earnest of the restoration of its visible and genial influence.

How comfortable, to the soul that longs for the light of God's countenance, to be informed, that the same God who is described in such colours of terrible and glorious holiness, through these three chapters, is yet " good, a strong hold in the day of trouble, and that he knoweth them that trust in him?"

But how can such seeming opposites, as we so very frequently meet with in the Old Testament, in the description of the attributes of God, be reconciled, and each maintained in full force with full consistency? Nothing can be conceived so tremendous as the character of God, when described in the pomp of his greatness, the keen penetration of his wisdom, the thunder of his power, and the awful dignity of his justice. Again, what can be conceived so benevolent and gracious as the same God, when represented infinitely merciful, that pardoneth iniquity, and that delighteth in mercy? Surely in Christ alone these seeming jarring views of the Divinity can be reconciled. God out of Christ is he, whom the whole human race have offended, since "the imaginations of the thoughts of men's hearts are only evil continually." His essential justice and holiness, then, form the basis of the tremendous descriptions of God; and such is God to the carnal and self-righteous, to those who remain in a state of nature. God in Christ reconciling to himself a sinful world, is that gracious and merciful Being, who to the believer is a loving and tender father, engaged to do him good.

In vain then shall the self-righteous, the careless, and the unhumbled take to themselves the comfortable views of God in the text. A God of absolute mercy to sinful men, as we are, would be a God unjust. When therefore we have such a view of God as this, "the Lord is good, a strong hold in the day of trouble, and he knoweth them that trust in him," let us cast our eyes on God sustaining this character, and exalted upon a throne of grace through the mediation of Jesus Christ our Lord.

To you, then, who desire to renounce yourselves, and are looking to and longing for Jesus as your portion and your ALL, I would, with God's blessing, exhibit this view of God in Christ which the text affords us. The Lord by his Spirit shine into our hearts, and give us to taste and see how gracious the Lord is.

I shall not spend your time in considering the particular occasion of introducing the passage of the text. Most probably it was intended to console the pious subjects of Hezekiah, who had lately suffered under the invasion of Sennacherib. Be that as it may, the view of God in Christ here is a general description, and therefore to be applied, by the people of God, in all ages. Let us be well assured, that God cannot consistently with his justice appear to fallen sinners in this comfortable character, but in and through Christ. Let us then endeavour to apply to ourselves, in the most profitable, that is, in the most general manner, the day of trouble here spoken of—the goodness of the Lord here spoken of—how he is a strong hold—how this goodness is applied by faith—and the happy privileges of the believer.—When we have done this, with the Lord's help, we may then very briefly draw a few inferences suitable to the cases of different persons.

Is there a soul here who has seen the character of God as set forth in the words a little before my text? " God is jealous, and the Lord revengeth; the Lord revengeth and is furious; he is great in power, and will not at all acquit the wicked." Then such a one knows what it is to be convinced of sin by God's Holy Spirit. He has been made to see the sinfulness of his nature, as well as of his practices. The tumult of restless guilt now fiercely disturbs the conscience. A broken law is continually calling for satisfaction. He finds all his efforts, to give peace to his conscience, vain.

Here is, then, " the day of trouble" indeed. Formerly, while the man was ignorant of the law of God and his own heart, he was at ease in false peace. His own righteousness, either acquired already, if he was a sober moralist, or intended to be acquired before he died, if a gross sinner; this appeared to him quite sufficient to give peace to his conscience, and such a hope to be saved, as satisfied his mind. But now he is humbled under a sense of his sinfulness; now he finds he needs a present peace, a present sense of forgiveness of his sins, not only in order for the present comfort and quiet of his mind, but also in order to love God, and enable him to obey his laws, in an acceptable manner. What shall he do? shall he hearken to men of this world, who advise him to stifle his uneasiness in carnal pleasures and sensual gratifications? His relish for these things is lost. They may be the means of continuing a state of stupefaction in them who are fast asleep in sin. They can give no ease to him, whose conscience feels the intolerable load of guilt, and who is incapable of pleasure, till guilt is truly removed. They may add to his trouble; they can do nothing to remove it. Shall he try to pacify conscience by amending for the future? Well assured, from God's word he his, that the very attempt would confound him.

Not only those that live in avowed contempt of the law, but those who are " of the works of the law," that is, labour to be saved by their works, are under the curse; for " cursed is every one that continueth not in all things written in the book of the law to do them." Shall he hearken to his worldly friends, who would dissuade him from real religion, through fear of losing his bread or his character? What is bread or character to a soul in distress like this? Of what consequence are all worldly advantages put together, to the man that stands on the brink of hell, and who is seeking for the favour of God, and longing for everlasting life? Shall he regard the reasonings of modern, unscriptural writers on divinity, who assure him, that man is not corrupt by nature, that he is very well able to save himself by good resolutions and endeavours? Let not worldly men be surprised, that all their reasonings are lost on the man we are describing. How can he believe himself able to save himself, when he finds he has naturally a will and resolution only to do evil? How should he have hope of salvation from sincere obedience, who finds, by palpable experience, he has no good thing in his composition, nor can have, till God give him a new heart and new spirit.

Such is "the day of trouble" to the convinced, thoroughly awakened sinner. It is the Lord's will he should feel himself beat off from every hope in himself, that he may look to the Lord alone for salvation, and give to him all the glory. If there is a man in this house who knows what this "day of trouble" means, let me assure him, that with his views of the law, of sin, and of himself, it is not possible he should ever be brought to enjoy that peace and happiness he thirsts after, by carnal pleasures, by a dependance on good morals, by pleasing the world, or by any endeavours to stifle his convictions. Let him despair of help from any of these quarters. Has not Jesus said, "in me ye shall have peace?" Yes in him, and in nothing else. " O thou afflicted, tossed with tempest, and not comforted;" in infinite mercy the Lord himself is pulling down thy strong holds, and bringing every thought of thy heart into captivity to the obedience of Christ. In attempting the right way of deliverance, thou wilt find thyself vehemently opposed by the united power of the world, the flesh, and the devil. But hearken diligently, notwithstanding, to what the Lord says concerning thee; for "he shall speak peace" to thee, that thou turn not to folly.

"The Lord is good." If he be GOOD, thou mayest come near to him with boldness, and pour out thy heart before him: it is the nature of goodness to be kind, accessible and bountiful to the needy. Be well assured "the Lord is good," and apply to him as good and kind, and thou shalt find him so to thyself. Only attend continually to the scriptural view of his goodness. The GOOD GOD which men in a state of nature look to, as one who allows men to live in sin and trample on his justice, no where exists. The GOOD GOD in Christ is to be thy God. O labour to see and know him aright, that thou mayest trust, and enjoy, and rejoice in him. For it is written, "they that know thy name will put their trust in thee; for thou, Lord, hast never failed them that seek thee. O put your trust in him alway, ye people pour out your hearts before him; for God is our hope. I will set him up, because he hath known my name." And, of such consequence is a spiritual knowledge of this good Lord, in order for a right faith, love, and enjoyment of him, that our Lord says, "this is life eternal, that they might know thee the only true God, and Jesus Christ whom thou hast sent." May the Spirit of God then shine into thy heart, " to give the light of the knowledge of the glory of God in the face of Jesus Christ;" for whoever is taught of God shall have the peace of his children.

GOODNESS is indeed essential to the character of God. While man was innocent, it was the glory of his goodness to deal bountifully with him. But the same goodness of his nature, if we consider his justice as an amiable attribute, required, that he should punish man when he rebelled. Yet mercy rejoiced over judgment here, by satisfying justice through Christ crucified; that so the goodness of God might shine to his creatures with more lustre than ever. O convinced sinner, look up then to this glorious goodness as it shines in the face of Jesus Christ. Be well assured that he offers to thee free and full pardon. What shall hinder thy obtaining it? Each of the Divine Three is exhibited in the most engaging and attractive light, to draw thy heart to a well-warranted peace with God by faith in Christ Jesus. God the Father, whose justice was offended, has received and declared his acceptance of a full satisfaction. God the Son has finished that satisfaction, and pleads it even now before the throne of grace. God the Holy Ghost has the office of quickening the soul, and applying this salvation to the conscience. Thus " the Lord is good," and thou who art thirsty, art called on and warranted, even now, without further delay, to come and taste this his goodness, by believing. Hear what the good Lord says to thee, even thee, " if any man thirst, let him come to me and drink,"

But further. "The Lord is a strong hold in the day of trouble." O troubled soul, make use of him as such; delay no longer to be happy. Thou knowest what thou wantest; and methinks I hear thee expressing thy desires in this manner, " O that I were delivered from a guilty conscience; that I had the enjoyment of redemption through Jesus's blood, even the forgiveness of sins; that I were no longer a slave, but free to enjoy God's love as a father, and serve him with a willing mind in love, walking with him in his holy ways: O that duty were a delight, and the ways of holiness a pleasure to me: O that I could come to Christ and find rest in him, and take his yoke upon me, and find it easy, and his burden light! But alas! I am so fast in prison, that I cannot get forth; guilt and unbelief, breed hardness of heart and unworthy thoughts of God, and I have no heart for duty, nor any strength to stem the corruptions and overcome the temptations that war against me."—Know, O soul, that the only remedy of all these evils is the Lord Jesus Christ believed on for all thy righteousness and strength. " The name of the Lord is a strong tower, the righteous runneth into it and is safe."

This is the " strong hold in the day of trouble." Thou canst not overcome Satan's temptations, nor enjoy the love of God, in duty, till thou flee into this strong hold. Thou hast a burdensome load of guilt on thy conscience. Thou wilt never find the load taken off, and peace and joy filling thy heart, but in one single way. That way must be God's, not thy own; and thou must depend only on God's wondrous way of effecting this. In truth Jesus is the peace. Thou must flee to him and trust him alone for it, and with all thy heart. Then guilt shall as surely be taken off from thee as it was laid upon him; as he bore it, and as he made an end of sin by his all-sufficient atonement. When guilt is gone, God's love will kindle thine. For "faith worketh by love." Then thy end and motive of duty will be the glory of God and the love of God. Then being one with Christ by faith, thou shalt share in his victory over the devil, the world, and the flesh.

Over the devil. Thy shield of faith shall quench his fiery darts, and thou shalt be able to repel his temptations. Over the world. The love of God shall shine to thee so sweet, so amiable, so soul-transforming, that thy affections shall be engaged to God, and deadened to this earth. Hence covetousness and earthly-mindedness shall be subdued, and in the school of Christ thou shalt learn the practice of charity, humility, and kindness to thy fellow-creatures. Over the flesh. For the power of God's Holy Spirit shall crucify it with its affections and lusts. Self shall be dethroned, and Christ shall reign in thy heart, and bring thy thoughts into captivity to himself. Thus the Lord Christ will be thy strong hold. Let thy guilt be ever so dreadful, when thou really receivest him, he shall give thee peace. Let thy corruptions be ever so mighty, they shall fall down before the power of his grace.

But further: There must be a closing act of faith in Christ, in order to receive and enjoy all this salvation. "He knoweth them that trust in him." That is, he owns and takes notice of such, and will surely give them the things they trust in him for. There is one of the collects of our church which very excellently illustrates the order of things in the plan of christian experience. Let us attend to it a little. " Grant, we beseech thee, merciful Lord, to thy faithful people, pardon and peace; that they may be cleansed from all their sins, and serve thee with a quiet mind, through Jesus Christ our Lord." You will find this to be the collect for the one-and-twentieth Sunday after Trinity. Here we see how well acquainted our Reformers were with that vital religion from which we have so dreadfully apostatized. For the profession of it in our days seems a strange, whimsical, singular thing in the eye of the world.

First, here is faith in Jesus supposed—" thy faithful people"—which is the same thing as what is called by the prophet " trusting in the Lord." Then here is " pardon" to the faithful, or believers, and pardon through the atonement alone of Jesus Christ. Then here is " peace," that is, the manifestation of this pardon sealed in heaven, to the believing soul, by suitable peace of conscience granted to the believer. For to the believer the Holy Spirit is granted, and the " fruits of the Spirit are love, joy, PEACE." Besides " PARDON and PEACE" being evidently two distinct things prayed for in this collect, and the meaning of the word pardon being doubtless the blotting out of all transgressions, as if they had never been committed, what could the composers of the prayer mean by PEACE, but the knowledge and sense of that pardon in the conscience; and so far were they from agreeing with those who describe good works as the cause instead of the fruits of faith, that they pray for this peace, to the end that they may be cleansed from all their sins, and serve God with a quiet mind: plainly showing that they would have people to look for the experience of this peace in the present life. Agreeable to this is the apostle's prayer for the believing Romans; " the God of hope fill you with all joy and peace in believing, that ye may abound in hope through the power of the Holy Ghost."

By this time the precious effects of believing in Jesus are plain and evident. Here is " pardon, peace, cleansing from all sins, and serving God" in all holiness of living " with a quiet mind." Thus does the Lord " know them that trust in him."

Since, then, O convinced sinner! " the Lord is good," and invites thee to come to him as " a stronghold;" and since these are the precious effects of believing in the Lord Jesus Christ, thou seest what thou hast to do, even to come to Christ without any delay. We set before you, brethren, Christ crucified as the sovereign remedy for all who are in spiritual trouble. We are warranted, by God, to exhort you to make use of him and to try him, and him alone, for the obtaining of true peace, joy, and holiness; of support in death, and in the end, everlasting life. There is no way of trying him and applying this Saviour but by believing, or depending on him; or to use the phrase of the text, by TRUSTING HIM. Receive him, then, O convinced sinners! Why tarry you? Arise, and wash away your guilt by faith in his blood. Do not put off this work of believing till to-morrow. Set yourselves earnestly to taste and see how gracious this Lord is immediately. " Blessed is the man that trusteth in him." Jesus also said, "he that believeth on me hath everlasting life."

Yes: You who have tried this remedy of trusting in Jesus, know its effects. You know this alone has purged your consciences; subdued your hearts; given you true joy and peace, and liberty; and enabled you to walk in God's commands with love. It has broken the force of your evil habits, and taught you to live soberly, righteously, and godly in this present world. It has made you to love and praise the Lord with all your souls.

I have now finished what I proposed. I have set forth the day of spiritual trouble; how GOOD the Lord is; what a "strong hold," and how he owns, and blesses, and sanctifies them that trust in him, and I have exhorted the convinced sinner to receive this Saviour without delay. But I fear there may be some here who despise this precious gift of faith in Christ; and the reason of their despising it is, because they are without spiritual feeling; they have no trouble nor care for their souls; they are dead in sin. If, however, there be any weight in the united testimony of the best and wisest in all ages, they should consider that the reality of such conviction and conversion as I have spoken of, has the sanction of the best witnesses. And to spare the mention of others at this time, I will only mention once more our Reformers, and repeat again that short collect of our church, to which they often say—Amen—" Grant, we beseech thee, merciful Lord, to thy faithful people, pardon and peace; that they may be cleansed from all their sins, and serve thee with a quiet mind, through Jesus Christ our Lord."

SERMON V.

THE SINFUL LUSTS OF THE FLESH OVERCOME BY FAITH.

2 Peter, i. 4.

Whereby are given unto us exceeding great and precious promises; that by these ye might be partakers of the divine nature, having escaped the corruption that is in the world through lust.

It is as true in spiritual as it is in worldly things, that the sense of want and necessity leads men to useful discoveries. In proportion as this sense increases, the soul is led on to acquire those advantages which may supply its wants, and in the natural progress of such exertion to obtain even blessings and conveniences, which were unexpected. Thus suppose (but I hope and trust it will one day be found to be more than a supposition) that there are persons here who, through the sense of guilt, and of bondage in sin, were led to Christ and the knowledge of his righteousness; that they, in wrestling with God, " obtained precious faith," whereby they received this righteousness; that they found " grace and peace multiplied on them through the knowledge of Christ;" had a soul-cheering view of " all things pertaining to life and godliness," being freely given them through this knowledge; and of the happy end, ETERNAL GLORY, " unto which they were kept by the power of God through faith:" Persons thus favoured of the Lord, must be sensible, that by the sense of want, which he kindly gave them, grievous though it was, they were led to pray, to seek, to inquire, "is there any rest; any light; any peace; any real victory over these devouring evils to be obtained?" That there is, and even much more than what is sufficient to supply their wants, the Lord has shown them by experience. Thus he led them to gospel-peace, and the enjoyment of divine love.

But now, since that time, especially if they gave way to pride, or to trifling, or to the love of the world, they have been led (still it is in a way of mercy on God's part) to a discovery of fresh wants. They have deeper views than ever of the enmity, idolatry, self-righteousness, unbelief, and rebellion of their hearts. Lusts and evil tempers, which, while God was filling them with peace and joy in believing, they fancied had been quite dead, or, at least, so subdued as never again to give them much trouble, they find, to their grief and astonishment, are strong and stubborn. Nay, from an increasing view of the nature of sin, and the extent of duty, they appear stronger than ever. Darkness also, and ignorance of God; of true pleasure; of duty; of all things which it concerns them to know, may overspread the soul. Temptations may harass; may overpower them at times, and if they have been looking more at the things done in them by the Spirit, and more pleased with the gift than with the source from whence all good proceeds, no wonder they are discouraged exceedingly, and give way to thoughts of much heaviness. Still however all will be well, notwithstanding their fears. They have brought forth true fruit, though defiled with far more evil than they were aware of during their pleasant experience: God is purging them, that they may bring forth more fruit. What they have felt of the plague of their own hearts, may help to cure that censorious spirit, that readiness to condemn, by rash judging, persons who were better christians than themselves. They will have less self-conceit, be less hasty in their determinations, have a less opinion of their own understanding, and in all respects be advanced in grace. The sense of wants still deeper and stronger than ever, should lead to deeper views of the riches of Christ their Saviour.

In a manner very suitable to the state of such persons, St. Peter goes on to show how they may grow in all sanctification, by faith, in the same manner as he had shown how we are to receive justification by faith. Hence we learn more and more of the riches of Christ. For it is not striving and watching, however earnest and sincere, that will give a man the victory over his sins, and renew him in the spirit of his mind. The world, the flesh, and the devil, will be too hard for him, unless he strive in the one only lawful way, set forth in the text; "whereby are given unto us exceeding great and precious promises; that by these ye might be partakers of the divine nature, having escaped the corruption that is in the world through lust." Here is the true secret of living happy, and above sin. Let us endeavour to illustrate the point a little; for the benefit of believers, and then apply it plainly to the unconverted.

You, then, who have known the Lord, do yet find your lusts and corruptions too hard for you, and till they are subdued you are miserable. Remember that a divine nature, by grace imparted, is that which is absolutely necessary for the overcoming the old. Give over depending upon yourself. Sit down in self-despair, and turn your eye simply to the true and only source of health. You have a High Priest in the heavens, the surety of the new covenant, which is established on better promises than the old. When the apostle says, " there are given unto us exceeding great and precious promises," remember that Christ is the surety of them all, engaged to make them good. By these promises, that is, by trusting in them, and expecting the fulfilment of them, you are to be " made partakers of the divine nature," with all its parts and members, in actual experience. You must believe then : yea : believe in Christ, and rest on him for the fulfilment of these promises, and they shall all be made good to you. When you want any particular lust subduing, or evil temper mortifying; strength, light, and comfort, in time of need, the way to obtain it is to fix on some passage of Scripture, which promises the blessing, in the name of Christ. Then look to Christ, and apply to him for it. As for the rest, it remains with our Saviour. When he shall cease to be faithful to his promises, and true to his character as Surety for all good to them who believe on him, then you will fail of the wished-for success ; but not till then.

There is the more necessity for this faith in

Christ respecting sanctification in all its parts, because though you may have trusted him, in general, for your whole salvation, yet if you do not actually depend on him for the mortification of particular besetting sins, you will find their power very formidable to you. The world you are in is evil. It corrupts you by its temptations through the lust, that is, the evil nature which remains even in the regenerate. In Christ there is strength and power promised, that sin shall not have dominion over you. And this is one of the most precious promises which belong to those who are not under the law, but under grace. You feel yourselves entirely unable to escape this corruption that is in the world, through lust. Reflect that in Christ there are "exceeding great and precious promises, that by these," by faith in these, "you might be partakers of the divine nature," the image of God, the mind that was in the man Christ Jesus, in all parts of his lovely image, and so escape this corruption of the world which tempts you through the lusts of the flesh. It remains then that you put the Lord in mind of these promises, and wait on him for their fulfilment. By this method you will find meekness to prevail over anger; patience over impatience; divine fortitude over cowardice; long-suffering over malice; kindness and liberality over covetousness and selfishness; heavenly-mindedness over the love of the world; and to say all in a word, love over hatred.—This is to put on the Lord Jesus Christ by faith, and to "make not provision for the flesh to fulfil the lusts thereof."

I scarcely know how to be sufficiently plain and

full in clearing up this point. However earnest we be against sin, and sensible of its evil and misery, yet without a real application for grace, to Christ, as the surety of the new covenant, with all its precious promises, which the text speaks of, we shall find we have no power to mortify a single lust, nor to bring forth one christian fruit. I suspect that some godly souls who look to Christ with simplicity of faith for pardon, do not with equal simplicity of faith look to him for holiness. They lose the sight of the Saviour here—May my text be the means of directing them aright. There is but one condition of our whole salvation from first to last: it is believing on the Son of God for it. Learn then, amidst the misery which your sin gives you, to prize Christ, and to make a simple use of him, by faith, for victory over the whole body of sin. Lust it will, as I apprehend; till death it will exist in us. But continued victory, by believing, is to be obtained. And, to this end, be well versed in Scripture. View all the precious promises which St. Peter speaks of: he means particularly the Old Testament promises. All these promises are in Christ, " yea and Amen, to the glory of God by us." They are all yours. Believe with respect to each of them, and you will find, as your wants lead you to them, each of them will be fulfilled to you.

I know nothing more needs to be said as to the practical and comfortable use of this subject. But it may be necessary to point out to you a few of these Old Testament promises, given for the purpose, that are remarkably precious and comprehensive. By exercising faith on these you may, notwithstanding the body of sin dwelling in you, obtain an established, comfortable frame of soul; a real and universal progress in all holiness, and a proof that the ways of wisdom are ways of pleasantness, and paths of peace. Nor should we rest contented without the attainment of such a practical establishment in Christianity, in this life, as well as the completion of it in the life to come.

A very precious promise you have, *Ezek.* xxxvi. 25, 26, 27. " Then will I sprinkle clean water upon you, and ye shall be clean: from all your filthiness, and from all your idols, will I cleanse you. A new heart also will I give you, and a new spirit will I put within you: and I will take away the stony heart out of your flesh, and I will give you an heart of flesh. And I will put my Spirit within you, and cause you to walk in my statutes, and ye shall keep my judgments, and do them." He only can conceive the preciousness of such a promise, who feeling, indeed, the miserable and vile idolatry of his nature, and his own helplessness in sin, comes to God in Christ with the promise, saying, " Lord, glorify this thy grace on me, let the Father be glorified in the Son," and who in patient believing finds, as all by patient believing shall find, the promise fulfilled in the conquest of sin and hell, and in bringing every lust and evil temper into captivity to the obedience of Christ.

Here is another promise made in Christ to believers. The apostle, in *Heb.* viii. where he is describing the new covenant, quotes it from *Jeremiah*. " I will put my laws into their mind, and write them in their hearts, and I will be to them a God, and they shall be to me a people; and they shall not teach every man his neighbour, and every man his brother, saying, know the Lord, for all shall know me, from the least to the greatest. For I will be merciful to their unrighteousness, and their sins and their iniquities will I remember no more." What an all-comprehensive promise! in which Christ the King, the Prophet and the Priest appears. How is this to be yours, O believer? By believing. There is no other condition. The nature of the thing shows it. In yourself dwelleth no good thing. You can bring nothing to God to merit his favour, or buy of him these great blessings. He is satisfied with Christ alone, who has discharged all conditions for you. What, indeed, is there in the way of condition, which you, in your own strength, are required to perform? Whatever you can conceive as necessary to be done, strength for the doing of it is here promised of God as a free gift. It is then by such promises as these, fully depended on, that St. Peter tells you, ye shall be "made partakers of the divine nature, and escape the corruption that is in the world through lust."

I will mention a promise or two more, which at the same time that they engage for your sanctification, ensure to you also your full and free salvation. "I will bring the blind by a way that they knew not. I will lead them in paths that they have not known. These things will I do unto them, and not forsake them." If, O believer, you are afraid that you shall not persevere in holiness, hear another passage in Scripture, in which the Lord promises that you *shall* persevere. He will prevent you, by his fear in your hearts, from abusing his grace in licentiousness. " I will make an everlasting covenant with them, that I will not turn away from them to do them good; but I will put my fear in their hearts, that they shall not depart from me." *Jeremiah* xxxii. 40. Oh! precious promise! I cannot but think St. Peter had such promises particularly in his eye when he wrote the words of the text. May every believing soul, in humble faith, drop all prejudice, and admit all the everlasting consolation, which should result from such a promise!

I add two more precious promises, delivered by our Lord, in the days of his flesh. " Whosoever drinketh of the water that I shall give him, shall never thirst, but the water that I shall give him shall be in him a well of water springing up into everlasting life." *John* iv. 13, 14. The use of such a promise is this: Do you find yourself weary, longing for happiness; wandering from object to object, yet restless? If you will drink of the water of life which Christ bestows freely on all thirsty souls, you shall find what will quench your thirst, and satisfy you. You shall live freely to God in holy, pleasant obedience, and enjoy him everlastingly. Again, " I am come a light into the world, that whosoever believeth on me should not abide in darkness." *John* xii. 46. Are you dark in your soul; uncertain what to seek after, what to do, what to avoid? Stick fast by Jesus, make him your confidence. This darkness shall not remain; you shall have satisfying light.

Having given, perhaps, a sufficient specimen of the manner of handling the " exceeding great and precious promises" of Scripture, by faith in Jesus, and set forth the pleasant and blessed effect of them in producing a healthy, victorious, divine nature, by which we escape the corruption that is in the world through lust; I would apply also to unbelievers, to careless people, the directions of the text. May God lead them also to Christ, that they may be real christians, and partake of the blessings of redemption. But how shall I speak to them? How shall they be made to feel their state, to own themselves unbelievers, and careless people? Ezekiel was bid to prophesy unto dry bones; and while I speak a few words unto them, the Lord can send them with power to their hearts; infix the arrows of deep conviction, and make them earnestly inquire " What must we do to be saved?"

Will you take notice of the text? There are " precious promises" given in Christ Jesus, " by which you may be made partakers of the divine nature, and escape the corruption that is in the world through lust." Will you see, that this corruption reigns over you; that you are slaves of sin? Some of you can scarcely speak a word without cursing and swearing. Others of you place all your delight in drunkenness and lewdness. Some of you, perhaps, come to church once or twice at this season*, who have lived, in general, all the year round without any attendance on public worship at all. You have not a spark of love to Christ, have no idea of thanking God, from the heart, for sending such a Saviour into the world. You care not for God; you pray not to him; you taunt those who do, and call them by reproachful names. Some of you may be rather in genteel and decent circumstances: God has given you success in this world, and the more

---

* Christmas.

you have prospered, the prouder have you grown. You have set your heart more and more on the world, become fond of its pomps and vanities, and are still greedy of gain, and as eager to get more money, as if you had reason to fear you should starve for want of bread. You have not, in life and conversation, shown gratitude and thankfulness to God; but have lived in your sins, notwithstanding all that he has done for you.

Others of you, O wicked, unconverted men! are poor, and perhaps have suffered many afflictions in your time; but they have not yet brought you to a stedfast, serious thought for your soul. You have not been thankful to God for the narrow escapes which he has favoured you with. It may be you have several times been in great danger of perishing by sea: then, in extremity, you prayed for mercy, and formed resolutions, in your mind, how good you would be, if you were spared. For if you thought seriously, you could not but think you were very unfit to die. Yet after you were delivered, you thought no more of it. You drank, you swore, and were as profane as ever.

Let me speak also to you who labour at the public works about this town, if there be any such here. Are not too many of you living carelessly, and defying the Almighty with the most shocking oaths and curses? Providence has brought you to this place, some of you, perhaps, from far. What a blessing if the word of life reach your hearts as well as your ears!—I would leave out no rank or quality of unconverted people, but would willingly engage the attention of all. Some of you, though young in years, may be grown old in wickedness. You may think, perhaps, that your wickedness will be excused, because you were never properly instructed by your parents. Perhaps you have not so much as learnt to read the Bible. If this be the case, you are objects of pity. But might you not find ways and means of learning to read still? This is not difficult for the young, careless sinners to whom I am speaking. Think not, however, that your want of conversion to God can be excused by these things: you hear, and you ought to hear the sound of the gospel; and if you would receive it, it will save you; if not your blood will be upon your own heads.

Now to all such, rich and poor, labourers and mariners, young and old, learned and unlearned, who remain unconverted, I say, there are precious promises made by God, in the name of the Saviour Jesus, who came to save sinners, as at this season, whereby you may be converted and live. But take care of thinking that you may be saved by God's mercy as you are. Indeed this false hope is the greatest enemy you have. Men must be partakers of a divine nature, and escape the corruption that is in the world through lust; if ever they get to heaven. While you continue such as you are, it is not possible for you to arrive there, nor, were this possible, could you be happy there. In heaven the employment of praising and enjoying God would be as disgusting to you, as the work of religion is now. Oh! then reflect, that you need new hearts; and unless you are determined to stand out against all the Scriptures of God, set it down as a certain truth, that " except ye be born again, ye shall not see the kingdom of God:

except ye be converted, and become as little children, ye shall in no case enter into the kingdom of heaven." If the corruption that is in the world through lust still prevail in you, and you die unforgiven and unrenewed, you will be "turned into hell, with all the people that forget God." And ye swearers, drunkards, whoremongers, sabbath-breakers, scoffers at religion, have ye yet thought what hell is? Where there is wailing and gnashing of teeth; where devils will be your companions and tormentors; where the worm dieth not, and the fire is not quenched; where you may beg in vain for a drop of water to cool your tongue! So often as you have called on God to damn your soul, have you yet thought what a horrible thing it is to be damned? How immense is his patience! You are still spared: and why will you die? For vengeance will overtake you at last, if you repent not. How many of you may be in another world, affecting thought! reserved in chains of darkness to the judgment of the great day, before the end of another year! Will you not now begin to seek the Lord, and, at the beginning of a new year, inquire how you may become new men?

Let me again remind you of this, that without conversion you cannot get to heaven. Deceive not yourselves. If there be a word of truth in all Scripture, you will be miserable, and must be miserable to all eternity. It is not possible for you to be otherwise, except you be partakers of a divine nature, and escape the corruption that is in the world through lust. Jesus Christ took on him human nature, as at this time, and, if ever we enjoy him, we must have his divine nature, with a set of desires, inclinations, dispositions, and affections, quite different from those we bring with us into the world. Do not think that giving up one or two sins, and still reserving others, will do your business. There is no change of nature, so long as we love any sin, and practise it. If you would be happy indeed, you must fall out with all sin, and war against the whole of it all your days. Oh! that you felt what misery it is to be enslaved in sin, what a curse and bitterness there is in it: Oh! that you were restless and uneasy to be delivered from it. Oh! that you knew how helpless you are in yourselves, and utterly unable, because utterly unwilling to save yourselves.

If you be indeed brought to feel your misery by reason of the state of sin, then observe what exceeding great and precious promises there are for you. "The whole," saith Jesus, "need not a physician, but those that are sick: come unto me, all ye that labour and are heavy laden, and I will give you rest; if any man thirst, let him come to me, and drink; I will give to him that is athirst of the fountain of the water of life freely." Hear the word of God, and the gospel promises made in Jesus's name, which promises exclude none but those who exclude themselves. Do not then turn away from a compassionate Saviour. He calls on you to be happy: if you give yourselves up to him, he will do all that for you and in you, which you cannot do for yourselves.

SERMON VI.

THE WORLD OVERCOME BY FAITH.

1 John v. 4.

Whatsoever is born of God, overcometh the world: and this is the victory that overcometh the world, even our faith.

The Apostle, in this verse, lays down an infallible method of overcoming the world; a method not consisting in war and violence, nor in making haste to be rich, with a view to become an independent man, and above the world, as it is called. These are the vain arts of vain men, which leave them the slaves of their lusts, and instead of lessening, exceedingly increase their misery. No: the method is entirely supernatural; far remote from all the schemes of men. It surely deserves our consideration; for what is so desirable as to be above the world, its cares, its disappointments, its fears, its evils, its desires? Let us then attend to the method laid down by God in this verse, and to this end, let us briefly consider the context.

The Apostle begins the chapter with observing that "whosoever believeth that Jesus is the Christ, is born of God." To believe thus is to receive him in all his offices as our Prophet, Priest, and King. This it is which makes a man new born; which conducts him out of the sinful state of nature into a state of grace; which exalts the son of Adam into a son of God; and gives him the privileges, blessings, and dispositions of a child of God. The words, " believing that Jesus is the Christ," have a particular respect to his prophetical character, by which he gives understanding to the believer. For as the work of conversion is a rational one, the understanding is first enlightened, that the will may freely follow its dictates, and take Jesus for Priest to redeem, and King to sanctify the soul. Here is then a new birth through believing in Jesus, and hence the man learns to love God, as his Father, and all the children of God as his brethren. For it follows, " every one that loveth him that begat, loveth him also that is begotten of him."

Now the very intent of this new principle of love engrafted in the soul, is, that the man may keep God's commandments; just as the intent of planting a tree is that it may bring forth fruit. " For this is the love of God, that we keep his commandments, and his commandments are not grievous." No: on the contrary, they are pleasant and delightful; and therefore all really good men speak the language of David, " Lord, how I love thy law."

But are God's commandments thus pleasant to us by nature? Let me appeal to the consciences of too many in this audience. O drunkard! is it pleasant, or grievous to thee to be debarred from the immoderate use of strong drink? O miser! is it a pleasant exercise to thee, to deal thy bread to the hungry? O careless soul! is it pleasant to thee to pray and to wait upon God in his ordinances? He that is " born of God overcometh the world."

You are overcome by the world; therefore you are not born of God; and if so, you are of your father the devil. "This is the victory that overcometh the world, even our faith." You are overcome by the world; therefore you have no faith. Men are apt to think that it is possible for persons to have good, sound faith, and that yet their works may be bad; taking that poor thing for faith which consists in a set of opinions. But my text declares that "faith overcomes the world." Happy then would it be for you, were you once convinced that you are without faith, and dead in your sins. Ask you, what you must do? Examine yourself. There is no hope for your soul, till you see its real state. When you are once brought to know yourself, you will pray, and the Lord will hear and guide you to Christ, to righteousness, peace, and joy in the Holy Ghost.

If any such self-despairing, heavy-laden sinners be here, let them hearken to the voice of Christ. "Come unto me, all ye that are weary and heavy laden, and I will give you rest." You are convinced of the impossibility of gaining true rest for your soul, but in Jesus Christ. You cannot overcome the world by yourself, because you are without strength. "In due time he died for the ungodly." Put in your claim as worthless sinners. Make free with this JUSTIFIER OF THE UNGODLY. Expect his loving kindness; for the gates stand open day and night; the fountain for cleansing is open. Go where your wants call you, even to Christ, and he will fulfil his promise.

The consciences of all unconverted men witness

that God's commandments are grievous to them; and yet his commandments are not grievous to those who are " born of God." " For whatsoever is born of God, overcometh the world; and this is the victory that overcometh the world, even our faith." Let me then beseech drunkards, misers, and all careless men, who hate the doctrine of the new birth, to consider the entire need they have of it, in order to render God's commandments pleasant to their souls, and enable them to overcome the world. Of regenerate men it is said, " ye are of God, little children, and have overcome them; for greater is he that is in you, than he that is in the world." While men remain unconverted, they hate the commands of God, which thwart their lusts. There is need then for all to experience a change of heart, (and let us try ourselves, whether we have had it or not) in order to live holy. The divine nature once received, will enable us to overcome the pollution that is in the world. For " who is he that overcometh the world, but he that believeth that Jesus is the Son of God?"

Oh! brethren, faith in Jesus is called a *precious* thing by St. Peter. It is the instrument that receives Jesus heartily, and by which the soul is justified. When the soul having seen her guilt, and felt her misery and helplessness, throws herself forlorn and empty into the hands of Jesus, as all her righteousness, there is faith, there is forgiveness of sins, and there is peace and joy in believing, and there is the gift of God, which is eternal life by Jesus Christ our Lord. Men who never knew what believing is, and who therefore are strangers to the power and fruits of it, say that this is giving men licence to sin. What kind of proof is there wanting, to the contrary, that the nature of the thing admits? The word of God declares, (and it declares so in my text) so far is real faith from being a friend to sin, that this is the very " victory that overcometh the world." Nay, the next verse goes farther, and by asking the question, " who is he that overcometh the world?" it challenges any man to produce any other way of overcoming the world and living above it, in the practice of all duties, but this way of faith. And it must be so, because by this way only a man is " born of God," and becomes partaker of that divine principle by which alone he can love the commandments of God.

There are three enemies to holy and virtuous practice, which every baptized person professes to renounce, the world, the flesh, and the devil. That, then, which alone can overcome these enemies, must be the only instrument to render a man good and holy in his life. But the " heart is purified by faith, and faith works by love." It is faith therefore which triumphs over the flesh. It triumphs also over the world, and by the " shield of faith, ye shall be able to overcome all the fiery darts of the wicked one." Thus it is written in the Scriptures of truth. Now then, whether are we to believe God or men with regard to the efficacy and tendency of faith? There is no doubt but if I am superior to the world, the flesh, and the devil, I must lead a holy life, and this very faith which rests on Jesus alone for all things, is that which gives the victory over them. Will ye say, the engine which extinguishes the fire, increases it? You might as well say so, as say that faith in Christ will not beget holiness of life. The Lord grant you and me this faith of the gospel, and that more and more. We shall then abound in good works. The experience of all believers proves this. Yours indeed cannot, who do not believe, for you must believe before you can have the fruits of believing, just as the seed must be sown before the harvest can be expected.

But let us now attend more closely to the text, as we have sufficiently illustrated the context. This same faith in Jesus that justifies, does also quicken the soul to good works, and particularly to such as evidence a victory over the world. When profession of religion begins to abound in any place, it may be expected tares will grow up with the wheat. By these fruits, then, let us examine whether we be in the faith, lest we deceive ourselves with a dead faith, as too many do. We will consider faith in Christ as an operative principle which overcomes the world, and then make application to the consciences of men.

1. The man, in whose heart Christ dwells by faith, overcomes the world. Though the flesh still lusteth against the spirit, he mortifies his worldly lusts more and more. He is so far from suffering them to have the dominion over him, that he is gaining a growing victory over them, till he comes to a perfect man, to the "measure of the stature of the fulness of Christ." This victory is evinced in his disposition and practice, particularly in these things that follow.

The believer is superior to the CARES of the

world. He sees enough in Jesus alone to make him happy both in time and eternity. He knows all things shall be made to "work together for his good," on the whole. Is he favoured with worldly blessings? His heart is not in them, but he enjoys them with thankfulness. Content with his portion, he is delivered from that eager, envious, impatient, anxious pursuit of them which marks the character of the mere worldling. Does the Lord try him with crosses of various kinds, losses in trade, family distresses, sickness, and various disappointments? He submits; he resigns with cheerfulness to the will of his heavenly Father. And that you may see the precious use of faith, in this, as well as in all other particular instances of overcoming the world, he is so firmly persuaded of the certainty and superior value of heavenly things, and of the love of his God in Christ, that he still trusts his wisdom, not his own, believing that he will make all things, in the end, turn out for his everlasting good. Thus faith in Jesus is the soul of patience, contentment, resignation, submission to the will of God, and all the graces and virtues which render a man superior to all the vicissitudes of human life.

One thing which particularly demonstrates a man to be a slave of the world, is the undue fear of his fellow-creatures. Many are led into ruinous sins by this. False shame, and a wicked modesty, lead some into drunkenness and lewdness, because they cannot bear the taunts of their more stout-hearted companions. How many feel convictions of sin, and wish to lead a godly life, but cannot hazard the inconveniences and reproaches which they must undergo! A most wicked modesty this must be called, which idolatrously worships the creature and respects him more than the Creator.

But he who, through faith in Jesus, is born of God, overcomes this fear of man. That expostulation of God by the prophet, " I, even I, am he which comforteth you : who art thou that thou shouldest be afraid of a man that shall die?" has on him its due effect. That faith which is the " substance of things hoped for, the evidence of things not seen," represents to him the glory and perfections of God his Saviour, and the real excellencies of a future world, in so strong and true a light, that by it he sees not only particular men, of whom he was once afraid, but all the world, in so low and insignificant a light, that he can say boldly, " the Lord is my helper, I will not fear what man can do unto me." Hence he is secured against that deceit and fraud, that insincerity and false complacency which springs from the fear of man. He learns in the school of Christ to be honest for God.

He learns also, by faith, to overcome the world in another respect. I mean what the apostle calls " overcoming evil with good." Is he ill treated, despised, and maligned? Patience, meekness, and charity are his arms. He commits himself to him that judgeth righteously, and endures the cross for the eternal joy set before him.

Lastly. The view of heavenly happiness procured for him by the blood of his Saviour, has won his heart, and secured his affections to him who " sitteth at the right hand of God," his forerunner, who has provided mansions for him. Hence he overcomes this world with respect to expectations of happiness from it. Man must have something to look to for his bliss. But he looks in vain, till, by the Holy Spirit revealing the things of Christ to his soul, he sees, and tastes how gracious the Lord is, and knows something of what he has laid up in store for him that waiteth for him. He is then effectually delivered from the love of this present evil world. He tastes the sweetness of that Scripture, " Jesus gave himself for us, that he might deliver us from this present evil world according to the will of God our Father." If he looks at the pleasures of this life, with which the natural man is enchanted, he sees their emptiness, and pities the wretched taste of those who are enslaved to them. At God's right hand, where his Saviour sits, he knows there are " pleasures for evermore." Hence he practises sobriety, temperance, and chastity, using this world, as not abusing it, and eats and drinks that he may live, not lives that he may eat and drink. The fashionable amusements in which vain men seek to kill time, have to him no charms. Truly he has no leisure for them; he has other employment for his time and thoughts. This all know, who know what true godliness is. If you say, what then, must no time be allowed for pleasure? He answers, yes. But these things can give him no pleasure. Since he was renewed in the spirit of his mind, his pleasures are heavenly. He reads the promises of his Saviour in his word, and that is an inexhaustible fund of solid pleasure. He meditates on the exceeding and eternal weight of glory, and there is joy which no man can take from him. He converses with his brethren in Christ, on the love of Christ, and that is a feast to his soul. He employs himself diligently in the duties of his calling, and labours to do good in his generation, particularly by supplying the needy with that superfluous money which others expend upon their lusts. This is glorifying his God, and this is also a pleasure.

Another way in which men show themselves enslaved by the world is, by seeking the honours and dignities of it. But the believer is made a king and a priest to his God, and expects one day to sit with Jesus on his throne, even as he also overcame and sat down with his Father on his throne—what can he want more? What honour or power like this? As to worldly honour, it is dross and dung in comparison of this. If he desires a good name, it is that his God may thereby be glorified among men. If it is not to be had but with the sacrifice of a good conscience, welcome to him contempt and reproach. He will rejoice that he is " counted worthy to suffer shame for the name of Christ."

But the love of money is that peculiar evil which makes a man a slave to this world. Nothing can overcome this, but faith in Christ and his heavenly treasures. Where this is overcome, there christianity triumphs indeed. For it must be confessed, that the love of money is an evil which sticks very close to the professors of godliness. The remnants of worldly lusts, in the regenerate, are here very stubborn, and obstinate, and the heart is deceitful here above measure; because this sober vice can deceive under the specious name of frugality and economy. Nothing, however, can overcome the world, in this respect, but faith in Christ. And where "Christ dwells in the heart by faith," he surely will overcome it. Hence the believer learns to be liberal of his substance, and delights to do good with money, as its proper use and end. He seeks "those things which are above," for his happiness is hid with Christ in God. Earth can never fill his desires, nor supply his wants. Jesus is all his salvation and all his desire: the world is as dross and dung compared with him.

Having thus shown how faith overcomes the world, with respect to its cares, its fears, its evils, and its desires, let me intreat you to search diligently, and not lightly and after the manner of dissemblers with God, man by man, and woman by woman, what you are, what is your state, and where your heart is. Are you possessed of what the apostle calls, "the faith of God's elect," or are you not? It is not worth while to inquire merely, whether you have changed your opinions and rectified your notions relating to matters of doctrine. Alas! you may do this, and be as far from God as ever. Faith does not consist in holding any notions whatever. There must indeed be an enlightening of the understanding where there is faith in Christ, and therefore doctrinal ignorance in the things of Christ is ruinous. But faith itself is a work of the heart. It is a cordial reception of Jesus Christ in all his offices. Let your notions of religion, then, be what they will, if you at this day live a slave to the world, you have no faith, you are yet in your sins, in the gall of bitterness, and the bond of iniquity. Ask again and again; does your heart love Jesus, or the world? One of the two is your state. There is no middle state.

Ask whether you are yet enslaved to the cares of life; so engrossed by them, that the soul is seldom thought of, that really your heart is so much taken up with worldly affairs, that you neither find leisure nor inclination to pray, and search the Scriptures? If so, you live for this world only; a constant prey to various anxieties; greedy, and discontented; now envying this man's wealth, and now that; impatient under crosses; and ever disposed to murmur and repine at your condition.

Again. Is it not more a matter of concern to you, to please man than God? Are you not overcome by all the evil you meet with? If you receive an injury, or an affront, do not you return it? Do not you repay railing with railing, and abuse with abuse? Are you still delighting in carnal pleasures? Still fond of the applause of men, and unwilling to lose your character for Christ's sake? Is your heart still bewitched with the love of money? Is it not too plain in your mean, ungenerous, hard-hearted, and avaricious conduct, that your love of self is excessive and predominant? Have you this world's goods, and do you see your brother have need, and can you shut up your bowels of compassion from him? If this be the case with you, your pretensions to christian faith may be brought to a short issue.

If you are sensible of the guilt and danger of your state, and wish to get out of it, beseech God to sprinkle your hearts from an evil conscience, and shed abroad his love in your soul, in such abundance as may overcome in you the love of this world.

Believers! whether strong or weak, your sins are forgiven you for the sake of Jesus Christ. In him ye are dead to the world, that you may live unto God. The remnant of worldly lusts, still remaining in you, is your burden and your grief. Resist it unto death, striving against sin, if you would live in godly comfort and spiritual joy. Be thus occupied till he who now is your life shall appear. Behold, he cometh quickly, and having burnt up this earth, to which so many are miserably enslaved, he will take you up to reign with him, in everlasting glory.

SERMON VII.

THE DEVIL OVERCOME BY FAITH.

Rom. xvi. 20.

And the God of peace shall bruise Satan under your feet shortly.

WHAT a comfortable assurance is it, to a person struggling under a severe contest, with a powerful and malicious adversary, to know beforehand, that the time will shortly arrive, when he shall have a complete and effectual victory. This encourages him to maintain the battle till that period, when he shall be no more subject to any assaults, but shall enjoy an uninterrupted tranquillity. Such is the comfort afforded by the promise of the text, made to the christian warrior of final victory over the devil. The promise comes in toward the close of an epistle, which lays open the peculiar glory, and precise nature of the christian religion. The faith and the conflict of the christian are described in the foregoing chapters, as they are felt and exercised in actual experience. And to cheer the spirits of those who are heartily engaged in those things, and who might be tempted to think they should never obtain the victory, he adds, " the God of peace shall bruise Satan under your feet shortly."

Let us, 1st, endeavour to illustrate the great

comprehensive promise itself, and consider what it contains, and what it implies, and then—2d, show the use and practical application of the promise.

If it should be asked, who the persons are who shall be favoured with this victory? They are undoubtedly christians; men to whom the name properly belongs. A fairer account cannot be given of their character than what may be collected from the foregoing chapters of this epistle, which I wish to be familiarized to all who profess the christian name. For this epistle is the best system of divinity that ever was published. The men here spoken of know, that the wrath of God has been revealed from heaven against all unrighteousness of men. Their mouth was stopped: They pleaded guilty before God. They gave over all hope of salvation by the works of the law; in hearty self-despair and self-abhorrence; for they have found themselves evil altogether in their nature, as well as in their practice. They have found Christ to be "the end of the law for righteousness." They have been brought to submit themselves to the righteousness of God. Righteousness was imputed to them, believing on our Lord Jesus Christ, who was delivered for their offences and raised again for their justification.

Indeed, the view of their own sinfulness might well fill them with amazement, and completely discourage them, if not attended with a view of God's inestimable love in redemption. But this "love of God is shed abroad in their hearts by the Holy Ghost given to them." This love, they find, is for enemies; for the ungodly; for those without strength. How suited is it to their wants! How divinely gracious is the propitiation made by Jesus; which God hath set forth; hath accepted; and hath invited them to partake of. Were any conditions proposed, that they should bring as a price to God; any quantity of meritorious works, or good dispositions of their own creating; they know this salvation could never be theirs. How could it? They are without strength; carnal; sold under sin. That it is free, and to be received by faith alone, is its peculiar glory. They take it as such, and have been emboldened to call God their Father, and to rejoice in hope of the glory of God. And whom he thus justifies, he will glorify.

But till the time of full deliverance, in soul and body, at the last day arrive, they hope for what they see not; in patience waiting for it. In truth, they groan in the mean time here on earth, within themselves; waiting for the glorious liberty of the children of God, then to be revealed. None but themselves know the conflicts to which they are exposed, not only from the workings of in-dwelling sin, but also from the rage and subtilty of Satan. He is vexed to think of losing his slaves. With what envy and spite may we conceive that implacable spirit to view a soul, now in a state of justification and peace with God, and in fellowship with Jesus, and walking in the way of holiness. How does he plot, day and night, to discomfort a child of light! What clouds of confusion; what distracting, terrifying, hardening, and blasphemous thoughts does he endeavour to inject into him! What difficulties does he lay in his path of duty! And what persecution from without does he raise! With what divisions, and schemes, and evil suspicions does he strive to oppress the whole body of Christ's church militant here on earth, during the whole of their pilgrimage!

Certainly, the child of God, who is most favoured with the joys of his Holy Spirit here, has his griefs often, and feels cause to long for his dissolution; for a state in which war and desolation shall no more harass his christian life, or seem to endanger the existence of his spiritual felicity. These are the persons to whom the promise is made. It is a cordial, brethren. The Lord enable you to receive it. " The God of peace shall bruise Satan under your feet shortly." It will not be long before you are brought to full peace. Time seems long to us, because we are naturally so full of the world, and so little moved with heavenly objects. But what is time to eternity? Here mark what Christian wisdom is. Get a christian frame; to live like pilgrims who have here no continuing city; but expect one to come. Dream not of rest here; set not the mark of your expectation too high in this life. You will be disappointed, if you do. Think more of what is to be hereafter, and let your conversation be in heaven. This will comfort you amidst the whole of your warfare.

God is a God of peace, and you shall find him, through Christ, *your* peace. This blessing of peace he will completely give his people in due time. Satan has been bruised under his feet, and he shall be shortly bruised under yours. " He shall bruise thy head." The first great promise is the same, and in part delivered in the same words, with the promise in the text. In the last day, christians shall be placed at their Saviour's right-hand, and with him shall judge the world; shall judge angels. What a mortification will it be to the pride of Satan to see himself condemned by those poor human worms whom he used in this life to harass, even after their conversion to God, and whom, before their conversion, he had held in complete slavery. Yes, christians, Satan shall " be bruised under your feet." He shall never more have the least power to hurt you.

At the glorious day of Christ, which you should often think of, there will be a resurrection of characters as well as of persons. To minds of just sensibility, it is often a sore trial, and a large exercise of patience to find themselves despised, maligned and censured unjustly. Often, in their most righteous and most charitable designs are they baffled, and that commendation, by a proud and misjudging world, is bestowed on ungodly men, which really is their due. The Son of God underwent all this to the full, and in the severest manner. His first followers were accused of the most horrid crimes without the least shadow of evidence. These cruel scenes of trial have often been repeated since. And though the complexion of the present times, and the spirit of civil liberty very much restrain these things, yet no man shall in our days serve God and his Christ faithfully, but " he shall suffer persecution." It always has been so; and it proves that the wickedness of man is naturally great.

But there is something more in it. Satan has a great deal of activity in all this. He, it is, who forges and encourages lies, deceit, slander, and reproach against true christians. Oh! what a change at that day. Every one shall be seen in a just light. The saints of the Most High shall enjoy the kingdom for ever. The wicked shall triumph no more. The " god of this world" shall be found a liar throughout. A lustre shall be thrown on the characters of those who loved the Lord Jesus Christ, in sincerity. They shall be found to have been wise and prudent, when they were proclaimed fools; just and righteous, when they were censured as hypocrites; meek and charitable in those very things for which they were accused of uncharitableness and bigotry. Their characters will be found honourable, before all the world; yet not so as to make them proud. They will say, " worthy is the Lamb that was slain." They know that their sins are washed away by the blood of Jesus; and if they have been enabled to live a holy life, they say, " not unto us, O Lord, not unto us, but to thy name give the praise."—However, a real glory will be seen in their character—be seen even by those who here despised them the most.

What a downfal will there then be of *other* characters. What numbers of proud, ambitious, false-hearted men, in whose praises history—as it has been managed by many admired writers—abounds, will be found mean, contemptible creatures, and not worthy to wash the feet of many poor, obscure, private men who loved the Lord.

Oh! brethren, what a thing will it then be found to love the Lord, and by a patient continuance in well-doing to seek for glory, and honour, and immortality?

Then, too, true christians shall be found to have been perfectly distinct characters from wild enthusiasts; deceitful hypocrites; and seditious, turbulent, persons; with whom it has often here been their grief to find themselves ranked by a censorious and undiscerning world. Yes: it will be then seen, what wicked men might have seen, even in this life, in many cases, had they been disposed to be candid and just, the real difference between the righteous and themselves. Satan's lies here will also be exposed, to his eternal infamy. And then, brethren, to meet with no company, hence forward, but that of Christ and his true disciples! This will be a scene of exquisite felicity!

There will be an inward victory, as well as an outward. You will have no more assaults, or buffetings of Satan; no more questionings of the divine truth and faithfulness, of your own interest in it. In a word: Satan you will find completely bruised under your feet for ever, and the God of love and peace will be with you.

We have now to consider the use, and practical application of the promise. Directly and immediately it belongs only to the children of God. It can belong only to them, who are delivered from the powers of darkness, and translated into the kingdom of God's dear Son, in whom they have redemption through his blood, the forgiveness of sins. God is a God of peace to you, christians, as soon as you have fled for refuge to lay hold upon the hope set before you. You have overcome Satan by the blood of the Lamb; for that speaks peace in heaven. God is the God of peace to you, and as such he will bruise Satan under your feet shortly.

You must carry on a warfare with the old serpent all your days. If you are walking closely and sincerely with God, in the faith, hope, and charity of the gospel, you may expect his assaults to be not of a flattering, but of a terrifying nature. It is the certain, decisive mark of a real child of God, who walks close with him in the real obedience of the gospel, that he will be very sensible of his imperfections, and very seriously affected, from time to time, with his manifold sins and transgressions. I do not mean his *past* sins only, committed in the days of his ignorance, and in his unconverted state; but also now in his best days, and best estate. He sees the extent and purity of the law of God. He loves holiness; and while he cultivates it in every part, and branch, and may even be admired by others for his attainments in grace, and his virtues, and his usefulness; he is daily ashamed of himself. He feels the workings of his sinful nature; and is grieved to think, that when he would do good, evil is present with him, and that though he delights in the law of God after the inward man, yet that there is another law in his members warring against the law of his mind, and bringing him into captivity to the law of sin, which is in his members. This makes him often cry out, " O wretched man that I am, who shall deliver me from the body of this death!"

Such a person is liable to be much assaulted by Satan with discouraging thoughts, and to be tempted to dwell too much upon his own vileness and unworthiness, which in truth should not be done; for a cordial you need, brethren, in such circumstances. See how St. Paul uses this cordial, in like circumstances. " I thank God, through Jesus Christ our Lord." Through HIM, brethren, you have perfect redemption, and are justified from all things. Your daily evils felt, and lamented—not allowed, not brought into practice, in life and conversation—these are all pardoned. This is the very use of the mediator Jesus. Thus you are to exercise faith in him. Be thankful for his redemption. Be always kept humbly sensible of your need of his intercession. Learn to call him Saviour; not as hypocrites do; in word, and name, and form, while they think well of themselves and trust in their own righteousness; but heartily; as knowing that to him you are indebted for your present acceptance with God, and your prospect of immortal bliss.

And is not this a consolation also?—to know, that sin shall not have the dominion over you? While you inwardly feel the load of sin, you are secured through grace from its breaking out into outward actions. How should this very consideration cause you to long for the glorious liberty of the children of God, to be revealed hereafter. A time is coming when you shall find the full accomplishment of the precious promise of the text. You shall soon be above the reach of evil for ever. These things have a mighty tendency to cheer and animate the souls of God's faithful and sincere people, amidst the worst of Satan's temptations, and the most subtle devices which he practises on them, in this life. Often think on these consolations. They will cheer your minds; and the more you look forward to the eternal state, the more you will bear with patience and serenity the afflictions of this life.

It is the misery of numbers professing godliness, that a future state makes so small a figure in their thoughts and meditations. To "rejoice in hope of the glory of God," is the very spirit of true christianity. To know that, one day, Satan shall be effectually bruised under their feet, will enable their souls to persevere, in the narrow way of faith and patience. While we complain of the difficulty of believing, and the want of just evidences of our state, we are apt to forget the use of the very means which would strengthen and encourage our souls. Let us rebuke our sloth, our doubts, and our fears; our heaviness of spirit, and our self-righteousness. Let us make more use of Christ Jesus, as our Saviour, by coming to him, and not giving way to those things which grieve his spirit, and prevent communion with him. Let us know ourselves to be poor, and mean, and sinful creatures; and yet let us know that the conqueror of our great enemy has in our nature and stead fully satisfied law, and justice, and opened the kingdom of heaven to all believers. Let us trust in him for happiness, not now but hereafter to be enjoyed, and to be waited for by patient hope here. In this frame you shall not grow weary or faint in your minds. And amidst your sharpest conflicts the promise of the text shall comfort your souls with power indeed.

If, brethren, you walk not close with God; but suffer your spirits to be carried away with the follies and spirit of the world; presuming on the grace of God, and not induced thereby to grow in holiness of heart and life, the consequence will certainly be, that Satan will, some way or other, gain advantage over you. You will not be able to draw those consolations from so rich a promise as that of the text, which it is, in its own nature, calculated to convey. In such a case, you must repent and believe the gospel afresh, and break off your sins by righteousness. If prayer has been neglected, you must practise it more steadily, and more patiently, and more earnestly. If reading, and meditation on the word of God, has been neglected, or slightly performed, you must set apart more time for it, and abridge yourselves of those less necessary occupations, whatever they be, which engross too much of your time, and steal away your affections from God. In thus waiting on the Lord, you shall renew your strength, and be able to draw comfort against Satan from the rich promise of the text.

I must now close this discourse with a word to careless, unconverted souls. But how shall I apply the consolation of the text to you? How shall I say to the ungodly and the sinner—" The God of peace shall bruise Satan under your feet?" You do not *desire* the extinction of his kingdom in your souls. You love sin as he does, and God is not the God of peace to persons of your character. I know nothing so difficult as the attempt to comfort wicked, unbelieving men, in the time of their trouble. There are no topics to ground consolation upon. For if God is their enemy, what ground of comfort can there be? " Are we then to be left comfortless?" you say. We cannot give the children's bread to the dogs. Indeed you do not seek comfort in God, but in the way of the world. The first thing you need is conversion. Your whole state needs to be changed. "Repent and be converted, that your sins may be blotted out." Consider that you are sinners, that your course is evil, and that you never yet thought it worth your while to acquaint yourselves with God, and be at peace with Him, in the gospel way. Study the Scripture way of salvation, and your own concern in it, till you are brought to hearty prayer and calling upon God.

Consider, if you attend to these things at all, that Satan will endeavour to prevent you from bringing any thing to good effect. He will strive to take the word out of your hearts, as our Saviour says, lest you should believe and be saved. If then, after finding a little uneasiness about the state of your souls, you can soon shake it off, and be as careless of your souls as before, be assured Satan is tempting you to your destruction. Awake then. The enemy is upon you. Pray, and watch, and use every means which God has appointed for your conversion. Cease not till you know that God is a "God of peace" to you in Christ. Then you may have the christian's comfort to know that He will make you conquerors, and more than conquerors, through Him that loved you.

SERMON VIII.

THE SELF-DECEIVER SHOWN TO HIMSELF.

Prov. xxx. 12.

There is a generation that are pure in their own eyes, and yet is not washed from their filthiness.

THESE persons think themselves to be clean. They have done something to satisfy their minds that they are so. They may own that they once were impure, and needed to be washed from their filthiness; but they have gone through certain operations for this end, and now suppose themselves to be made pure. Yet the filthiness of sin remains in all its poisonous impurity, and they are in reality no more washed from their filthiness than if they had done nothing.

As there is a way in which a man may walk, in a confidence of walking right, which may nevertheless end in death, so is there a washing which a man may give himself, and yet remain filthy and unclean. The first is the case of those regular characters who are content with outward religion; and morals without christian principles and affections. This proverb may be applied to another kind of character; men who own and profess to love, and to embrace the real principles of the christian religion; the fall, regeneration, justification by Jesus Christ; and who yet are themselves unacquainted with the new birth unto righteousness, and are not justified by the grace of Jesus Christ. This is but one of the many proofs that abound, of the deceitfulness of the heart of man. The Scripture is full of cautions on this subject; and yet how easily do mankind impose on themselves, and one another, with regard to the goodness of their state! Till the principles of the gospel be known in any place, and while men go on without Scripture light and knowledge, such sort of self-deceivers cannot be found. They are apt to grow numerous, in proportion as light increases, and the more fashionable true religion grows, the more of this counterfeit sort makes its appearance. The enemy of God and of souls, who has laboured to keep men in utter ignorance, and prejudiced them against Scripture-truth altogether, finding this post no longer tenable, changes his plan. He persuades those whom he can now no longer induce to despise conversion altogether, to suppose themselves converted, when they are not so.

I fear, this is a growing evil among ourselves. Blessed be God! there is good fruit to be found—I hope in great abundance—which will appear in the last day. But there is also much chaff and false profession; the counterfeit works of Satan; by which he would disgrace the genuine work of God. It is of these I am then to speak at present. May it please God to enable me to say something that may be the means of undeceiving those who are deceived; and also of quickening and stirring up the really sincere, to shake off, and cleanse themselves from all false mixtures they may have imbibed, from the torrent of temptation, in this bad world, and to become more guarded against Satan's snares, and their own besetting sin.

I must first give as clear a description as I can of the case itself, and then speak a few words of exhortation.

False professors do not take all one course; there is a large variety in their cases. I can only undertake to point out some of the most common, and the most striking. These men heard the doctrine of the gospel. They attended to it. Their consciences were, probably, stirred up and awakened. Their curiosity was excited. They were gratified with a new fund of knowledge. Salvation by grace grew a pleasing sound. The comforts of free, and full justification by Jesus Christ, which contrite and humbled spirits, who have the most right to them, hardly dare venture to make their own, are fearlessly grasped by these arrogant spirits. Nay, they are even encouraged, from hence, to cast off the fear of God; and though they live uncharitably, selfishly, carelessly, and proudly, they suppose they shall still be saved by the grace of Jesus Christ. There are many ways of proving to them how they abuse the grace of God, but one is so obvious that it may seem a wonderful instance of the power of Satan's delusions, that it does not strike their minds.

You know, O false ones! that "the tree is known by its fruit." As you know more of the Scriptures than the ignorant Pharisee, you can prove to him, and justly too, that the faith of the gospel, which justifies a man through Christ, teaches him to live soberly, righteously, and godly. You can tell him that a man who really believes in Christ, will live holy, though not perfectly so, yet that he will live holy, and be a new creature, in all his dispositions and practice. This you can show from the Scriptures, and also from experience, as there want not living seals to confirm it. For you can point out to them real saints, who believe on Jesus so wholly for salvation, as to renounce all works for that end, and yet, by the force of love, are led to be as careful of all good works as if they expected salvation from them. You can also add, that these alone of all men live to God.

Now this, you, O false professors, maintain to be true. "Thou then that teachest another, teachest thou not thyself?" Look at your life since your fancied conversion began. You are not called on to examine your conduct, before that period, with this view, but since. Is it not astonishing that you should not see, that your life is no more according to godliness, since your religion began, than before? Is it not as fruitless as ever? What good do you more than formerly? Are not your tempers as violent, your dispositions as worldly, your conversation as trifling, your views as selfish, and your taste as earthly as before? Name any one essential alteration that has taken place in you. A NEW CREATURE! a great change indeed! if any man be in Christ, he is one. "Old things are passed away; behold, all things are become new." So great a change must be visible in the temper and conduct. The whole course of the desires must be altered, and this cannot be, unless it is followed by a very great alteration in the practice. Now as no such change has taken place in your case, as you are what you always were, it is certain you are deceived. "This is the victory that overcometh the world, even our faith." You are still like the rest of the world, and therefore are not in the faith. O that this plain state of the case may lead you to know yourselves, and bring you to seek God afresh, and as for the first time.

And yet, sometimes your conduct is so flagrantly unchristian, so prayerless, so negligent even of the forms of religion, that you cannot support your false confidence. But then, what do you do? From Antinomians you turn Pharisees. You show how little you know of believing in Christ, when conscience afflicts you sore. You do not come really to Christ. You betake yourselves to some duties, while the pang of conscience is on you. By a great quantity of praying, reading, and hearing, you endeavour to pacify conscience. Still to Christ you never come in all these things. The flattering, confused, distant notion of his doctrines of grace have no practical influence. Your heart never approves of, and embraces, and rests on Christ himself by faith. So that when you have comforted yourself with the performance of some Pharisaical duties, you relax again, through love of the world, (for God you love not) into your former indifference, and the Antinomian spirit takes possession of you.

Thus you may go backward, and forward, many times; one while taking Pharisaical pains in duties; another while sinning on the Antinomian presumption of grace. You resemble the pendulum of a clock, moving backward and forward; and yet like other vibratory motions, you may at length gradually settle in a state of rest. If you do, your state is more dangerous than ever. The 6th *Heb.* points out such cases of persons much enlightened, and yet never bringing forth the least fruit. If you happen to attain a considerable degree of some sort of light, and have some gifts of prayer, or ready utterance, and are much praised by weak, though well-meaning judges, it will help to maintain a false confidence. Then if you should be persuaded to join some sect of Christians under a notion of greater purity of profession; as for instance, if you be induced to enter into the views of those who call themselves Baptists, and be re-baptized, in these and such-like cases your false confidence, buoyed up by pride and self-conceit, may fairly overcome you with the most flattering delusions. You become "pure in your own eyes, and yet are not washed from your filthiness." Nor do I say this from ill-will against any particular sect of men. I know men may love our Lord Jesus Christ, who are of very different persuasions in lesser matters. And all who do, should be honoured, and loved sincerely. Yet I do think that the great zeal with which some go about to proselyte men to their own sect, is little, if at all, better than that of the Judaizing teachers, who, by circumcision, led souls from trusting in Christ. And I mourn the case of some who, I fear, have this way been seduced even to their destruction, and I warn others against such snares. The true faith of Christ is a tender plant, and men, indulging foolish scruples, may soon be beguiled out of it, and brought, by one means or other, to rest in a false peace.

You may think that your faith is good because of certain opinions, and your works good because of moral decencies. You may suppose yourselves even to be eminent Christians, because of some gifts, and some zeal for smaller matters. Ah! brethren, what shall I say? Where is Christ? Where is the broken heart; the honest, humble cleaving of the soul to him? Where the panting after heavenly things? Where the tender, affectionate spirit, that in lowliness of mind loves all the brethren of Christ, and rejoices to do them good? Ah! if you are stony, selfish, unfeeling, Christ will say to you, "I know you not, depart from me, ye workers of iniquity."

You are just such saints as king Saul, who was always either boasting or clearing himself, disputing instead of obeying, following his own headstrong passions and humours, yet wanting to be honoured as a good man. You are just such christians as Judas, the traitor; keeping up a course of profession, while you love the world above all things; and were you, like him, to be hurried into a very black sin, might show, with him, that you knew nothing of trusting in Christ, and with him die in despair.

I will now show for the comfort of sincere souls, as well as for the conviction of false professors, what they want amidst the most flourishing profession. They may in gifts and some showy qualities seemingly far excel true christians; but mark, our Lord says, "repent and believe the gospel." I shall show they know nothing of either.

1. It is a most essential quality of true repentance, that a man be convinced altogether of his sinful state by nature and practice. The very nature of true religion, and of our circumstances, requires it. We all begin the world wrong. Born in sin, and children

of wrath, we show from the most early life a mind alienated from God, disliking his government and authority, setting up an independent spirit, and following ways of our own. We do not seek happiness from God, but, however unsuccessfully, from the creature. Let any man truly try his own heart, and see what is its most natural bent and taste. It certainly does not carry him to God, nor has he any idea of " delighting himself in the Almighty." To perform some religious services, from a sense of duty, now and then, but to give the heart to the world, in some shape or other, is the universal spirit of mankind. Indeed the wisest of men, without that spiritual conviction which is from above, feel not this to be their case. Some wrong actions they are conscious of; but the enmity of the heart against God they understand not. Now this conviction of our sinful state lies at the root of all true repentance. Man's chief and governing delight should be in God. There should be nothing so pleasant to him as the service of his Maker. It was the meat and drink of our Lord, in the days of his flesh, to do his Father's will. This is what should be the case of all men. To be brought to a decent compliance with some religious forms, and then after satisfying conscience with the duty, to return with delight to worldly things, as those which mainly engage our affections, is a religion common indeed, but fitter to be paid to an idol, than to Him who is a Spirit, and ought to be worshipped in spirit and in truth. Now this " generation who are pure in their own eyes, and yet are not washed from their filthiness," notwithstanding their judgments are better informed of christian principles, than those of the common sort of Pharisees, yet like them they feel nothing of their sinfulness.

Here is, then, an essential distinction between true converts, and false professors of religion. The former know by undoubted experience that in them (in their flesh) "dwelleth no good thing." They feel their nature evil, altogether evil. They measure sin by the contrariety of the heart to God. Of this they are sensible continually. This they see the evil of. They loath, and cannot but own themselves worthy of being thrust into the society of devils, because, like them, they are at enmity with God. The risings of this evil principle, in one shape or other, they feel continually. This is conviction of sin, and it ceases not; it grows with them all their days. But he who is not washed from his filthiness, feels no such thing. A terrifying pang of conscience he may have had, now and then, and this he calls conviction of sin. Or he may be distressed occasionally for some particular sins. An abiding conviction of universal sinfulness, by nature, he has not. He knows not what St. Paul means, when he says, "I know that in me (that is, in my flesh) dwelleth no good thing."

2. There is a necessity that every true convert should learn to despair of himself altogether, and as Paul divinely speaks, to "suffer gladly the loss of all things, to win Christ." Generally some remarkable turn or other, in the course of experience, will take place, when the true penitent finds himself in such a state, that he is baffled, confounded, beat off from all hope, and has done with all schemes to help himself. He has no resource left, but to wait on the Lord, to see if he will help him. "O Lord," says

he, "I find my nature so desperately wicked, that it is sure to disappoint all devices of my own to save me. Take me, Lord, worthless as I am, I beseech thee, and save me for thy own goodness sake. But do not leave any thing to me, for I am helpless and poor. I desire to give all up to win Christ, and be found in him." We scarce ever read or hear of any real child of God, but he had the substance of this experience in his soul. Some remarkable occasions in life led him to this, in a very emphatical manner, perhaps, several times. This is indeed to be a patient in the hospital of Christ, and to verify his words, "they that be whole need not a physician, but they that be sick." And unspeakably gracious is God, and for ever blessed be his goodness for such a physician as Jesus!

But the patient, you see, must be brought to give himself wholly, as lost and helpless, to the physician. Here the false professor fails altogether. He has always something or other, which he will not give up. He is not so helpless as to be a perfect dependant. For want of an entire conviction of his lost state he will not come into the hands of Jesus Christ; and it is a fixed point that Christ will be all to us, or nothing. Therefore he never comes to Christ.

3. There is a point of faith in Christ, a point of all others most essential, and by false professors, and by all, but true saints, most neglected. It is the act of a convinced and self-despairing person putting himself into the hands of Jesus Christ, and committing to him his whole salvation. It may seem amazing how slightly this matter is passed over by mankind, even those of the Christian name. Some-

thing of repentance many have a notion of; something too of the fruits and good dispositions which flow from faith. But what faith itself is, and how in that a true convert is distinguished from a false one; here is the trying point. A true convert is certainly one, who under conviction of his lost state, and in despair of all things else, freely trusts himself (and the more assuredly and the more confidently the better) with Jesus Christ, for all his salvation and happiness. This is that faith by which the heart is purified, and therefore, this man shall be "washed from his filthiness." While he lives under an abasing sense of his natural pollutions, he is nevertheless, "through the Spirit, mortifying the deeds of the body" more and more. He puts on Christ; is renewed in the spirit of his mind; and attains that real purity of heart, which he who has is blessed, and shall see God. *Matt*. v. 8.

I hope it has appeared what the false professor wants. He may have many showy qualities, and if he have good natural faculties, that will give him great advantages. But he wants a true conviction of sin, a true self-despair, and a real trusting in Jesus Christ, according to the promises of the gospel. He was always an unbeliever. He never would humble himself, despair of himself, or venture wholly on the credit of the promises on Jesus Christ. Hence he remains unrenewed and unpurified, however high he may be in his own eyes. I shall conclude with a word of exhortation to different sorts of persons.

1. False professor of Christianity! Thou hast this day been weighed, and found wanting. Thou knowest how to prove the gospel doctrines, as truths of

God's word, and to distinguish them in a measure from false doctrine. But look inward, and see how thou hast received them. Never hast thou mourned for thy inbred guilt and pollution. Thou art not burdened, nor distressed for sin, nor ever hast been, so as to make thee come truly to Christ. A faith grounded on the promises of the gospel is what thou art a stranger to. Thy life and conversation show what thou art: worldly-minded, selfish, proud, without tenderness of conscience, without any practical communion with Christ in thy soul, from day to day. Thy eagerness for the world, and the ungoverned state of thy passions and lusts, too plainly show what thou art. It is certain that the truly regenerate are entirely distinct from men of the world. They are " the salt of the earth and the light of the world." Now do recollect since thy supposed conversion, if thou canst, what fruit has appeared in thy life superior to that of persons who make no profession of religion at all. What dost thou for God, and his Christ, and his cause in the world, more than they do? What honour dost thou bring to the gospel by thy words, or deeds? What victory hast thou gained over thy passions? In what one instance art thou materially changed for the better? And if thou art at a loss what to answer, if no one can see thee more charitable, more humble, more heavenly-minded, more conscientious, more upright than thou wast formerly, or than those are who profess nothing, what shouldest thou think? Oh, but thy heart is hard! It is more difficult to move thee, than those who never heard the gospel sound. But get thee to thy closet, and pray in secret, and see if thou canst profit by these hints, and be affected with thy danger. God may meet thee with true conviction, and give thee repentance unto life.

I must also warn you who are careless of all religion, not to exult over "the generation that are pure in their own eyes, and yet are not washed from their filthiness." You wallow, as swine, in your filthiness of sin, and will ye exult over those, in the same condition, who yet are not so impudently revelling in it as you are? They are restrained by some degree of religious reverence: you do not think it worth while to profess any regard to God. Their very profession of religion evinces some respect to the righteous Governor of the World. But you despise him openly. The very profession of serious religion excites your contempt, and can ye justify this even to your own consciences? You are glad to find false professors disgraced. But remember true religion loses none of its excellencies by their hypocrisy and ill conduct. There are counterfeits in all things. If a man is to treat true experimental religion with contempt, because of false profession, there is not one thing in the world that he can value; for there never was a good thing but it had its counterfeits. Instead of treating all religion with reproach on this account, it would be your wisdom to *study* true religion, and learn to distinguish it from false. A glass toy may glitter, and seem as valuable, to one who is no judge of such things, as a diamond. Yet on being shown the deception, he would not conclude there were no such things as diamonds. But he judges as foolishly who despises all religion on account of hypocrites.

A word to those that are poor and of a contrite

spirit, and whose hearts stand in awe of the Divine word. I hope you may have heard, this day, not only something that may condemn the false professor, but comfort the true. That self-knowledge and self-despair which makes no part of the hypocrite's character, is a strong feature in yours. That entire dependance upon Christ alone, and increasing sense of his strength, and of human weakness, which the false professor is an utter stranger to, forms a distinguishing part of your religious experience. The more you thus " grow in grace, and in the knowledge of your Lord and Saviour Jesus Christ," the more you will be washed from your idols, and from your filthiness, and enabled to perfect holiness in the fear of God.

SERMON IX.

THE DIFFERENT MANNER IN WHICH THE RIGHTEOUS AND THE WICKED DIE.

Proverbs, xiv. 32.

The Wicked is driven away in his wickedness: but the Righteous hath hope in his death.

HAVING considered in some former discourses the way of obtaining righteousness and sanctification by faith in Jesus Christ, I need not say to those who know them by experience, how necessary to their well-being, both here and hereafter, it is, that they should be established in the truth of these doctrines. But now, methinks, I can conceive the opinion which many form of such discourses, if in truth they think it worth while to think of such subjects at all. They wonder why one should deal so much in abstruse speculations, and refined notions of things. They see no use, or importance in them, but think it would be better to confine our discourses to plain moral subjects, which the vulgar can understand. These thoughts are so suited to the perverted state of nature, that I wonder not that so many are duped by them. Indeed all will, in general, think thus, except persons with whom religion is matter of heart-work. These will pity the ignorance of such objectors, and assure them, that Jesus " made of God righteousness and sanctification," is no such abstruse subject as to require any depth of human learning to comprehend it, since it is taught of God. The proudest scholar must learn it of the Holy Ghost, or not at all; and the simplest and most unlettered soul, when taught of God, can comprehend it as well as the brightest scholars.

These subjects are christianity itself; necessary to the being of a christian, and among many most valuable purposes, which I stay not now to mention, this is one fruit of a spiritual understanding of them, that they fit a man for death. Yes: in that awful hour the soul who knows Jesus as his righteousness and sanctification, can rejoice and leave the world in triumph, as one who is going to enjoy his true rest, while all who are destitute of this knowledge either die in terror, in stupidity, or at least in false peace. To be fitted for death is reason enough for learning any thing. What should the grand business of life be, but to prepare for death?

Do thou, good Lord, infix a real solemnity in our hearts, while we weigh this subject. Do thou place death with proper weight on our souls, and deliver us from levity and carelessness of spirit. Thy truths always prevail where men are serious. Do thou, therefore, give seriousness to us who are here, while we consider the usefulness of Christ in the heart to a dying man, and the misery of the soul that in death is destitute of this knowledge, whatever it may know besides.

Solomon observes the different manner in which the righteous and the wicked die. " The righteous hath hope in his death:" therefore he dies in peace, and resigns his breath into the hands of his Saviour with joy. Would you see the righteous man thus die in peace? Behold Stephen, the first Christian martyr. The fury of his enemies and the volley of their stones disturb not, at all, the heaven within him. He sees the glory of God, and " Jesus standing at the right-hand of God." He says to his Saviour and his friend, " Lord Jesus, receive my spirit." He prays heartily for his enemies, and then falls asleep. For his hope is full of immortality. Generally speaking, it is in the article of death that the light of God's countenance, more particularly, shines on the saint. However he may have been tossed with tempests, darkened, as to his evidences, and chastised by his heavenly Father for his sins, while in health, yet in death the Lord remembers him, and favours him with the manifestations of his grace, that so he may take up the Apostle's song, " O death, where is thy sting? O grave, where is thy victory? Thanks be to God who giveth me the victory through Jesus Christ my Lord."

Thus " the righteous hath hope in his death." But it is not so with the wicked: he " is driven away in his wickedness:" Led captive indeed, and hurried along by sin and Satan all his life, so that he moves not like a free man, but eminently in his death is he " driven away." You can conceive how the condemned malefactor is driven away to death, when against his will he is carried to the place of execution. But not he only, all who die in their wickedness, unpardoned, unreconciled to God, are hurried out of life against their wills, divorced from that which makes their heaven—this earth's enjoyments—to appear before God in judgment, and be sentenced to everlasting fire. There may be different degrees in which this unwillingness of the wicked to die shows itself; but in general, this, I apprehend, (and surely experience proves it) is the true note of distinction between the righteous and the wicked, in their death, that the righteous die willingly, and move freely out of this world into a better, while the wicked die unwillingly, and would rather remain here than depart.

Let us, then, endeavour to illustrate a little farther this important sentiment, and show the reason why the righteous and the wicked are so different in their deaths. That there is such a difference is matter of fact; and though in some cases it may be difficult for the living to form a proper judgment of the spiritual state of their fellow-creatures, yet that a judgment may be formed is plain, from our Lord's rule of knowing men by their fruits: a rule altogether impertinent, if always incapable of being put in practice. Suffer me, then, to set before you, (so far as man can form a proper judgment) the different manner in which, generally, the righteous and the wicked die. I have visited many sick-beds, and taken notice of the different consequences of different sorts of religion on the minds of men, as they show themselves at that awful hour. Let it only be granted that those religious principles and affections must be the true ones which support a man, with a solid hope, in the hour of death, and in the view of eternity.

Now from all the experience we can collect, on this subject, it appears, that wicked men "are driven away in their wickedness," that is, die unwillingly, in the sense in which I set forth the text. They die like persons dragged out of life. Some, indeed, bear the summons with a better grace than others, and it is hard to say how far pride, and self-deceit may impose on a man at this solemn hour Yet plain it is that no wicked men are in St. Paul's state, " desiring to depart and to be with Christ, which is far better." They see, and know nothing in Christ or in heavenly things that should make them objects of desire. They see *that* in the world which draws their love to it. They wish to enjoy it longer, and are loath to leave it. Hence while in health wicked men make death no part of their serious meditation or discourse: They hate the idea: They shun the society of those whose serious discourse might bring it into their minds. When haunted with such thoughts, they strive to rid themselves of them, as enemies.

It is the working of natural guilt, and enmity against God, in their minds, which causes this uneasiness at the thought of death. Amidst all their self-righteousness, carelessness, and worldly avocations; amidst all the pride, and stupidity which the Fall has occasioned in the human race, conscience will be heard. The wicked man understands, or regards little what she says; but this she says, " thou art a sinner, and if thou be not reconciled to God before thou die, death will bring thee no good; but send thee a condemned malefactor to the justice of God." Hence the fear of death: Hence wicked men are struck with a gloom, if death be named in a serious way. They may, now and then, get the better of these thoughts, but they return after a time with increasing violence.

The article of death itself makes no essential alteration in their views of things. Death was disagreeable at a distance, though it is still more so as it approaches near. For it appears then like a grim executioner of vengeance. " They are driven away in their wickedness." They may be weary of pain, or adversity, and so in that sense be weary of the world. But if health and prosperity were granted them, the wicked would rather live than die. Their sensations (by what I have observed) on the near approach of death, distinguish them into three sorts.

1. The despairing sinner, who sees himself, indeed, to be in a guilty, dreadful state, and dies without the gospel hope. I need not say how he is " driven away in his wickedness." No words can paint his horrors. Hell is begun on earth. The Lord grant us, brethren, never to experience his misery.

2. The self-deceived wicked man, who dies in a false peace. He has not a doubt but that he is a good man, and consequently he is in a calm, quiet, and what people often call a resigned frame. He sees every thing in a false light. He expects that God will pay the same regard to his worth, that he himself does. This man lays the grand stress, for his salvation, on his own imagined goodness; and therefore, if his life has been decent and regular, it is no wonder, with his views, on comparing himself with others, that he should say with the Pharisee, " God, I thank thee that I am not as other men are."

He may, also, think himself somewhat obliged to Christ; but he might just as well be a Deist. Whether men talk of the mere mercy of God, or of the mercies of Christ, there is no difference at all in God's account, where they depend, at bottom, on themselves. For " Christ is of no effect to as many of you as are justified by the law : ye are fallen from grace." I mention this, to show that this second sort must rank with the wicked, by the Scripture rule; though too many who belong to it think themselves righteous.

But how does it appear that these are " driven away in their wickedness?" Not so plain as the former sort; but yet " driven away" they are still. For they have no relish for heavenly things. They do not leave the world with delight, because they have no delightful objects before them. All that can be said of their supposed resignation is, that they make a virtue of necessity. But this is not christian resignation. The real christian, in death, not only dies resigned, but with such a hope before him, that it is *his* choice to die, as well as the Lord's, and because it is the Lord's. This can be said of no wicked man, either in life or death. A christian, the same in death that he was in life, chooses what the Lord chooses, and is pleased with that which pleases HIM. How terrible hell must be to the self-deceived, I need not say. The Lord grant us such a view of all delusions here, that we may be delivered from them while time remains.

But I apprehend that by far the major part of wicked men belong to neither of these extremes. They die, neither despairing nor confident, but hardened and insensible. Ask them what they ground their hope on. They know not what to answer. Eternity has not cost them a serious thought. This world fills their heads to the last. It is dreadful to think how many, in this, which calls itself a christian country, die with no understanding, or religious affections at all. They may think it needful for the

Minister to pray with them or give them the Sacrament, placing much the same confidence in this as the Papists do in extreme unction; but this is all they suppose necessary. Many, if possible, are still more stupid, and die with no more thought, or concern, than if they expected nothing more after death, than the beasts that perish. Tell them of the necessity of conversion or the new birth, ever so often, they regard it not. Alas! how dreadful is this! that so many pretended christians should die with no more regard for Christ, or knowledge of the work of his Spirit on their souls, than if they had never heard his name! The next life will awaken them out of their stupidity, to feel their misery. These however, like the rest, are " driven away in their wickedness." They would rather live, if it were possible. For they see nothing beyond death that engages their affections.

This belongs, only, to the righteous. He dies in hope: he sees the glory of heaven, the glory of the Saviour; he has a love for them, and therefore he moves freely out of life, because he is going to what he loves. Understand you this peculiar happiness of the dying christian? I might dwell upon his other amiable qualities, his resignation, his patience, his brotherly kindness and charity; but I mention that particularly in which he most evidently differs from the wicked. He moves freely, and with pleasure out of life: he would not have it otherwise with him: but " the wicked is driven away in his wickedness." None can conceive how happy the righteous are in death. I have seen what is very wonderful and glorious, at such a season. But none can understand, save they that feel, what it is to be just on the threshold of heaven. Ask you what is the cause of this difference? The influence of gospel principles alone. Let us, then, consider this a little. The excellence of the gospel is not to be tried by its making a man great in this world, but in fitting the real receivers of it for death.

Permit me, with this view, briefly to refresh your memories with the subjects of some late discourses. He that believes on Jesus Christ, in reality, receives him for all justification unto life. Here is, then, the foundation of the difference between the righteous and the wicked in death. The righteous build for their acceptance not at all on a life well spent, as too many speak—Gracious God! Deliver us effectually from the soul-destroying delusion!—but they build on a perfect righteousness, on pure grace, unmixed with any of their doings. They separate entirely their works, both good and bad, from this affair of their dependance for eternal life, because " the law worketh wrath." It requires perfection, and they, in themselves, are all sin and imperfection. Of course, if they built on any thing but Jesus alone, who is " the Lord their righteousness," they would build on what is defective; on that which worketh wrath. Go to the bed-side of the dying person, who is really a righteous man, and he will always tell you, though he may have lived many years in the practice of real good works, " Christ is my only plea; as a sinner I expect salvation through his blood, who loved me and gave himself for me." Should any tell him of the good things he has done, he cannot endure to hear them named, as at all procuring him the favour of God. No: he counts them all as " dung" for Christ's sake, and he knows that laying any weight on them, for this end, would be rejecting Christ, and ruining the soul.

I need not say how different wicked men, whether they be decent moralists, or not, are in their dependance for life. They hold fast their dependance on their own goodness too well. However little good they may have done, they expect their salvation from it, if from any thing. Now need it be wondered at, that the righteous have a sweet hope in death, which makes them go willingly out of life, and that " the wicked are driven away in their wickedness?" The first build on the perfect righteousness of their God and Saviour Jesus Christ. The second build on that which they themselves know to be imperfect, their own works. Conscience, with the first, is satisfied; with the latter it cannot be satisfied.

Pride and ignorance will go a great way to procure the wicked a false peace; but were it not for their stupidity with respect to eternal things, they would be all in terror. They labour therefore, in general, to keep themselves from thinking deeply about eternity, and so do their friends about them, with cruel kindness. Thus, most commonly wicked men die in an insensible way. But the Christian builds on the LORD HIS RIGHTEOUSNESS. Hence he can think of death, judgment, and eternity with delight. His foundation is firm, and his comforts will bear examining into.

He who believes on Jesus for righteousness, believes on him also for sanctification. Being " one with Christ," he lives to God, and dies to God. He has a true relish for the heavenly things to which he is hastening.

He goes as a beloved son to the house of a kind father, with joy. He delights, on the bed of death, to be thinking, and talking of the love of his God, and expressing his desire to be at home. Whatever good thing, in life, he has been enabled to do, he will find none of it to be lost, when he arrives at heaven. For we shall all be rewarded according to our works. But he eyes Christ alone as the door of eternal life.

Now whatever appearance of good, in their death, wicked men may have, this intercourse of love with God, as a father, this sweet view of heavenly things, they cannot have. They go to God merely as a judge, against whom, at bottom, their hearts are at enmity. Therefore they are all " driven away in their wickedness."

If, then, brethren, persons who have visited sickbeds, and taken notice of the consequences of different doctrines, can discern such an evident difference in the deaths of those who build on Jesus for all their righteousness and sanctification, and of those who build on their own false repentance, or what is wrongly called a well-spent life; if the first die in love, in joy, and in liberty, and the latter in terror, in stupidity, or at least unwillingly; has not God set a mark on his own doctrines, to teach what is truth and what is not? If dependance on ourselves, either in whole or part, cannot give solid peace in death, what may be expected from it but destruction after death? Ought men to be content with it while in health?

The application of the whole is obvious, and shall be short. Men and brethren, consider yourselves as dying, and ask what you build on for eternity? Have you gotten a perfect righteousness, "Christ in you the hope of glory?" How will you face death without it? How can any thing of your own, all imperfection at best, stand before a holy and sin-hating God? Ponder this truth. God hath given his son, that we might live through him. Turn ye then to him while there is hope, and receive him for your all. So shall you die in true peace, and have that prospect, and that relish for heavenly things which shall make death delightful. But if ye will not receive him for your all, you receive not the real Christ. You build on the law, and " the law worketh wrath," and will send you, after death, to everlasting destruction.

I beseech you, brethren, to consider what has been said, with a serious view of death and judgment before you. Then you may both understand and receive the record of God, that he hath given you " eternal life, and this life is in his Son." Then may you have " Christ in you, the hope of glory." When this is accomplished, you will be delivered from the inordinate love of this present evil world, and from the fear of death. You will be enabled to meet your last enemy without dismay, and find, not a difficult, but an abundant entrance administered unto you, into the everlasting kingdom of Jesus Christ.

SERMON X.

SAINT PAUL'S DETERMINATION TO KNOW NOTHING ELSE, SAVE JESUS CHRIST AND HIM CRUCIFIED.

---

1 Cor. ii. 2.

For I determined not to know any thing among you, save Jesus Christ, and him crucified.

This is the determination of the Apostle of the Gentiles. It requires, indeed, wisdom and strength more than human to be brought to such a resolution. There were many things besides Jesus and him crucified, to which a mind like the Apostle's would be tempted to cleave. In proportion as the endowments of the mind are rich, and various, this temptation is strong and inviting. The philosophy of the Pagans would solicit his penetrating understanding. Their poetry, their rhetoric, and their elegant taste, would be apt to seduce his warm and vigorous imagination. The Jewish politics, antiquities, and ceremonies, would quite fall in with the habits of his youth, his early imbibed prejudices, and his natural spirit and ambition; especially as he had made a proficiency in them from his youth, above many his equals. But from the time that the Lord had met with him in his way to Damascus, he conferred not with flesh and blood: The Son of God was revealed in him; and he saw such a sweetness, suitableness, and glory in the discovery, that he "counted all things but loss and dung in comparison." In the cross of Christ he found the true solid refreshment of his spirit; however contrary to this world's taste, spirit, wisdom, and righteousness. Though of all things the most unpopular, the most contrary to this world's course of things, he found it meat indeed, and drink indeed. He knew no other pleasure but the cross of Jesus, and it was the capital theme of all his ministry among the Corinthians, though it was " to the Jews a stumbling block, and to the Greeks foolishness."

And, brethren, to this day, all who are just and righteous in their own eyes have no idea of being saved by the grace that is in Jesus; and all who are wise in nature's light, and on that depend for their instruction in the way to happiness, see nothing tempting in Christ crucified. So far is this from being in their eyes the most glorious and refreshing discovery of the wisdom and goodness of God, they can see nothing in it desirable, or pleasant; and it is the last thing they think of going to for pleasure, joy, liberty, and happiness.

Here is, then, a subject which will try us what manner of spirit we are of. Undoubtedly if we mean to be christians indeed, and not to content ourselves with the name and form, our taste ought to be the same with the Apostle's. Every minister of Christ should, in his ministry, have the same theme at heart; and he is likely to go on with little pleasure, or spirit in it, unless his own soul feel the same relish for the cross of Christ. Every private person, also, who means to travel to heaven, should be like minded. " Know ye how ye are affected toward Christ Jesus?" Let this question go round the congregation. If, indeed, "Christ crucified" be your delight and your glory, you will make sure of him as such. You will know where to seek in times of difficulty and trial: You will go and find him the very thing that you want. Happy are they with whom this is the case! They prove, indeed, that they "live by the faith of him," because they use him as a Saviour.

But if you make no use of "Christ crucified," either in worldly troubles, or in your religious; but lean on an arm of flesh for the first, and on a round of duties for the second, Christ is only a name with you, a name without power. Deceive not yourselves. You are not in the faith, nor do you yet know the way to God by him. You are in the darkness of a heathen nature, and the " sun of righteousness" has not arisen upon you " with healing in his wings."

Oh! that my audience were now brought to fair and honest dealing with themselves! Were I to say no more than what has been said, it would be a useful Sermon. For if indeed "Christ crucified" be our grand object: If it be the fire that kindles our love, the medicine that relieves our guilty souls, the balm that heals our corruptions, and the refreshment that cheers our spirits, what ail our hearts that we cannot know that it is so? Ought not many, who have no earnestness in religion, or, if ever earnest, are never brought to Christ for comfort, to know that Christ and they are not united by any means? Let such persons say, "I need to be made a new creature, and this must be in Christ Jesus. O crucified Saviour, I will seek thee till I find happiness in thee, as others have done."

It were an unfair, an unjust use to make of this text, to prescribe from thence to ministers, that their whole discourses must directly relate to nothing else but the wounds, and agony, and sufferings of Jesus Christ. For a man may, in a natural way, be much affected with his sufferings; just as he would with seeing a stage representation of an innocent person suffering under cruel indignities; with no other consequence than the stirring up of natural pity and compassion. It is the DOCTRINE and USE of " Christ crucified," not merely the history of it, which is to make us holy and happy. And, therefore, the preaching of the law, and of repentance, as leading men to feel their need of Christ; and the preaching of good works, and duties as the fruit of faith, are necessary. But still you see Christ is the grand subject: all is referred to him: the design of all is that he may be endeared to us, and honoured by us, and may form our capital enjoyment. The subject before me will give an opportunity of enlarging on these hints, and if I am enabled to point out to you the just and weighty lessons learnt from " Christ crucified," or even the most material of them, you may see that the Apostle said not without reason, " For I determined not to know any thing among you, save Jesus Christ, and him crucified."

Perhaps, we may see that some things, which may be learnt by other mediums, are yet more powerfully learnt from the doctrine of Christ crucified; that many very necessary lessons of instruction are not to be learnt by any other way; and that there is no one thing, of any importance in religion, but it is taught by the cross of Christ.—Oh! may the spirit of the Father only be with us; take of the things of Christ, and show them to us, with marvellous light, and victorious energy!—" Thou art engaged, O Father of mercies, to honour thy Son, and to fulfil his great promise of sending the Holy Ghost the Comforter! Send him, O God! on this congregation, and on me, that all who look unto thee in thy son's name may find thee gracious, and that others also may be moved to inquire the way to heaven. Oh! display thy glory in Christ this day: Point out thy only-begotten Son to us as crucified for us, and let us see, and find, and actually make use of him for those holy purposes for which thou gavest him to us. Dispose us to child-like attention and submissive obedience to thy truth. Let it sanctify us, O righteous Father! and let us sit down at the wellspring of delight, even Jesus; find it a substantial reality, even happiness itself; and feed on him to thy praise and glory, through all eternity."

One of the most natural lessons to be learnt from the cross of Christ is the evil of sin. There is nothing mankind are slower to comprehend than this: " What harm do we do to God by our indulgences and vanities?" This is the language of the heart. " Is it not hard that he should punish us with hell for them?" Now stand and see this great sight, the cross of Christ. What read you there? What does this teach you? Consider who it is that suffers. You see a man like yourselves, and so he was in all things, sin excepted. But it is also God manifest in the flesh that you see. The Son of God, who has the very nature of God, as much as the son of man has the very nature of man. He is one with God, so that "whosoever sees him sees the Father, whatsoever the Father doth, the Son doth likewise." Think you that God's own Son, his only-begotten Son, in whom from eternity he had such delight, is not most dear to him? Must not HE whose name is LOVE, love his dear Son, his own very image? But see, he has poured the vials of his wrath upon him; he treats him as under the curse, and makes him bear the curse due to sin. He spares him not in his agony. He suffers him to be the victim of malice, both infernal and human, and empties his whole indignation upon him. You see the Son of God a willing substitute for guilty man. The strength of the Godhead enables him to endure the load of divine vengeance :—for what he suffered in his soul is inconceivable—and the merit of the Godhead enabled him in a little time, to expiate our guilt, which would have consigned us to endless misery.

When you lay all this together; who the sufferer is; what relation he stands in to God the Father; how beloved by him; how sorely suffering; you have the strongest argument that can be formed to evince the evil of sin. No creature's sufferings, not even the highest archangel bleeding on a cross, could have shown so clearly the evil of sin, as his sufferings did, who is "very God of very God." But indeed comparisons are lost. The highest archangel is but a creature, and there can be no proportion between the creature and the Creator. Oh, then, how provoking must sin be in the sight of the holy

God, who thus punishes it! Shall men dare to trifle with oaths; with the Scripture; with the name, and ordinances of God; with the obligations of justice, and mercy, and truth; and say they see no great harm in these things? Look at him whom you have pierced. Behold his sorrow, and agony extreme, and say, " My sins wrought him this pain, can they, then, be trifling?" Christian principles are not those trifling points of opinion which many fancy. I am persuaded were they planted in our hearts, they would be found to produce the most powerful practical effects.

A man may argue many ways to show what a base thing it is to sin against God, and very justly; nor do I mean to set aside any useful rational way of learning it. Our natural conscience teaches us something of it. There is that within every man, not fancy, but the voice of God, sober and still, yet soft and clear, which will tell the scorner, would he listen to it, something very different from what he may have learnt from infidel books, or profane company. It whispers, that sin is a serious evil, and calls for just punishment from the God of truth. The effects of sin, in the miseries it brings on us in this world, afford no feeble lesson to the same purpose. The revealed law of God, especially as expounded in our Lord's Sermon on the mount, teaches us also to see our sins in a very different light from what we are all apt to do. But the suffering Saviour teaches it the most powerfully of all. It is well to learn the evil of sin by all ways that we can; for there are a thousand ways, in this bad world, by which men teach one another to make light of it. But we shall learn true conviction of sin more forcibly from the cross, than from any other way. If your sins were trifling, would God thus expose his Son to suffer? If he made him a propitiation for the sins of the whole world, as he doubtless did, we are a part of that world which required to be thus redeemed. Even you who may rank with the better sort, and suppose you have merited little punishment, must yet own you have done what has exposed the Son of God to the Cross. Will you not be suitably affected with this? Must you not be a monster of baseness to do all this mischief?

"The fear of the Lord is the beginning of wisdom," and it lies mainly in feeling the evil of sin. No religion can be worth the name that teaches not this. Oh! let each look, then, at Christ, and learn to feel his own sinfulness. We cannot go a step in the way to heaven, if we are not thus convicted. Nay, I would not part with you coldly assenting. I want your hearts to be pricked, to be rent, to be humbled. You should feel that you are not only sinners—all will own this—but vile sinners. May the Spirit of God, by the cross of Christ, teach you this, and you will learn the other lessons which it teaches with ease and comfort.

I remember in the account of that wonderful work of God's grace shown to Colonel Gardiner, related by Dr. Doddridge, an author of approved good sense and veracity, these words which he heard from the vision, or whatever it was, of Christ crucified which was shown him, "O sinner, did I endure this for thee, and are these the returns?" The immediate effect, with him, was a saving conviction of sin from this vision of the cross of Christ alone.

"They shall look on him whom they pierced, and mourn." May our hearts feel the strength of this text, and understand its power.

2. Would you know what sort of a character GOD is? It may be learnt from the cross of Christ more powerfully than from all other considerations. It was a work of matchless power, indeed, to conquer hell and all the works of darkness, by so contemptible an instrument as the cross. "The weakness of God," in this way, appears "stronger than men." It was a scheme of amazing wisdom to reconcile justice with mercy, holiness with compassion, both in complete perfection, and to bring the greatest good out of the greatest evil.

Without enlarging on these topics, I would ask, how are our hearts affected with them? See you not what sort of a God he is who made us? Wisdom and power we all allow him. Indeed the works of nature show them abundantly; though you see them in Christ crucified also. But holiness and justice we are reluctant in ascribing to him. We would have him be all mercy, and yet the mercy which is in him is immensely larger than the heart of man can conceive; but it is exerted in a way different from what man could apprehend. Suppose ye that a kind God will never send rebellious sinners to hell? See his own son suffering actually the severest tortures of body and mind. When you think of the infinite dignity of him who suffered, and behold him in his agonies aright, you must correct your false idea, and learn to tremble for your own sins, before a God thus hating and punishing sin.

And when you are once brought to penitence, and true contrition, look to the same cross, and see what mercy is there displayed; that for you the Son of God should suffer! It will astonish your minds, and gladden you with prospects far brighter than nature would ever have allowed you to imagine. God appears, on the one hand, most holy, most just, most inflexible in his hatred of sin, most righteous, most true, and faithful; on the other hand, most compassionate, gracious, and merciful beyond all imagination, and conception. Nature, and our reason can form no such God as this. Either we presumptuously vacate his holiness, crying up his mercy; or, if frightened for sin, we vacate his mercy, looking on him only as a terrible judge. An awful judge, or a mere idol of mercy, "these are thy gods," O natural reason! We are sure to form to our minds one of these, and God is neither. In "Christ crucified" the lines of justice and mercy are both drawn with strength, and colouring inimitable. If you understand it not, go to the cross, and while you pray for spiritual light, look there, and know the true God, whom none know but men truly converted, and born again. Learn to worship him with confidence and with reverence, and remain not in the idolatrous ignorance of nature.

That this lesson may not lose its due influence, I desire my audience to examine, if they know what God is. It is not calling him by the name of God, and believing there is a God, who made all things, that constitutes this knowledge of him; and yet, if we serve and worship him, we should know his character.

Men of vicious lives, and downright carelessness, you know him not. Look to Christ crucified, and see him there, holy, and just, and hating your sins, with infinite hatred. Blind Pharisees, who mean to obtain heaven by a heartless course of duties, you know him not. Look to the cross, and see heaven freely bought by that which your works can never purchase, and let both sorts learn to know his character, and thence be prepared to serve him aright.

3. Christ crucified points out, indeed, the propriety of that name of God which St. John gives him, " God is Love." Here is love to enemies, to rebels, to the worthless, and the vile. Here is free love, nothing to solicit, or purchase it. " God commendeth his love to us in that while we were yet sinners, Christ died for us." What a God is this! Love is his nature. All his perfections centre in this. He loves not our misery. He calls us affectionately to turn to him and live. He has proved, indeed, it is his pleasure, seeing he gave his Son to suffer for us. He withheld not his only Son. What a jewel was that which he parted with, to save a vile worthless world. " As I live, saith the Lord God, I have no pleasure in the death of the wicked." Want you still further proof than my oath? Look at my bleeding Son—bleeding for you.—The honour of my government is this way restored, and justice is satisfied. I can consistently with my own character show you mercy. Turn unto me by Jesus Christ, and I will receive you. Why, why this averseness? Is Love so disagreeable a thing? Can any thing make you happy like Love? "He that dwelleth in Love, dwelleth in God, and God in him."

4. While you behold " Christ crucified," and consider, that as Ministers of the Gospel, we are to " know nothing else:" while you remember what

is written, " how beautiful are the feet of him that bringeth glad tidings," learn, I beseech you, to respect aright the Ministry of the Gospel, and be candid enough to believe that we mean no self-exaltation, but your benefit, while we press you to regard us as Ministers of Christ, and Stewards of the household of God. The word of God " preaching peace," by him who hung on the cross, shall not return void to God, it shall accomplish what he pleases, as the rain and the snow that cometh from heaven accomplish the designs of Providence. The Ministry of the Gospel setting forth Christ crucified, and calling men to receive him for life and salvation, is God's own appointed way of turning sinners to himself. The efficacy of the power is of God, not of man. If you say you can read and judge for yourself without Ministers preaching, I think it may be safely affirmed, that no instance can be brought of any man, who despised the Ministry, being brought to the true faith and love of Jesus; that you cannot succeed while God is not with you; and he is not with you, if his ordinances be despised. The contempt of preaching in our day, among the richer sort, is lamentable, and it is always joined even with the contempt of Christ crucified. But, certainly, if you see him aright, and know why he suffered, you must respect, and attend to the errand of the Ministry as the errand of God to you concerning your salvation.

I could enlarge further on the uses of Christ crucified, but shall close with one simple use to be made of this most endearing of all objects by every contrite soul. I would speak as God's ambassador to you, and ask, is there a man or woman in this congregation, at this present moment, unhappy, feelingly unhappy, because of sin; sensible they are lost for ever, and undone, if God alone do not relieve, and save them; despairing of help from riches, pleasures, their own righteousness, wisdom, and every resource; and only kept from total despair by the hope that God may, by a way of his own, step in and save them? Have I hit your case? Look then to Christ crucified. What did he bear all this for, but for your relief? You are the very persons who are welcome to receive all the benefit of his sufferings. Who else can they be? Will you say, those who have received them already? *They* shall receive more; but they were just as you are at present, when they began to receive. Are they persons better disposed than you? Away with this selfrighteousness. It will hinder your sight of Christ, and your rejoicing in his cross. What can all your guilt be, which the blood of Christ cannot expiate? Are any excluded from the benefits of redemption, but those who exclude themselves by unbelief? There is every encouragement given to penitent sinners, of every description, to believe on the Lord Jesus Christ, that they may be saved. Receive, then, the record of God, that he hath given you eternal life, and this life is in his Son. Trust in him, and be not afraid. So shall good come unto you, even peace of conscience here, and glory everlasting.

SERMON XI.

THE DIFFERENCE BETWEEN A CARNAL AND SPIRITUAL KNOWLEDGE OF CHRIST.

2 Cor. v. 16.

Wherefore, henceforth know we no man after the flesh: yea, though we have known Christ after the flesh, yet now henceforth know we him no more.

The Apostle is here describing the effect of conversion. "The love of Christ," says he, "constraineth us." We were dead, but now we live, and " he died for all, that they which live should not henceforth live to themselves, but to him who died for them and rose again."

So powerful an alteration as this, which takes place in every real conversion, gives a man a taste and spirit quite different from that which he had by nature. He no longer knows things " after the flesh," that is, according to the spirit of the world, which is natural to fallen man. Persons and things are now beheld with different eyes. A real christian " knows no man now after the flesh." He sets a quite different value on objects from that which he did before. What was once pleasing is now become insipid; what was once disgusting is now become agreeable. His prejudices are removed; his affections have a new direction; his will is turned to God from sin and the world: and the sense of his vast obligations to Christ, who redeemed him from the just damnation of hell, constrains him to suffer and to do whatever he is called to for his sake. It is but little that he can do to show his gratitude; but he does that little: he gives himself up to him who died for him and rose again to be his for ever. Hence he must know, regard, and estimate persons and things no longer "after the flesh, but after the Spirit."

When a man acts according to the course of this world, with no higher or better principles than mere nature furnishes, he is said to "live after the flesh;" and even the fairest shows of virtue, unprincipled with the love of Christ, are merely FLESHLY according to the Scriptures. But when a man comes to have a new nature, and Christ dwells in his heart by faith, he then is said to "walk after the Spirit;" meaning the Spirit of Christ which now rules in him. And if a man before his conversion had known Christ after the flesh, that is, had conceived of Christ after the manner and spirit of the world, yet the change which now has taken place in him, leads him henceforward not to know him in that manner any more. He now knows Christ spiritually; beholds his real glory; loves him with spiritual affection; conceives of his character, person, offices, and kingdom, according to their real nature. And all this is not to be wondered at: for being "in Christ," he is "a new creature, old things are passed away, behold, all things are become new."

It has been thought that the Apostle alludes to the mistaken notion which Peter and the other Apostles had formed of Christ, when they thought his kingdom was of this world, and that he was come to be a temporal Prince and a worldly Conqueror. And indeed this mistake of theirs affords us an instance, and gives a good illustration of what it is "to know Christ after the flesh." But the meaning must by no means be confined to this. To know Christ and every other object, "after the flesh," is to know and value them according to the spirit of fallen nature, and is quite opposite to the knowledge and estimation of things "according to the spirit." These two sorts of lives, tastes, tempers, and dispositions, called FLESH and SPIRIT, the one the fruit of mere nature, the other of the Holy Spirit in regeneration, are so spoken of in St. Paul's writings, as to leave no reasonable doubt, that the general idea I have given is the true meaning of the text.

Nor is it in knowing Christ only, but all men, that the Apostle speaks of this fleshly principle. His great object is to teach us, that the new creature views, feels, loves, estimates every possible object, in regard to his ends, motives, and pursuits, in a manner quite different from the way of mere nature. Doubtless the spiritual views which the Apostles had of Christ's kingdom, so opposite to those of the Jews, and to those which they themselves had on their first acquaintance with Christ, is a good illustration of the general subject before us. But I cannot think it was the main thing intended, nor even particularly alluded to by the Apostle: for it should be remembered that the Apostle Paul was not one of the twelve. Such a sentiment was therefore more likely to have proceeded from Peter, James, or John.

The general idea of the text being stated, I purpose to describe two sorts of Persons—1st, those who know Christ, and estimate both him and all other objects after the flesh—2d, those who know Christ in that manner no more, but who know him after the Spirit. And I must beseech my audience to examine their own consciences, that they may see whether they are real or only nominal christians. It also behoves me to speak plainly to the consciences of each according to the Scripture—"O God of grace, who hast given us thy Son to be our Saviour, send thy holy Spirit into our hearts, to give us a right judgment in all things."

1st. He who knows Christ after the flesh, was bred a christian; was baptized, and pays some attention to christian forms. Nor has he totally renounced the worship of God on the Lord's-day. In that he will go so far as the prevailing custom and fashion prescribes. When it was reckoned an indecent thing, as it was in the days of our fathers, to neglect public worship, on either part of the day, he would conform to the allowed rules of propriety. But now that the fashion of violating the Sabbath in the afternoons is grown strong, he does it without shame; for he is kept in countenance by numbers.

I mention this only as one instance; for it may stand as a good sample of the whole character. He who "knows Christ only after the flesh," or in an external manner, moves by the rules and customs of the world. He thinks nothing shocking, nor does he feel any thing grievous to his conscience, which has the sanction of the multitude. With the same loose ideas of religion which he has, he would have been a Mahometan, or a Pagan: He would have professed any religion which happened to be the fashion. He has no deep, serious, abiding concern for eternity. His soul is to him an object of small magnitude compared with the riches, the pleasures, or the honours of this world. Hence you never find him ready to deny himself, to bear the cross of Christ, to put himself to any cost or trouble for Christ's sake. So far is he from being constrained by the love of Christ.

He professes, all this time, a regard for Christ and the christian religion, but he lives not to him who died for sinners. If christian profession abound, and the doctrines of the Gospel be fashionable, where he lives, it is not to be wondered at if he also profess evangelic truth. And he will use some of these phrases concerning religion, which are common among his neighbours. But he only knows Christ "after the flesh:" he has no lively ideas annexed to the words. His soul cleaves to the world, and in business, in conversation, in company, he goes on just like a man of the world. If he meet with a godly man alone, he may honour and own him; but in public he is quite ashamed of him. He takes care never to expose himself to contempt and reproach for Christ's sake. He knows how low and mean a christian looks in the eye of the world, and he never suffers himself to be aspersed as a professor of godliness in the sight of persons of rank and figure.

There is a reason why he is thus ashamed. He has not "Christ in him the hope of glory." He never felt a wounded spirit on account of sin; the burden of guilt never lay heavy on him. It has always cost him far more pain and trouble of mind to gain the good-will of men, and to compass his worldly views of riches, or success in trade, than to obtain a persuasion of the pardon of his sins and the favour of God. And though he may not have been without stings of conscience, his character among men is of more consequence in his eyes than the love of God. He obeys the commands of his Maker no farther than is agreeable to his carnal reason or lust. "Honour me, I pray thee, before the elders of Israel," he will say with Saul to the prophet, and make a parade with him of worshipping the Lord, while he has spared Agag and the best of the sheep. He has no notion of being moved by the plain weight of divine command, to do this or to avoid that. If he can see no worldly, interested views, why he should do so or not do so, he disobeys or disputes, extenuates or cavils, but will still be thought religious. He never had a broken heart; his inmost soul never trembled before the Divine Majesty. The evil of sin he feels not, nor is Christ precious to his mind as a Saviour. He will defend the christian religion, in general, as a thing decent and reputable, as a matter of politics or of party. His own personal concern in it is little considered. When he is called to look at himself alone as a sinner before God, who must shortly appear before him in judgment, he feels nothing. Eternity weighs not with him: He is wrapped up wholly in the objects of time and sense. He has no delight in communing with God by Christ in secret prayer, or in meditation on the world to come. There is no intercourse maintained between Christ and his soul. He has heard of the burden of sin; but he feels it not. He has heard of the pleasures of godliness, and of delight in God; but he has no notion of it.

How should he? He is full of the world, and has not an idea of any delight in heavenly things, nor would all the riches of heaven give him an atom of comfort. He may assent to the general doctrine of salvation by Christ; but he never felt any need of salvation. The new birth is to him an empty sound, and justification by faith in Christ is either not believed at all, or perverted to the purposes of sin, and to encourage himself in wickedness. The whole of the divine life, and the influence of the Holy Spirit on the heart, and the various trials and conflicts of godliness with the world, the flesh, and the devil, are to him unknown. Nor has he, by experience, any real insight into any part of practical godliness, described in Scripture. Let him take christianity in a general view, and he will stand as a christian; but bring him to the test of any one plain essential truth, which enters into the heart of christianity, and he knows nothing of it.

His notions in religion, and all that he understands of the subject, are confined to things moral and prudential; to maxims of conduct, which respect this life, and to such general ideas of virtue as a heathen philosopher might expatiate on; but he has nothing in him peculiarly christian. That he is without the cross of Christ is because he never showed those dispositions, essential to real christianity, which bring the offence of the cross.

Now, conscience, do thine office. Let not this

man go away self-deceived. Let him consider that he may die this day. Death is to him always at a prodigious distance; he is too full of worldly objects to think of being removed hence. Think not, nominal christian, to avail thyself of a general notion of being a christian, and of being received as such into heaven. Thy heart must be detected. Has this man " known Christ after the flesh or after the Spirit?" Is it merely by an outward show, with some decent christian phrases, that he has imposed on himself, or does he " know Christ after the Spirit?" His heart being laid open, behold! it is enmity against God. It is all alive for the world. It has no humility, no feeling of the need of Christ's righteousness, to justify him before God, no desire at all after acquaintance with Christ and conformity to him.

In particular: the offence of the cross is not to be found upon him. Blow off the thin varnish of christian phrases, and outward observances, and you see nothing but what a Pagan moralist might assent to; nothing answerable to the description in the passage before us. " The love of Christ constraineth us—living to him who died for us—being a new creature—old things passed away." With him all is the same as it ever was. No change of heart at all. He was always ashamed of Christ, and never had an idea of professing religion but in a crowd.

Repent, O man! Christ will be ashamed of thee, when thou appearest before him, as thou hast been ashamed of him in this world. There is no family-likeness between him and thee. Thy life shows that sin has had dominion over thee. Know, then, before it is too late to remedy thy case, that there is a knowledge of Christ " after the Spirit" very different from any thou hast to boast of. Search the Scripture, and thy own heart, and pray for light, that thou mayest be made "a new creature in Christ," and not be ashamed before him at his coming. " Knowing the terror of the Lord, we persuade men," says the Apostle. Think, O ye nominal christians, of the terrors of divine justice to be laid open at the last day. Here you sheltered yourselves in a crowd of christians, as it were, and were able by some shows of religion to deceive both yourselves and others. But then you will be laid open; for the secrets of all hearts shall be disclosed; and it will then appear, that you had no real love of God and his Christ at all : that you made use of certain christian forms to impose on your own conscience and on the world, while you lived in the constant breach of the divine commandments, following a multitude to do evil, and conformed to the world in its pomps and vanity, pleasures and luxury, covetousness and earthly-mindedness. The furnace of fire, the wailing and gnashing of teeth, the everlasting fire prepared for the devil and his angels, these things mentioned by our Lord in the gospels, set forth the terror which the Apostle knowing, was induced to persuade men to repent and believe the gospel while time remains. And, nominal christians, if you would not be confounded as hypocrites at that day, if you would escape the wrath to come, be persuaded now, while it is called to-day, not to harden your hearts against the call of God to your souls. Examine yourselves by the rule of the divine word, and not by the fashions of the times and the ideas of the company which you keep. See how far removed you are from the spirit of real christianity; how destitute of that lively faith, patient hope, and genuine love, which the gospel requires. Consider what a difference there is between form and spirit; between death and life; between a shadow and a substance; and assure yourselves that the applause of your misjudging companions will be no shelter to you from the penetrating eye of him who seeth not as man seeth. Fall low before his footstool, and humble yourselves under his mighty hand, and seek for illuminating grace, that you may know Christ no longer "after the flesh," but in a spiritual manner, that you may live as christians, and die in peace.

2d. Consider we now what it is "to know Christ no longer after the flesh." This and the two foregoing chapters instruct us very strikingly on this subject. But the New Testament abounds in such instruction, and he who has had a name to live and yet has been dead, if he desires to be delivered from his errors, may read in abundance and learn the distinction between the two sorts of characters. And is not the distinction obvious in real life? May you not see two persons, who both profess the christian religion; nay, who may express their creed much in the same manner; who may attend the same ordinances and means of grace, and yet are so totally distinct from one another, that you shall plainly see them to be living on quite opposite plans? The one has a heart for God and his Christ; the other a cold formality. The one is broken and contrite in spirit, and humbled before God for his sins; dreads, and hates, and forsakes sin; loaths it as the pollution of his nature, and groans under it as the burden of his life: The other confesses himself sinful for form's sake, and because he knows his religion requires him to do so; but it is evident from the ease with which he can mix with all sorts of company, and even be entertained with the sinful practices of others, instead of being concerned or grieved at them, that sin is no burden to his mind. The one has a delight in God through Christ; rejoices in the cheering manifestations of divine love to his soul, and praises his God for the light of his countenance; or he mourns for an absent God, and cannot rest under his frowns: The other is unconscious and unconcerned about the favour of God, and is uniformly alike in religion, because he is dead, and the work of the Divine Spirit is to him unknown. The one has joy and sorrow, hope and fear, pleasure and sadness, exercised on soul concerns, from time to time: The other has all these passions as a man, but in religion they have no place. They are exercised on the world.

In short, I would appeal to the common sense of mankind, whether you may not observe this most important distinction exemplified in real life; whether, notwithstanding the doubts which involve some characters, you cannot see that there are persons, even in this bad world, plainly alive in the christian religion; loving the Lord Jesus, and his ways and people; studious to make as many as possible acquainted with him; grieved that he is so little inquired after, and so little regarded in the world; delighting to converse with one another, and to improve and quicken one another in godliness; and careful to promote all good works. These have plainly their joys and their hopes derived from the promise of eternal life made to sinners in Christ Jesus, and rejoice in hope of the glory of God, to be revealed hereafter. They are men whose taste and turn of mind you see to be moulded by the doctrines and precepts of the written word; and therefore it SPEAKS to them; encourages, rebukes, directs, and warns them continually.

Now these are the Christians; and when you read of those who are " dead," and whose " life is hid with Christ in God;" and to whom Christ is " the life," and who expect that " when he shall appear, they shall appear with him in glory," and who therefore "mortify their members which are on earth," and having Christ " in them the hope of glory, purify themselves even as he is pure," you see in these persons living examples of what you read. In others, who bear the Christian name without life; who live for this world and not for the next; who are led away by worldly and carnal lusts; who are covetous, proud, high-minded; living in malice and envy; lovers of pleasures more than lovers of God; and who yet join to all this some christian forms and rites, you see an image of the Scribes and Pharisees, who persecuted the real church of God, and who were very studious of being applauded as the people of God, though they were void of the love of God. By this distinction you see what it is to have the FORM, and what it is to have the POWER of godliness, a difference that began to appear even in St. Paul's days. You see with what propriety real christians are said, by our Saviour, to be " the salt of the earth, and the light of the world;" and that they are as evidently a distinct people from the men of the world, though these may bear the christian name, as they are from professed Pagans.

And here one peculiar sign of the christian character is to be marked—the scandal of the cross; the offence, which however undesignedly, they give to the world, by their religious singularity, and their conscientious abstinence from the sinful ways, customs, and fashions of the world.—They particularly provoke all persons who pride themselves in their moral virtues; because they are necessarily bound to count their own righteousness as filthy rags, and glory only in the Lord Jesus; gladly suffering the loss of all things, that they may win Christ, and be found in him: Because they live righteously, soberly, and godly in this present world, and yet after all count themselves unprofitable servants; knowing that there is sin enough in their *best* deeds to deserve wrath and damnation, (how much more in their *worst*) and thankfully embracing the redemption from the curse by Christ Jesus, who was made a curse for them.

This part of their spirit and character is unintelligible to all persons whose religion is mere form, who neither have, nor desire to learn true humility; and who therefore are not fitted to sing salvation to him that was slain, and that redeemed them to God by his blood.

But as those who know Christ only " after the flesh" find themselves condemned as wrong by real christians, not only because of their vicious lives and earthly-mindedness, but also because of their self-righteousness, and their trusting in their own works for acceptance with God, hence a bitter hatred and enmity must arise, which has led, in all ages, those who " are born after the flesh to persecute those who are born after the Spirit." Hence the cross of persecution. Hence so much is spoken in the Scripture of the duty of christians to bear with patience the evil things said and done against them ; to show meekness and long-suffering under the ill treatment to which they are exposed, " not returning railing for railing, but overcoming evil with good;" and to consider the Lord Jesus, " who endured so much contradiction," lest they should be faint and weary in their minds. Hence also the many comfortable promises of inward strength and guidance given to christians, to keep them from being swallowed up with the spirit of heaviness; and the directions to keep themselves unspotted from the world, and not to be ashamed of Christ in the midst of an adulterous generation. This is their duty, though the cross of Christ be foolishness in the eyes of the world, and the choicest truths and excellencies of the real religion of Christ be scoffed at, and the persons of those who espouse them be held up as the most ridiculous and contemptible of all characters.

From this circumstance of contempt, a great trial arises to a real christian. It is no little matter to bear the contempt of all around us. They may call it a little matter, who have never been tried with it; but those who have, know what it means. When the outward profession of religion abounds so much, as to take away, in a great measure, this cross, the evidences of christianity grow less easy to be seen. Such sort of converts as join themselves to a great multitude, or very large party, which keep them in countenance, have no idea of the trials of those who were not ashamed of Christ crucified, when they stood almost alone. It therefore highly behoveth those, in our days, who begin to profess godliness, to see that they have a different ground for glorying, than in a numerous sect or party, by whatever name it be called. Let them examine themselves whether they "be in the faith," and whether they can bear the cross of shame and contempt, when called to it. If men can do so in a right manner, it must be because they are alive to God. But men void of life have no idea of the duty of bearing this cross, nor do their circumstances point out to them the propriety of patience under persecution and ill usage for the name of Christ. They say that such things belong only to the first christians. They might just as properly say, that all the consolations of godliness, and even heaven itself, belonged only to the first christians. But let it be remembered, that Christ, his Gospel, and human nature, are the same in all ages, and therefore that all Scripture was written for our learning, as well as for that of the first ages.

Let the real christian consider the nature of true religion as it is described in this, and the foregoing chapters of St. Paul's 2d Epistle to the Corinthians.

He who knows Christ spiritually has the law of God written, by the Spirit, on his heart. He feels his own insufficiency; knows the SPIRIT of the New Testament, and is sensible that the LETTER will not save, but destroy men's souls. He is delivered from the ministration of death, rejoices in Christ Jesus, and has no confidence in the flesh. He beholds heaven opened, and God reconciled through Christ. The veil is removed from his heart. The god of this world holds him no more in blindness. What a difference between the state of the earth when in darkness, and when God said, " Let there be light, and there was light." Such is the difference between his state, as now renewed and illuminated, from what it was in a state of nature. He rejoices in the prospect of being with Jesus and sharing in his resurrection. He can enter into the full meaning of the Apostle's words, in the close of the foregoing chapter, with which I shall conclude —" We also believe, and therefore speak, knowing that he which raised up the Lord Jesus, shall raise up us also by Jesus, and shall present us with you. For which cause we faint not; but though our outward man perish, yet the inward man is renewed day by day. While we look not at the things which are seen, but at the things which are not seen: for the things which are seen are temporal; but the things which are not seen are eternal."

SERMON XII.

THE CONVERSION OF ST. MATTHEW.

Luke, ch. v. ver. 27—33.

After these things he went forth, and saw a publican named Levi, sitting at the receipt of custom: and he said unto him, Follow me, and he left all, rose up, and followed him. And Levi made him a great feast in his own house: and there was a great company of Publicans, and of others that sat down with them. But their Scribes and Pharisees murmured against his disciples, saying, Why do ye eat and drink with Publicans and Sinners? And Jesus answering, said unto them, They that are whole, need not a Physician; but they that are sick: I came not to call the righteous, but sinners to repentance.

THIS story is full of instruction: Very much of the power of true grace is displayed in it; of grace as it is in the Most High, effectually converting one dead in trespasses and sins; and grace as it is experimentally exercised in the heart and practice of a true convert. The holy, meek, condescending, and gracious character of the divine Saviour is exhibited, to the great encouragement of needy, broken-hearted sinners. The nature of true repentance also evinces itself in a renunciation of all self-righteous hopes, and in a hearty, thankful embracing of so suitable a Saviour as Jesus is briefly, yet strongly, declared to be. We likewise see the Pharisaic spirit of those who are too good to need the Son of God to shed his blood for them, and too righteous to want converting grace, exposed or rebuked.

These topics have all, from time to time, been laid before you; but there are different lights and views in which the same things may be exhibited; and variety may yet be displayed, even on those gospel subjects which have the greatest unity and simplicity. Our present plan then shall be to go through a plain expository view of this narrative. It may please God to impress us as we go along with views adapted to each part of the story, and to furnish us with suitable matter of comfort, instruction, rebuke, and correction.

I said " a plain expository view." To be very studious in quest of the ornaments of speech ill becomes, in general, a Minister of Christ, and is ill adapted to christian subjects. But in what relates to heart-work, to the application of divine things to the conscience, it is peculiarly unsuitable. " My speech and my preaching," says the Apostle, " was not with enticing words of man's wisdom, but in demonstration of the Spirit and of power." A negligent plainness will most powerfully reach those hearts, who are likely to be benefited by thoughts which are purely spiritual. As for those who love to have their ears tickled with smooth language, and are looking only for entertainment in well-turned periods, instead of desiring the words of eternal life, they ought not to be gratified; nor can they but at the expence of divine truth itself. For such is its nature, that it cannot endure an ornamented style. It loses much of its strength, generally speaking, when clothed in such a dress. The Holy Spirit will have nothing at all to do with the laboured oratory, which is calculated to raise that kind of sensations in which many persons think the feelings of true virtue consist.

" He went forth and saw a publican named Levi."—The Lord of life is just going to display one of those godlike acts of mercy and power, in which he chiefly delights: To open a sinner's eyes, and turn him " from darkness to light, and from the power of Satan to God, that he may receive forgiveness of sins and an inheritance among the sanctified by faith" in himself.—To raise the dead is an astonishing display of divine power; but it is neither so powerful, nor so gracious an act as this, to quicken a soul that is " dead in trespasses and sins." We are all so by nature: as soon as we were born, we went astray and spoke lies. To know God; to love him; to delight in him; to put our whole trust in him; to glorify him; and to place our eternal happiness in enjoying him as our portion, for these things man was created; but these things he lost in the Fall: We were in Adam when he fell: We lost them by that event, and matter of fact shows, that not these, but very opposite dispositions prevail in us from the womb.

Some are of quick, others of slow parts: some by nature are vigorous and active; sanguine and choleric: Others, as naturally, inactive and slothful; mild and timid. But with reference to God, amidst a thousand constitutional differences, we are all exactly alike. We do not seek after him: we do not know him. His real nature and character is to us a secret. We have no notion of placing our happiness in him. Natural conscience may compel us, at times, to do something in a religious way; but surely we had rather from the bottom of our hearts have nothing to do with God. When men come to feel what lies deep in their souls, they find there is a principle of enmity against God. Melancholy we think is connected with religion. Not that we have any thing to follow that we can say makes us happy: it is impossible. God never meant that we should find happiness, nor is it possible that we should, out of himself. Therefore, some in one thing and some in another, seek for that which satisfieth not, and man walketh in a vain shadow, and disquieteth himself in vain. Still he will not turn to God; he will try one thing after another; but the vacancy remains still. The various pursuits of life may a while divert; but none will say that they are happy in them. Guilt, distance from God, and blindness of heart, keep them still the slaves of misery.

This is the way of all men by nature. But God has not left us without hope, if we indeed be brought to fall in with his way of salvation. There is, there is in this life, a saving change, and restoration to the favour of God to be obtained. Observe! in this life it must be found. Deceive not yourselves with the thought of finding it in the next, though to your dying hour you go on unacquainted with it. This is a fatal mistake—Oh! what numbers of souls have perished eternally through it. *There* at least they find, " he that is filthy, let him be filthy still."

My brethren, be persuaded, ye who have any concern for your precious souls, to attend to these things; to seek after God, that your souls may live; to hearken to the Lord's words, " ye must be born again." Consider the importance of this change. Though careless men think it an easy and slight thing to obtain forgiveness of their sins, yet that there is, indeed, forgiveness with God, is a great, an amazing thing, not easily believed with the heart, in a due manner, however professed with the lips. The fallen angels can tell you this: They once sinned, not " keeping their first estate," and behold! they are " reserved in chains" to everlasting darkness. They have not found forgiveness, nor ever will find it. Forgiveness, in a certain way, is offered to us men, it is not so to them. Sin is not that trifling thing you think; nor is God that idol of mercy you imagine. Behold! he gave his Son to procure forgiveness for us; to make justice and mercy meet together. And HE found it dreadful work indeed! Witness his unheard-of agony in the garden at Gethsemane; his cross and passion on Mount Calvary.

This, then, should both make you serious in seeking for salvation, and encourage you to seek. " If other sinners have found mercy, I may also." Levi is " sitting at the receipt of custom." He is a publican, doing the duties of his office. It is no hinderance to a man in religion to be following the duties of his calling. But then what sort of a calling was this? A calling that exposed a man to the guilt of extortion, oppression, deceit, profaneness, and the keeping of bad company. No Jew of credit would keep company with a publican. He is joined with sinners continually in holy writ. Now this should be an encouragement to the vilest and grossest sinners, not to remain in the practice of their sins; but to seek for the grace of Jesus to be forgiven and made new creatures. Matthew the Publican (for he it is who is also called Levi) became afterwards Matthew the Apostle; the writer of the first gospel; the beloved disciple of Jesus; the faithful preacher of his word; and a choice saint now reigning with Jesus in glory. No doubt he would find, as we do, sin very strong and powerful; his lusts exceeding violent, and old habits, oh! how hard to be eradicated. But grace did all for him; and why not for us also? yea for us, above all that we can ask or think. This is the use that we should make of this instance of divine grace.

I remember Cyprian, Bishop of Carthage, tells us, in his account of his conversion, that he had thought it impossible that he should become a new creature, to love what he before hated, and to hate what he before loved. But when he experienced the washing of regeneration, he tells us what grace did for him; that it made every thing new, easy, delightful, and pleasant in his soul, which he could not before have imagined. He suffered martyrdom for the faith of Christ in A. D. 260. But in every age the case is the same with all who are turned to God.

Be it observed, however, that this is no work of man, but of the Lord God, as much as the creation of the heavens and the earth are. Admit that Matthew might have had dawnings of grace in his heart, before this, preparing him for what was to happen—which whether he had or not we cannot tell—yet what cause could there then be in the man, after all, to bring about such a change? He is attending to the publican's office. Many of you know what a distracting thing the business of the world is: how it causes the heart to cleave to the earth, and to forget whether you have a soul, and whether there be a God or not. Now for a man to leave so sinful a calling, merely on our Lord's saying, "follow me;" to leave all; rise up, and follow him; and count every thing as nothing compared with Christ; to cleave to him, and become a despised, persecuted disciple of a poor, despised Master—what could bring this about, but effectual grace?

A great point is gained, if men be brought to feel this: That it is not in themselves to turn to God; that the turning point is with the Lord; that the thing is impossible with man, but yet possible with God. Till men know this, the little they do in religion will be heartless and weak, through some poor resolution of their own. But when this is known, they will look out for grace, effectual grace, by faith and not by works, and in this way will surely thrive. Could the bare word "follow me," effect this, think you? We exhort and cry unto sinners again and again; but they are not persuaded. You may say it was the word of Jesus. But had we then lived and seen Jesus in that poor, mean condition in which he was pleased to show himself on earth, those who now slight his gospel would have slighted his person, notwithstanding they call themselves christians.

The word spoken to Levi was a word of power: It came with the Holy Ghost: It reached his heart: He saw the glory of God, by it, shining in the face of Jesus Christ: His holy and glorious character as a Saviour was manifested to him: Divine things, in their beauty, won his inmost soul. He felt his sin, misery, and undone condition: He saw now, in heavenly things, what appeared worthy his regard. Therefore he freely and cheerfully "followed" Jesus; ready to give all up for him. And this is to follow Jesus in the regeneration. This is the light of effectual grace: This won Matthew to God; and you and I must experience this; and for this, and the continuance and growth of this, should seek and pray. Indeed we have no business worth attending to in comparison of that one thing needful, without which we shall in no case enter into the kingdom of heaven.

Admire we, then, for our encouragement, and to the honour of our God, the riches of his grace in this transaction. It is but a word, " follow me," and this publican "leaves all, rises up, and follows him." Matthew, after this, walks as "a new creature in Christ. Old things are passed away, behold, all things are become new." He never had any thing near such delight in counting his bags of money, as now in contemplating the unsearchable riches of Christ. The forgiving love of God constraining him to love, to spend, and be spent for Christ, is now more to him than thousands of gold and silver. He has the true riches laid up sure in heaven.

How strong that power must have been which thus changed his heart, judge ye, who feel the bewitching influence of the love of money. If you wish for deliverance, " the pitifulness of his great mercy," exercised in Almighty power, can loose you also. Look to him and seek his face. How kind that free grace is which forgives the sins of a Miser, judge ye, whose extortion and oppression have grinded the faces of the poor. But the blood of Jesus can wash you also. Seek him, and do no more presumptuously.

Behold! the effects of this grace on Matthew. If you read the same story in his gospel, *Matt.* ix. 9, you will find he says " he arose and followed him." He does not say, " left all :" a great significant expression. Luke says so. But Matthew, who feels what indwelling sin means, and is not studious of his own praise, suppresses it. For the conjecture is not unlikely, that humility and poverty of spirit prevented his mentioning it. This is right. Let the effects of grace be admired and taken notice of by others : Let him who is the subject of it, as it were, see them not, but be low and contrite in spirit; admiring the grace of the Saviour alone.

But a still more striking instance of this nature occurs. " Levi," says Luke, " made him a great feast, in his own house; and there was a great company of publicans and others that sat down with them." See how rich this man appears to have been! What a wonder, to see a rich man, so heartily embracing a poor despised Saviour! Ye rich men, think of this. Consider the danger and deceitfulness of your riches, and learn to become poor and humble in your own sight, that a poor despised Saviour may give you the true riches.

How natural is it for those who have tasted that

the Lord is gracious themselves, to long that others may taste also! "Come, see a man which told me all that ever I did: is not this the Christ?" "The Spirit and the bride say, come." Oh! go to Jesus; I found him a merciful and a gracious Saviour.— Matthew, whose bowels now yearn over his former companions, the publicans and sinners, invites them to hear Jesus, that they might also partake of his grace.—But see the modesty of his own narrative "as Jesus sat at meat in the house." He does not tell us, that he "made a great feast" for Jesus, at his own house: but Luke tells us so. If true Saints love not to speak of their own excellencies, it is fitting that others who see them should not be silent concerning them.

This humility, and this sincere compassion for the souls of former comrades in iniquity, then, are the immediate effects of grace. Who among us know the like? What evidences of conversion like this of Matthew, have we experienced? But "their Scribes and Pharisees murmured"—not against our Lord— there was an awfulness in his character that kept them at a distance, but "against his disciples, saying, why do ye eat and drink with publicans and sinners?" This is the true Pharisaical spirit. These *holy* men were too good to be touched by a publican. They would have thought themselves defiled by such company. They see not the filthiness of their own natures. The least insight into that, will always dispose a man to think no otherwise of himself than as the vilest of the vile; for it inclines a man to think none so vile as himself.

Thus when a man is brought quite low in his own eyes, he will thankfully embrace Jesus as his Saviour;

glad now to live out of another's life; to act from another's strength, and to rejoice in another's righteousness. And this is that "mystery of godliness, the life of faith in Jesus," which we preach; and which when I forget, as the grand theme of the gospel, call me no more a Minister of Christ.

But, oh! this principle of self-righteousness! How strongly does it work in many decent, regular moralists! They may envy the happiness of those gross sinners, whom grace has humbled, and enabled now to live a life of holiness, to which they themselves are utter strangers. They can have no idea of such love of God! Pride, and malice, and self-sufficiency, all under a decent show, and all unknown even to themselves, set them farther from God than the grossest sinners. To such how hard to learn this lesson, that "by the works of the law shall no flesh be justified," and that they must be saved by mere grace, as much as the greatest criminal in the world. Theirs is a hard case, and very discouraging to think of, if one look at human means and probabilities. But "is any thing too hard for the Lord?" He can make the proudest to feel their vileness; and enable the most haughty and the most stubborn of Pharisees to read, in legible lines, their own character; find themselves vile sinners, and gladly submit to be saved by Christ alone. Saul of Tarsus was one of this stamp: and yet who, more than he, after his conversion, saw into the evil of self-righteousness, and glorified more simply in Jesus Christ?

To be plain, we must drop all hope of this kind, I mean from comparing ourselves with others, or we are on a wrong foundation for life, and are not come to Christ. And what think you is the way to bring men thus low in their own eyes, and make either Publican, or Pharisee, gross, or decent sinners, feel their absolute need of salvation by Christ alone? I will tell you by experience: For I surely have reason to know this matter, having been once righteous in mine own eyes. Only be serious, brethren. Whether you rank with Publicans or Pharisees, humbled to the point before us you must be, or never know what rejoicing in Christ means. Do not deceive yourselves with notions of religion. It is a thing that must be felt in the inmost soul. What I was going to tell you, will be done from the words of the text. "And Jesus answering unto them, said, they that are whole need not a physician, but they that are sick." Yes, Pharisees, if God make you feel your sickness, and let in light into your souls to know how and what manner of persons you are, no sick man ever applied more earnestly to a physician than you will to Christ. Why does the word come so cold to your hearts? You are not sick: You understand not, you relish not the gospel, because you feel not the pangs of conviction. Pray then to be awakened. Examine your lives by the rule of God's commands, and seek till you do feel and know what vile and condemned sinners you are.

The pain and trouble of true conviction is great when God makes a man to know what he is. How foolish, then, *foolish* as well as proud and wicked, appear his former high thoughts of himself. But conviction of sin is not given to be rested on. It is from the Saviour: it should lead you to him.

I trust there are some here who know what peace and rest is, through faith in Jesus. But do not many still remain at a distance, pining away in conviction, or wearing it off and relapsing into a trifling state? Think! The issue should be healing by Christ the physician, and through the application of his blood. That can do for Pharisees and for Publicans what they want, and nothing else can. How long will it be ere many half-earnest professors come to a point in this business, and find healing through the blood of Jesus? Will you go to hell, then, at length with your eyes half open? And will not ye who once knew these things, but whose eyes are now grown dim through sloth and worldliness, return and be revived with grace before you die? And ye who say all is well with you, and who yet are unacquainted with these things—may one ask when began your soul concern? When had you acquaintance with Christ? When experienced his healing power? Go ye and learn what that meaneth, " I will have mercy and not sacrifice, for I am not come to call the righteous, but sinners to repentance."

The spirit of the law is to be preferred before the letter. Self-righteous characters are always nice in trifles, and negligent in the life and soul of religion. Happy for us Christ is not so: HE has mercy on poor humbled Publicans. Yes, and on Pharisees also, when they become humbled. Behold! in the text, a lovely picture of grace, condescension, pity, loving-kindness. Sink down in your own sight, ye sons and daughters of men, or you cannot see it. HE came to save sinners. The righteous who think themselves so he abhors. Submit yourselves to him and be happy.

SERMON XIII.

THE HAPPY EFFECTS OF FEARING ALWAY, AND THE DANGER OF PRESUMPTION.

Prov. xxviii. 14.

Happy is the man that feareth alway: but he that hardeneth his heart, shall fall into mischief.

THERE is not a more common description in Scripture of godly men than this, that they fear the Lord. In the text the constancy of this fear is recommended: "Happy is the man that feareth alway." It is never safe, while we live, to be without such fear as causes us to suspect ourselves, and to watch over our steps that we go not astray. The man will be always safe who does this. But he who rushes on without watchfulness and suspicion, will certainl bring himself into great evils, and if he cease n from his folly, into hell at last. "He that hardeneth his heart shall fall into mischief."

Such is the general instruction of the text. It is my design to apply it more particularly to se cases. In doing this I see, methinks, four sort characters to be attended to.—1. The man of world, who has no fear of God before his eyes, and who professes no principle of religion.—2. The man, whose religion only affects his head, but neve reached his heart.—3. The man, whose heart h been touched with religion, but a religion either entirely, or at least partly false.—4. The blessed man, who fears the Lord indeed, and that alway, as the text directs.

I beseech you, brethren, receive with charity, what with charity I hope shall be delivered for your benefit. Some of you may possibly find you can heartily agree with me in condemning one sort; but when I proceed to condemn another sort, there you may find yourselves disposed to make excuses, and to palliate, perhaps to be angry with me. Then is the time to suspect yourselves to be the very persons who are wrong in that particular. It will be worth while to examine your own heart, and God's word, and compare both with the account that shall be given. Let what I shall say be submitted to the authority of God's word, and by that let it stand or fall. Only let no one condemn or reject, till assured that it is contrary to God's word. There is no other safe rule; all things else ought to give way to this.

It is the business of the Gospel Minister, brethren, not to flatter, nor to amuse, not to set up one sort of religious professors and to cry down another, but to act with strict impartiality, as one who pleaseth not men but God. It is his duty to expose the faults of all sorts and kinds of people; to point out the way, the only way, in which they ought to walk; and to distinguish it, continually, from all false ways; and to rebuke and exhort with all long-suffering, and doctrine. To this end, I beg the prayers, the hearty, and constant prayers of all that fear God, that I may be so qualified, and now, and at all other times, may my ministry be to your edification!

The man of this world, who has no religious principles at all, shall first be spoken to. He hardens his heart against all fear, by such considerations as these. "Sin is too slight a thing for God to punish it so severely. He is too merciful to damn us for our faults. God is good, and has done us much good, has given us success in our worldly business. He surely will not destroy us at last; he will not consign us to everlasting burnings." Had I the voice of thunder, and the keenness of lightning, I could not sufficiently lay open the tremendous horror of your situation. How dare you be easy in your souls, on such false reasoning as this! I may well call it *false*, because matter of fact speaks otherwise. Is not the world full of misery? Where do you live that you cannot see it? If the scourge has not yet reached you, what reason have you to think that your time will not come ere long? Is God a respecter of persons? See you not numbers very miserable, who are not more wicked, it may be, than you? At this very time one part of the world is the seat of dismal confusion, and the horror of war. The hand of the Almighty is in all this, and it is certain that he is punishing sin. He is teaching thee, by thy neighbour's experience, what thou mayest expect by and by in thy turn because of sin. Surely a God of pity, of goodness, of Love itself, delights not in our misery. He says himself, " he does not afflict willingly, nor grieve the children of men." There must be a cause then, a necessity, of which he alone, in his infinite wisdom, must be the judge, for his punishing sin. The pride of reasoning against such evident matter of fact, when the character of the Lord is considered, is intolerable, and equalled only by its folly.

But where do you live, that you cannot see the hand of God punishing sin? Not a newspaper can be read, but marks of it appear. In private life, and among your neighbours, the same thing appears. Perhaps dress and diversions; gaming or business; grandeur or trifling; gaiety and laughter, so take you up, that you are drunk with folly's cup, and kept in such a state of intoxication, that you cannot see matter of fact every where and every day crying aloud, " O men, repent and flee from the wrath to come." God is jealous, and the Lord revengeth, the Lord revengeth and is furious." Every where may be seen objects oppressed with poverty, or the prey of loathsome disease; distracted with pain, or benumbed with lethargy. It is folly to draw a veil over these scenes, and talk of every thing going on in a smooth, agreeable way. You that talk so may be of those whose hearts are hardened against the cries of the wretched; or who are so otherwise engaged, as not even to know, or to take notice what misery many suffer in the world. But it is fit that things be stated as they are. The world is a miserable, sorrowful world; and the sin of it in every age has made it so.

Take you your share of affliction, ye insensible ones! It ill becomes you to laugh in jollity, while the world weeps in woe. Have you obtained the pardon of your sins, and a sure title to glory through believing in Jesus? You will not say this: for religion has never yet cost you a course of serious thought. To repeat one prayer at rising, and another at night, with the attendance of your bodies occasionally at this house, this is your religion. Long have you been called on to repent and believe the gospel. But you have not so much as yet understood what repentance and faith mean. It then becomes you, in your present state, to mourn, and weep. " Let your laughter be turned into mourning, and your joy into heaviness."

If any on earth have a right to rejoice, it is those whose sins are pardoned, and who through Jesus have God for their father, and heaven in reserve for their portion. They possess the true sweetener of human woe; yet their joy in this life must be mixed with sorrow. The hand of God at this day chastening us as a nation should affect us all, independent of other causes of grief. To be totally unconcerned, and to go on still in wickedness, must be dreadful indeed, and may provoke the gracious Lord to display his wrath in an uncommon manner against us.

But whatever may be your present lot, O ye careless ones! your prospect beyond the grave is dreadful. Not a passage of Scripture speaks comfort to you. All, all the book, like a thunderbolt, is pointed against you. The present dispensations of God, in his providence, speak what a God he is, holy, jealous of his authority, and surely punishing sin. They are so many harbingers which foretel, against all the lying insinuations of those who cry false peace to themselves, that impenitent sinners so dying shall be thrown into the lake that burneth with fire and brimstone. You think God will be kind to you always, because he has blessed you in temporal concerns: but did you never read, "the prosperity of fools shall destroy them?" You grow proud, insolent, unfeeling in prosperity. You will not bear reproof, no, not from God himself. You should know that the goodness of God leadeth you to repentance. "Is God so good, and shall I thus vilely grieve his Spirit from day to day, requiting evil for good?" This you do by despising the gospel. You have heard it long, and have been entreated to receive it, but in vain. Christ is not your's, nor does his Spirit rule you, nor have you peace through his blood! God is not your delight and portion. You trifle all the day about your soul. Instead of fearing always, as the text directs, you fear not at all. You join any company, you follow any diversion that helps you to forget God. You have no idea of husbanding your time for God: You hear sermon after sermon, but you apply none to your consciences. You are curious to hear of the faults of this and that professor of religion: You apply, perhaps, the sermon to others: even the parts particularly meant for your good, and therefore discourses from the pulpit, which once you heard with anger, now you hear with cool unconcern. Alas! have you no souls? Are you not to appear before a holy God in judgment? Is it necessary for others to appear there, and not for you? To win Christ is as weighty a concern to you as to others. Flee to him, and pray him to impress your heart with what has been said. Learn the lesson of the text, lest you "fall into mischief." Learn to fear God, and continue fearing him and giving him his glory: so shall you be guided unto Christ and rest. If you will not, mark it, I speak on the authority of God's word in the text, you will "fall into mischief." A sudden death may bring you quick into the hell of divine wrath. Your children may suffer, in this world, miseries which you may live to see. You, or others may suffer, even in this world, horrible evils, which will convince you that "there is a God that judgeth the earth." I beseech you harden not your hearts. Make the christian religion your business, your supreme business, or never think of being happy.

But I must speak to a second sort.—You deceive yourselves, and live without the fear of God, by a vain hope of being saved, because you have gained some gospel light, and orthodox doctrine, though you are not yet converted! Worldly cares, pleasures, company, business, eat up your souls; you have yet no love of Christ, and therefore the faith of God's elect is not yours—" Am I in Christ? Are my sins forgiven? Am I born again?" This, this should be your grand object. This is to put the doctrines to use; to get life and salvation by them. But you have not this; for you never felt the burthen of sin as the deepest of all defilements. Oh, then, pray and seek for real religion. You trifle from day to day; no prayers, no watchfulness, no fear of getting wrong in your practice; selfishness and levity mark your conduct. The world cannot see you different from others, except, in this, that you like such and such preachers, and such and such opinions. Shame on such religion! Pure religion, and undefiled before God, is set forth in the Scripture, and in those in whom it is real, as consisting in righteousness, peace and joy in the Holy Ghost; but your religion is vain. A truly godly man " feareth always," lest he be wrong in this, or in that matter. Ah! you know not, you know not sin, nor God, or his fear would not be strange to you. Repent and begin religion afresh. Say, " Lord, hitherto I have had a name to live, and have been dead. Thus far I have had religion in my head; Lord give it me now in my heart. Give me Jesus, the true life, to live in me and walk in me, that I may find his words to be spirit and life."

There are those also who are earnest in religion, but who deceive themselves with a false religion. I am tender in speaking of these, though fully convinced that such cases have been and are. St. Paul met with such among the Corinthians, and such are described in St. Jude's Epistle. But the reason why I am tender in speaking of these is, that some are notwithstanding the children of God, by faith in Christ Jesus. They are not deceived in the foundation of their faith, and they prove that they love the Lord Jesus Christ, but they build hay and stubble on the foundation, and thus their progress in real holiness is hindered. The reason seems to be this: After the attainment of their first joy and comfort in religion, they ceased to fear ever going wrong. They neglected the very positive direction of the text, " happy is the man that feareth alway." They could see that others, men of the world altogether, were wrong for living without fear, and that those who thought their salvation secure, because they had right notions of religion, were wrong also. But they see not (and in this they are much to be pitied) that they themselves are not observing the rule of the text, in another way. They live not under a constant suspicion of themselves and of their own spirit, and temper, and aim, as every watchful christian will. Just as if the whole body of sin was extirpated in them, they indulge their self-will; and whatever they have a strong inclination to, they are apt to fancy it is the will of God, and the direction of his Spirit. Hence self-denial makes, in this view, no part of their religion. What they like, must be done; for they suppose it is the suggestion of the Spirit of God; and what they dislike, however fitting to be done, they neglect. They disregard the only supreme rule of good practice, the written word, and lay themselves open to the workings of an irregular fancy. Did men learn to *fear always*, they would suspect their own hearts, they would watch more narrowly, and what they felt themselves strongly inclined to, they would not be so ready to suppose was the voice of God's Spirit. Influenced by right views of themselves, and the wickedness and deceitfulness of the heart, they would rather suspect such inclinations to proceed from an evil than from a good quarter. They ask, " by what then are we to be ruled in our conduct?" I answer, God's word is the rule; and they that desire so to be led, giving up their will to God's, shall be directed. This is the true leading of the Spirit of God.

However, there is hope, that those who are involved in this delusion, if they are the real people of God by faith in Christ Jesus, may be delivered from it, even in this life. Let them pray for humility. Pride, self-will, and ignorance of themselves deceive them. I have spoken, in charity, a few words to remedy, or to prevent such evils among ourselves. As for those who are righteous in their own eyes, and wise in their own conceit, a miracle of grace only can deliver them. I know none whose religious situation is more deplorable than those who think themselves arrived at the very height of christianity, so as to look down with a kind of pity, mingled with contempt, on inferior christians, and who yet are in the gall of nature's bitterness, and in the bond of iniquity. But this and every other evil in the way of the godly is prevented by observing the direction of the text, " happy is the man that feareth alway."

I would now show you in the last place the character and the blessedness of him that does thus.— May it be my choice, may it be yours, to follow the rule in the text, and we need never want happiness.—When it is said, he " feareth alway," lest any should suspect that constant fear must render his life constantly miserable, I would observe that the fear of the godly, is not that fear which hath torment. It is his privilege, not to be afraid of condemnation, but to rejoice continually in the Lord his righteousness and portion; for " there is no condemnation to them that are in Christ Jesus, who walk not after the flesh, but after the Spirit." I go further, and say it makes no part of the fear before us, to live under the dread of the possibility of falling into destruction at last. For his God has provided against this very expressly: " I will make an everlasting covenant with them, that I will not turn away from them to do them good; but I will put my fear in their hearts, that they shall not depart from me*." Agreeably to which St. Paul tells the believing Corinthians, " the Lord Jesus shall also confirm you to the end, that ye may be blameless in the day of the Lord Jesus Christ." This holy fear, then, is consistent with a constant sense of God's peace, and a certain prospect of eternal salvation already secured through the grace of Jesus. In the promise in Jeremiah, this fear is mentioned as one of the blessings of God's everlasting covenant, and therefore surely consistent with it; being indeed the very means of God's fulfilling it. The children of God, by this jealous fear, are kept close to God and preserved to the end.

But the fear recommended through Scripture is a *filial* fear, such as a dutiful child has of a kind parent. This is so plain a state of the case, that a better illustration of it cannot be given. A christian is one whose sins are forgiven, and who by adoption and grace is taken into God's family. It is his privilege to call God his Father, and to approach him as such, at all times, with boldness; because " the blood of Jesus Christ his Son cleanseth him from all sin." He is not under fear of being disinherited, or turned out of doors. His Father will be his Father still. But if he behave ill, he is liable to be chastised by his Father, and by various ways outward and inward, to have communion with him cut off. How disagreeable is this to

* Jer. xxiii.

a good child! and how agreeable also to live under the encouraging smiles of his heavenly Father, which is the consequence of watchful obedience.

Nor is this all: to obey, brings happiness itself along with it: there is no other road of bliss: " In keeping God's commandments there is great reward." A froward child, by stubbornly refusing to obey his parents, brings woe to himself, in the necessary course of things, because he has not skill to keep himself from dangers, and his wisdom is to follow his parents directions. From these considerations there arises in the hearts of his children a fear of displeasing the best of fathers. The covenant provides, as we have seen, that by this they never shall depart from him. Those who neglect this are said to "harden their hearts," and they shall "fall into mischief:" "but happy is the man that feareth alway." Let the believer always keep up this fear, because there is always occasion for it.—A word or two may be spoken concerning his manner of doing this, and of its happy consequences.

Having once tasted the sweets of communion with God, as a Father in Christ Jesus, he is jealous to preserve his relish for it, and to keep up this communion. It is carried on by the prayer of faith in Jesus. Besides his diligent attendance on public means of grace, he attends constantly to private prayer, meditation, and searching of the Scriptures. He fears, by the least neglect of these, to grieve his Father, and to be shut out from pleasant communion with him in his soul, and every day brings with it so many wants, cares and trials, that he finds he has constant need to pray. The more sweetness of communion he has experienced, and the more powerful answers to his prayers, the more is this jealous fear increased. For the more we prize, and feel the goodness of any thing, the more careful are we of preserving it. This communion, then, he keeps up by praying without ceasing; a praying frame, a spirit hungering and thirsting after righteousness, and a cautious fear of displeasing God in any thing great or small, it is his business to preserve through life. All the forms and duties of religion and morality are, he knows, a mere carcass, the outside of godliness, without the heart.

This same fear of the Lord obliges him to be constantly watchful and wary in all his conduct. In word, and conversation; in promises, bargains, and all his dealings, this godly fear will lead a man to an exactness which will distinguish him from the careless professor of religion, whose religion is only noise and opinion, but has no place in his heart. But the man who fears the Lord indeed, knows that he has three enemies to fight with as long as he lives; the devil, the world, and the flesh. And as they are always against him, he is obliged to fear always.

He is forced to strengthen himself continually with the whole armour of God against Satan, and to be jealous that he constantly use it, lest Satan get an advantage over him, by throwing him into despondency, or into presumption, or into some delusion: for he is not ignorant of his devices. He is constantly obliged to watch against the world, that the love of it may in no sense get the better of the love of his Father; and as he daily feels and will feel till death, if he continue to know himself aright, a treacherous, deceitful, and wicked heart, the working of corrupt nature, hence he suspects his heart continually. He watches it. He calls himself to task to examine his own spirit perpetually, lest he deceive himself.

This is he that feareth alway: but it is his privilege to be bold as a lion for God, and to maintain a knowledge that God is with him, and will be with him to the end. He fears himself the most: but this very fear has this blessedness with it, that neither godly nor ungodly persons can find any blot in him, any thing in his walk inconsistent with his profession of godliness. He stands in awe of the majesty of God, and sins not. He communes with his own heart, and keeps it with all diligence. Thus he escapes the mischiefs that fall upon the heads of the careless and presumptuous, and is preserved blameless unto the coming of his Lord and Saviour Jesus Christ.

SERMON XIV.

THE FOOLISHNESS OF MAN PERVERTETH HIS WAY, AND HIS HEART FRETTETH AGAINST THE LORD.

Prov. xix. 3.

The foolishness of man perverteth his way; and his heart fretteth against the Lord.

To persons, at all acquainted with Solomon's Proverbs, one need not say, that the sentences are single, and unconnected; containing weighty truths or precepts, written by the direction of the Spirit of God, for the use of his people. The sentence which, with God's assistance, I would consider at this time, is a very important one in its nature; and if the Lord assist us in comprehending, and using it aright, we shall see very much useful matter in it, that will deserve the attention both of sinners, and of saints. My intention is to apply it to both distinctly, after having briefly illustrated its meaning.

" The foolishness of man." As if he had said, such is the blindness and folly natural to man, that of himself, without any sort of influence from above, he perverts his own way; he makes himself wicked and miserable. God would have him do otherwise, that he might be happy; but he will not be ruled by his heavenly Father. He will follow his own foolish, headstrong ways; by which he involves himself in misery. This then is one instance of man's natural corruption, viz. his FOLLY. "The foolishness of man perverteth his way."

The second is another instance of his depravity; consisting in his enmity against God. " His heart fretteth against the Lord." The original word is the same that is elsewhere used to represent the raging of the sea in a storm. His heart then boils against God, as the angry sea in a tempest. How impudent this! how ungrateful! how unreasonable! It is man's own " folly that perverteth his way." He should properly accuse himself only; but he accuses God, and chides with him for that misery which he has brought upon himself. This bitterness of heart shows itself, in some, by angry invectives against their fortune, and the like: In others, by a fretting, murmuring, repining frame of spirit: In others, it preys upon itself, and inwardly gnaws the soul.

But you ask, " of whom is this true ?" I answer: this folly, and this impiety is natural to all. For all are gone astray from God's ways like lost sheep, as holy Scripture, and the experience of all who know themselves, bear witness. In the converted only this temper is subdued, and though it is still felt, an opposite, spiritual temper counteracts, and reigns, over it. But in all the unconverted this temper reigns, and is sure to show itself under suitable temptations and occasions.

The words of the text lead us, also, by no means to confine the evil spoken of, to some particular men. It is said, " the foolishness of MAN." The word for MAN, in the original, is ADAM, the common name of man ; intimating, it must seem, both the universality of the disorder, and also the first sin of Adam as the introducer of it. Thus, on the whole, we are told that man naturally makes himself miserable, by his wilful folly, and is so base and proud, that his heart—if he restrain his tongue—fretteth or rageth against the Lord in an impudent and unreasonable manner.

Let us see first how the unconverted are perverted in their ways, by their own folly, and how their heart fretteth against the Lord.—There is that in natural conscience, besides the effect of the more extraordinary motions impressed on it at times by the Holy Spirit, which tells every man that the law of God is good; that he ought to obey it; that for the breach of it God will bring him to judgment. Therefore he cannot break away entirely from God, and give up himself to sin without remorse, and control, till he has first stifled some, nay perhaps, many convictions. He has had some plain intimations, that in true religion only can be true happiness. He may have been flattered by the love of pleasure, riches, or honour, but these things did not fill and satisfy his soul. He has felt that all these things leave a sting behind them, and will at last expose him to the wrath and vengeance of God.

Now, notwithstanding the loud calls of lawless inclinations, yet—canst thou say—can any of us say, that we have not had fair warning, that if we took such and such steps, we should, persisting in them, finally ruin both body and soul? But did we obey the warning?—Conscience! be faithful in the breasts of each of us.—Ran we not into wilful sin? Nay some of us, perhaps, hardened our consciences by degrees, and sold ourselves to do evil in the sight of the Lord.

" Thou shalt not indulge in lewdness and drunkenness. They are sins against God, and provoke his displeasure." How often has conscience said this to thee, O drunkard, O unchaste soul! Yet hast thou dared to commit fornication, and to be intoxicated with strong drink. The first time thou wast guilty of either of these, how did thy conscience smart for it! How didst thou promise, while the pang was on thy soul, that thou wouldst not be guilty of the like again! Yet hast thou repeated the offence. Thy remorse was less and less; and after a time thy sensibility wore off.—But we need not confine our subject to lewdness and drunkenness. Of gaming the same may be said very eminently.

If thou wast of a graver cast, thou employedst thyself earnestly in seeking to obtain money, or honour, or agreeable worldly connections. Conscience at first assured thee (more honest then than now, that she is stupified with long ill usage) that the world had too much both of thy time and heart; very far beyond its due proportion. She remonstrated that thou scarce leftest any time for prayer; searching the Scriptures; and serious meditation on eternity. Thou resolvedst, over and over, to amend; but instead of this thou art farther and farther involved in the world; and less and less disposed to seek the best interests of thy soul. And now, lover of money! that which befel the drunkard, the gamester, the careless profligate, has befallen thee. Thy own "foolishness hath perverted thy ways," for it hath hardened thy heart; stupified thy conscience; given Satan an advantage to draw thee into many hurtful, and evil practices. It hath made thee averse from religion. It hath entangled thee in sin, to such a degree; that now when thou art told how dangerous thy state is; in a peevish manner thou criest, " How can I help it? How can I do otherwise, in a world like this? I cannot amend my heart and ways; it is out of my power. 'Tis very hard one must have passions, and be condemned for gratifying them." Stop, O foolish man! thou hast perverted thy own ways; and now thy "heart fretteth against the Lord." Thus thou fulfillest both parts of the text. Hadst thou not fair warning of the evil consequences of sin? Did not God tell thee all this that has happened, in his word, and in thy conscience?

Now sin has led thee into many worldly inconveniencies. It may be, thou hast hurt thy health, or thy character by it. Thou hadst set thy heart on many worldly things, in which thou hast met with many disappointments. " Sure," sayst thou, " none has such hard fortune as I." Foolish man! Again thou art boiling in thy mind against God, according to the text again. Thou shouldst have sought the " kingdom of God and his righteousness," and then thou hadst a fair promise that " all other things should be added to thee." Then thou wouldst have met with no disappointment. Thou didst not choose God's way; but a way of thy own. Misery, and vexation is the consequence.

Restrain thy fretting against the Lord—accusing fortune is nothing less—Lay all the blame, where it belongs; on thyself.

But to come still closer to the case of many. Thou hast been entreated to be reconciled to God, through Jesus. His dying love has been set before thee, with assurance of obtaining pardon, and of being conducted into the true way of happiness, by giving thy heart to God in him. Thou hast hardened thy heart against this, the most moving of all scenes. Thou hast sinned against the gospel, as well as against the law. Thou hast stifled thy convictions: and if the effect has been to harden thy heart, and give Satan more and more power over thee, who is to blame but thyself?

Perhaps, then, some one here present may cry out, "all this is true, and my heart has vilely accused God for that which I ought to accuse myself of. I am guilty; but is there any hope left still?" Oh! yes. Humbled soul! "I will heal thy backslidings," saith God. Look at the last chapter of Hosea. It exactly suits thy case. Only acknowledge thine iniquity, and "believe on the Lord Jesus Christ, and thou shalt be saved." That is the gospel still. Jesus's blood will cleanse and sanctify. Only come now, and prove its power by turning to the Lord with thy whole heart. But thou sayest "God has given me a view of these things, and I have prayed again and again in Jesus's name; but still find darkness and bondage." Take care thy folly pervert not thy way here, by peevish quarrelling with God, and fretting against the Lord, and so adding to thy offences. How often, and how long did God call, and thou didst not answer? Be patient. If the tables be turned upon thee, for a season, be thankful; because if thou seek with perseverance thou shalt find.

But the subject of the text belongs also to the converted. In nothing does the old man, still remaining in them, prove his existence, and demonstrate his power more sensibly, than in this "foolishness of perverting the man's ways," and then causing the heart " to fret against the Lord." Let us, then, consider some instances of this: the very consideration of which will naturally lead us to give suitable advice with reference to them.

One thing by which the " foolishness of the heart perverts the way" even of believers, is, a mistaken apprehension of freedom from the cross after conversion. When the soul, that was burdened with guilt, was set at liberty, by a believing view of Christ crucified, and was enabled to " joy in God through our Lord Jesus Christ," she fondly thought that, henceforward, she was to live in ease, and triumph; always basking under the smiles of God's countenance. The lusts of the flesh seemed to be extinct; Satan seemed for ever put to flight; and Heaven itself appeared just at hand. The new convert indeed might in his judgment deem otherwise: nevertheless, in his heart, he viewed things in this false light. By degrees, he finds his lusts return with violence; the devil to rage vehemently; a burden he has to carry; and severe war against himself rages all his days; attended often with pain of mind, and much disagreeable depression of spirits. Then it is that " the heart fretteth against the Lord." The soul inwardly accuses God of unkindness, and cruelty; and stubbornly stands out against the yoke which the Lord would have her to bear. It had been happy, indeed, had she learnt a better lesson from the first. Much uncomfortable experience might have been saved. But whoever know that this has been their case, if indeed they be the people of God, they will be glad to learn wisdom from the past.

They see now, after a while, that the Lord was not unkind. Over and over, in his word, he exhorted them to take his yoke upon them. Nay they see that all the sons of God are partakers of chastisements; for " as many as he loves, he rebukes and chastens for their profit, that they might be partakers of his holiness." They are told that all the Saints in Scripture met with this; but none so heavily as the Captain of their salvation, " who though he were a Son, yet learned he obedience by the things which he suffered." Why then should his members refuse to tread in his steps? It was their own folly to expect to meet with nothing but what was pleasing, after their conversion. For is it not written, " no chastisement is joyous, for the present, but grievous?" though afterwards it yieldeth the peaceable fruits of righteousness to them that are exercised thereby. To bear, and to endure is, then, what they are seriously to set themselves to learn. In Jesus there is strength sufficient for this; and by the prayer of faith they may acquire it. There is a kind necessity for manifold trials here. And they are assured that by these trials their iniquity shall be purged, and that this shall be the fruit of them, to take away their sin.

Let the believer look forward, and anticipate the time, when he shall " come to Zion with everlasting joy upon his head." Let him consider in what a cheering light he may at last view his present crosses and burdens. Methinks, it will then afford no pleasing thought to his mind, to reflect, that " his heart fretted against the Lord," for those very kind crosses which were necessary to keep him from ruining himself. Nay even now when he looks around him, and views the dreadful falls of once flourishing professors of religion, he may certainly see, in the light of God's Spirit, a kindness exceeding great, in ordaining these trials, and laying on him these burdens, which check his wild schemes; clog his natural activity in doing mischief to himself; and prevent those impetuous sallies of passion, which in those who are bastards and not sons do so much hurt to the cause of God. On a just review of these things, he should learn patience, thankfulness, and resignation. Then the yoke of Christ will be easy, and his burden light; and divine peace, and comfort, will sweeten all the way, narrow though it be, to the everlasting kingdom of the Lord Jesus.

Another way in which the " foolishness of man perverteth his way, and his heart fretteth against the Lord," is in not avoiding the occasions of evil. Many converted souls, who tremble indeed at evil itself, are by no means studious, as they should be, of avoiding occasions of evil. They content themselves with avoiding what is itself sinful in conduct; but do not avoid those things which *lead* to sin. Hence their folly very often "perverts their way" in wounding their consciences. Whenever they fall, they grieve, and abhor the sin; and because they feel that they abhor the sin, they are ready to wonder, why they fell into it. Hence, their " heart frets against the Lord," and charges him with unkindness. Another exercise, this, of the immense patience of the gracious and merciful Lord to his people! We know that it is very provoking to us for persons to do themselves a mischief, and then to lay the blame on us. But so the good Lord is most unreasonably dealt with every day. The mention of an instance or two may clear up this matter.

You know, by experience, you scarce ever come into such and such company, but you fall into evil passions, or in some other way wound your soul. You never divert yourself, in such and such a way, but your mind is quite unfitted for prayer a long time after. Then why do you frequent that company, and follow that diversion which you know is to your hurt, whatever it may be to others? The question is not, is it sinful in itself? If you will abstain from nothing for *fear* of sin, you take a very likely way to ruin your soul. To you it is a manifest occasion of sin, first in " perverting your ways," and then causing you unreasonably " to fret against the Lord." The advice belonging to this head is plain and short. Avoid what experience tells you to be, to you, occasions of evil.

An excessive attachment to the world is another fruitful source of the evil mentioned in the text. You are disappointed in your family comforts; in your trade; in your connections; in a variety of pursuits; and "your heart frets against the Lord." What a mercy it is to you to be cut off from all your schemes of bliss, in every quarter, but one, time will show. In the mean time, submissively wait the event, and recollect what you daily pray for, that God's "will may be done on earth, as it is in heaven." Consider it is "your own foolishness that has perverted your ways." Why did you expect great things from the world? When the Lord told you, "in the world ye shall have tribulation," saying also "in me ye shall have peace:" When he has taught you by the Apostle to the Hebrews to live as persons "who have here no continuing city, but who seek one to come."

Unreasonable expectations of divine comforts in this life form another fruitful source of the evil mentioned in the text. That all God's children shall have peace, great peace, is promised. But when, and to what degree, is entirely an affair of God's pleasure. Many, hearing of the extraordinary consolations of some, pray for the same, and obtain them not. Hence their "hearts fret against the Lord," and they feel a spirit of envy against the brethren. Thus do they miss of that which they might obtain; because they expect that which the Lord has not promised. He that would live in peace, and fruitfulness here, will do well to refer the quantity, and degree of his comforts to the Lord's pleasure; to be ever jealous, and watchful to be found in the way of duty; and to derive his *strongest*, because they are the most *solid* comforts, from the prospect of the exceeding and eternal weight of glory which he shall receive, when Jesus who is now his life shall appear, and he shall appear with him in glory.

The self-sufficient spirit natural to man is another exceeding fruitful source of the evil under consideration. Such and such difficulties lie in the believer's way: he is tempted by the flesh to help himself. Impatience, and unbelief, and self-confidence direct all his steps. Nor is he, by repeated experience, reclaimed; though the result of that experience uniformly is always bitter disappointment, and vexation of spirit. He thinks his case hard, and blames the Lord; but, in reality, it was his own folly that "perverted his ways" from the first. He should have "committed his ways to the Lord," as a poor blind helpless creature, and then, as it is written, "his thoughts should be established." But in order to this, there is need for him to grow in the experience of his own nothingness, and of the Lord's all-sufficient grace.

Thus, brethren, we see, in various cases, how apt even converted men are to lead themselves into mischief, and in their hearts "to fret against the Lord." What a view does this give us of the goodness of the Lord to his people! Surely, when, notwithstanding all their self-sufficiency and unwillingness to be directed by him, he has at length perfected that which concerneth them, and received them with glory, one most fruitful source of everlasting praise and admiration will be, this unwearied patience of the Lord amidst all their perverseness.

Persons, who know nothing of themselves, may wonder that we should charge so many mistakes, so much impiety of heart, on the Saints of the Lord. Nevertheless so it is: and so you will find it, if ever you awake out of sleep, and come indeed to know the Lord and yourselves, and to taste his grace. When you begin, indeed, to live aright to God, you will entertain a vile opinion of yourselves, and discover infinite depths of wickedness in your hearts by which you are at present enslaved, although you are not conscious of it.

What a state then must you be in now! How do those, who by believing in Jesus "have passed from death unto life," pity your blind, dead, stupid condition! Will you not, at length, pray for divine light, by which to see yourselves? Will you not, at length, take notice of those alarming hints of your own conscience which whisper to you the truth of those charges which in very charity I am making against you? O Saviour of sinners! whether we are converted or unconverted, do thou pity and spare us. Teach us to flee, indeed, to thee, as our strength and refuge!

To conclude. Till we are impressed with a sense of our prodigious sinfulness, an Almighty Saviour and deliverer can appear to us no suitable foundation of hope. However, through him, and by faith in his blood alone it is, that the guilt of all the perverseness and impiety we have mentioned can be taken away, and the souls of men brought into a state of acceptance with God. Thus are they taught that meek, submissive resigned temper, whereby alone they can enjoy God's salvation in their souls here, and at length enjoy it to perfection hereafter.

SERMON XV.

THE FOLLY OF ATTEMPTING TO MAKE THAT STRAIGHT WHICH GOD HAS MADE CROOKED.

Eccles. vii. 13.

Consider the work of God: for who can make that straight, which he hath made crooked?

The great design of this book of Solomon is to enable us to form a just estimate of human life, and thence to teach us how to pass through it in the most prudent manner, so as to obtain the greatest comfort from it possible in our way to a better. On this account the wise author was divinely directed to inculcate the vanity and emptiness of all worldly things, which he does repeatedly. He confirms and illustrates his point by a variety of cases and instances, to teach us—what we are all very slow to learn, what young people have scarce any idea of—that the world is a world of emptiness and misery. This is absolutely necessary to be known, not only to dispose us to seek for the blessedness of the next life, but to enable us to pass with any tolerable cheerfulness through this. For if we expect nothing else but vanity, and a variety of crosses, we shall be prepared to use those wise rules for their mitigation, of which this book of Ecclesiastes is full, and may make the care of the soul the one thing needful. But if we have a wrong estimate of life—as most have during the greater part, if not the whole of their days—and keep continually expecting happiness from it, what must be the effect? Surely bitter disappointment will ensue, besides the unspeakable misery of losing our soul for ever.

But, I say no more of the plan of Solomon's book. He who, under a divine influence, attends to it carefully throughout, may see, that one thing runs through it. It teaches us never to expect any thing from the world to set our heart upon. Solomon has written another book, commonly called his Song, to teach us what the heart ought to be set upon, even Christ Jesus as the true husband of the soul, in whose supreme, and unrivalled love, we may here taste the beginning of bliss, and be led to the fulness of it hereafter. The Lord is a jealous God, and as he will not fail to bless us, if we cleave to him in faith and love; so if he see us shy and cold, and more disposed to cleave to other persons and things than to him, we shall be sure to suffer for it. But let us now dwell upon the peculiar doctrine of the text. "Consider the work of God: for who can make that straight, which he hath made crooked?"

The world, and our lot in it, is not straight, but crooked. There is always something rough and perverse in all its concerns. We can meddle with nothing that fully answers our wish. Most people, upon finding this in some particular object of desire, try some other scheme; but every fresh trial leaves them just where they were, always disappointed. They are ready to blame this and that hinderance. " If it had not been for such a person's folly, or such an unlucky thing happening, I should have been happy." Would you so? Indeed you would not. Something else would have set you at a great distance from happiness, if that did not. The hinderance does not arise from particular occasional things, but from the general nature of things. And what you call LUCK, is the PROVIDENCE OF GOD.

" Consider the work of God." Men are apt to be Atheists practically, and to forget God, as if he had no business in the world, though " in him, and through him, and to him are all things." He has ordained it thus, and "who can make that straight, which he has made crooked?" The great misery of men in this life, and which will awfully prepare them for the misery of the next life also, if it be not cured here, is, that they are passionately set on having their own will gratified, and fondly expect that to be *straight* which God has made *crooked*. Do not you see what numbers blunder through life in this way? And as far as appears, after having taken pains in their own way to be happy all their lives, lie down in sorrow at last? But " consider the work of God." He has appointed this course of things. It is in vain, then, to resist it. All that you should expect—and a great ALL it is, more than I can express—is to be supported in patient cheerfulness, by divine grace, through life, and then to be landed in perfect, everlasting rest hereafter through his mercy in Christ Jesus. The same sentiment occurs in the fifteenth verse of the first chapter of this book, " that which is crooked, cannot be made straight; and that which is wanting, cannot be numbered." The Holy Ghost is still teaching us, that it is not owing to any particular misfortune, but to "the work of God," that human life is so full of vanity. You cannot make a crooked thing straight. And if there be a real want, you can never by numbering make up for that want. I fear, many are not accustomed to think of things in this light. If they did, it might, under God, help to teach them two things. One is, to bear with patience what is not to be remedied; and the other is, to seek more earnestly for the kingdom of heaven.

Since the use of the subject is so great, let us in the sequel endeavour, 1st, to illustrate a little more particularly this work of God in the crookedness of human life; and 2d, point out the complete felicity of the next life. A word of exhortation may follow to two sorts of persons.—Be with us here also, O God of compassion—and teach us wisdom in the greatness of thy mercy!

1. You will more firmly believe this account of human vanity, if you attend to the general cause of it. It was not the first original plan of the world. "God beheld every thing that he had made, and behold it was good." So Moses tells us, in the 1st chapter of Genesis. Man fell, and then behold the change! "Cursed is the ground for thy sake. Thorns also and thistles shall it bring forth to thee." In the same manner misery has reached all other objects of sense. Sin is the most dreadful evil. It has filled the world with evil. In the wisdom of God it is ordered that thus it should punish us in its consequences and effects. And indeed so wicked is human nature since the Fall, that we cannot bear prosperity. Adversity seems needful to keep us in any tolerable order.

Such is the unavoidable lot of humanity; but the adorable goodness of God has not left us to despair in this state. He has given his beloved Son to restore us from it to life everlasting. This is the constant joyful theme of our Ministry. I would hope there are few of you so very inattentive to what you continually hear, as not to know something of the gospel remedy. I need not, therefore, go out of my way to enlarge upon this theme. But it is of consequence to know the way and manner of applying the salvation of Jesus. It is not meant to put us into heaven while here; nor to exempt us from feeling the vanity of the world. Indeed to true believers there is peace of conscience, and a sweet and joyful hope beyond the grave, and godliness alone can bring some real pleasure into the soul while here. But I say it exempts us not from afflictions either inward or outward. On the contrary, afflictions are much made use of as means to keep us in the right way to heaven. Lay all these things together, and you will see how impossible it is that what God hath made crooked we should be able to make straight. So long as God hates and punishes sin, and the creation remains in a fallen state, there must be death and misery in it. Even the salvation of Jesus itself is not meant to take away sufferings here, but to sanctify sufferings to us, that they may prepare us for heaven. Hence this " work of God" must remain. Strive to bear it, and get good from it for your soul: This you may, you ought to do; but remove it you cannot. By striving against God, you only add to the load instead of lessening it.

Look a little at the state of things in the world

at large; in families; in a man's own body, and mind; even in that of a truly converted person, as well as of the church of Christ in general, and you will see, every where, abundant proof of "the work of God" thus punishing a rebellious and fallen race. Among mankind at large, what a view have we of misery and vanity! All history is full of it, and were you to take away the account of wars of nations with one another, and among themselves, little history would be left. Surely this is not the very good world which the Lord at first created. It has lost its dignity and birthright. We now see a mere wreck, and only the fragments of what it was.

But, perhaps, it may be more instructive for us to attend to what passes in private life. Are not all families full of vexation? Is there not, commonly, in every family some one, or more, a plague and vexation to all the rest, by their bad conduct? You are delighted with your children, when little. This is generally the best time that parents have with them, though by their fond indulgence, and neglect of bringing them up in the nurture and admonition of the Lord, they often lay the foundation of the bitter sorrows that follow. Bitter, indeed, are the agonies often inflicted upon parents by their children in after-life. Few reward the kindness shown them, by proper returns of gratitude.

But look at yourself. "Consider the work of God" there: "who can make that straight which he has made crooked?" What diseases of the body; severe, and afflicting! What infirmities, and those likely to grow with age! Young people, though almost arrived at the stature of man, are generally as ignorant of real life as infants. Their imagination represents every thing in a gay, pleasing light. Bitter experience convinces them of human misery, at length ; and it will be well if they learn, that this is not an occasional thing ; but fixed, and steady, from the wise appointment of God, thus frowning on a lost and guilty world, and conducting through much tribulation the true members of his Son's body to a better world. The want of right views of the fall of man will throw all your ideas, in religion, into a wrong channel. If you look on the present state of the world as the original state, you will find the constant course of human events to confound you. If every thing be so good, and among the rest, man's heart so good, why so much evil? It is astonishing that a good soil should produce nothing but weeds for ages. On this plan you lose all sight of the divine purpose. You will be always apt to deceive yourselves with false hopes of happiness, and what is worst of all, will be kept from Christ the true hope of rest and glory. On this account it is most useful to attend to our subject, melancholy as it may seem.

But let us not forget our minds. Are they not loaded with distracting cares, mischievous tempers, evil imaginations, darkness and confusion? Many persons are never at home ; look not within, at all ; have an ear for every thing, but what tells them something of themselves. The more miserable will it be to discover the truth, when it is too late. One trembles to think how men, dying in a thoughtless state, will feel, when, in the next life, they awake in that state of wailing and gnashing of teeth, of which our Saviour speaks. But the more a man knows of himself, the worse he will appear in his own eyes. The best men have always had the lowest opinion of themselves. Every real christian feels this plague of an evil nature, and *must*, in the wholesome warfare against himself, till death.

And if there be so much evil in a single person, as his own inward experience convinces him, what may not be expected from a number? Need we wonder, then, that the church of Christ, God's own garden, planted in the wilderness, (though surely as preferable to the rest of the world as a garden is to a wilderness) that the church itself, I say, should, in this life, have something crooked in it, which no man can make straight?

It does not seem so in the beginning of things, in any place, when it pleases God to pour out his Spirit, and to attend with success the simple, and faithful preaching of his word. It often seems, then, as if a nation were " born in a day." Many appear to set their faces towards Zion; and such light, such power, such tokens of the divine Presence are seen; there is such a spirit of prayer; such kind visits of Jesus are afforded, as he walks in the midst of the churches, attended with such evident fruitfulness in holy living, and such rooting out of former vices, and evil customs, that heaven seems brought down to earth. What tender love then appears between the pastors, and people; and how do the members of Christ's body love one another, as if they had all one heart, and one soul; and how are they separated from the world! Many precious saints, who have seen such sights, and they are the most charming sights upon earth, have fondly expected that this would continue and increase, till the earth should " be full of the glory of the Lord, as the waters cover the sea." But in a few years there is often a decay of simplicity, faith and love. Many backslide. Numbers forsake their first love. The church, once so simple, and beautiful, and full of love, is rent into factions and parties. Even perverse doctrines, and heresies are started, to the stumbling of many; and one standing heresy, THE LOVE OF THIS WORLD, gradually pours in its mischief, and throws a damp on all this beauteous scene. You may then see persons, once all on fire for the kingdom of heaven, very cold in religion, and choked with the cares and covetous pursuits of the things of this life.

Now here we are still to " consider the work of God." What he has made crooked we cannot make straight. If there be so much evil lurking in individuals of the best character, it will be apt to show itself in the multitude. There is, indeed, to be expected a glorious time of the universal spreading of the gospel on earth; but we seem not to be near it. Probably we shall all be the food of worms before it take place. Many have written, and spoken concerning it, things, which they did not understand. I would rather, therefore, draw your minds, and my own, to what the Scripture holds out as solid comfort against these evils. This I was to do in the second place. May we conceive and embrace it aright, and it will do good to our hearts as a medicine.

Brethren, the glory of Christ's kingdom does not appear, in this world, generally speaking. The best things in the church of Christ are inward and secret.

The fervent groaning of spirit; the sincere struggle against sin; the self-loathing of the humble soul; the grateful acknowledgments of the forgiven soul; the delight, and peace of the saint; the sweetness and power of the word on the heart; these things are precious, but you see them not. Unconverted sinners appear better in public than they are in secret. With good men it is just the contrary. In secret their best is shown; but to God, not to man. In public what they do has a mixture of the world, and is soiled by that mixture. And though the decays I spake of will take place, yet Christ's church is not lost. Amidst many false professors the Lord still "knoweth them that are his," and they drop off from the stage one by one, (in a few years numbers are swept away) and if a succession of new converts arise not in their stead, the fine appearance of godliness, in any place, will wither of course. But in the next life this crookedness will effectually be removed. The spirits of just men made perfect will know no more of the miseries of mortality. When Jesus, at the last day, shall appear—the first-born among many brethren—a great multitude which no man can number, of all nations, and ages, will stand before the throne. "They have washed their robes and made them white in the blood of the Lamb, having come out of great tribulation. Therefore are they before the throne of God, and serve him day and night in his temple: and he that sitteth on the throne shall dwell among them. They shall hunger no more, neither thirst any more, neither shall the sun light on them, nor any heat. For the Lamb which is in the midst of the throne shall feed them, and shall lead them unto living fountains of waters: and God shall wipe away all tears from their eyes."

This glorious view of heavenly happiness I have drawn from the latter end of Revelations. It is a precious passage, and deserves to be meditated on with tears of joy, by those who love Jesus Christ. Such a prospect entirely, and fully suffices to remove the melancholy which a view of the text may give us. There is an end, a bliss for christians; but let them not expect it too soon. We are all apt to be impatient. We must live by faith, not by sight. This present life, and it is a short one, is for suffering, rather than enjoyment. And sufferings, rightly undergone, do " work for us a far more exceeding and eternal weight of glory."—I conclude, then, with a few words to two sorts of people.

Are there not here some real believers; men who have fled for refuge to Jesus the hope set before you? Have you not found a sweetness there which is to be found no where else? Does He not give " living water," which satisfies the soul? Be thankful. That you have had a taste for the least measure of what is called the " earnest of the Spirit," calls for thankfulness; and you will believe so, when you think of your own great unworthiness and of the love of Christ, which " passeth knowledge." Be thankful, and be content. Remember, that you walk here by faith. You must walk by sight hereafter. You must here fight against the world, the flesh, and the devil, all your days. What God hath made crooked cannot be made straight. You must, through life, feel the consequence of sin; a corrupted nature, a tempting devil, and an evil world. Your frames will vary. Even your bodily infirmities will have a great effect on your minds, and keep you far from a state of perfect enjoyment; and your worldly affairs and connections will subject you to various crosses. Your wisdom, then, lies in the practice of that divine sentence, " if we hope for that we see not, then do we with patience wait for it." You will meet with many disappointments, not only in the world, but in the church also, many, perhaps, unexpected falls, and backslidings of religious persons. Some whose kindness you once made too much of, will by their ingratitude and estrangement from you, be apt to give you more grief and surprise than it ought. For, " consider the work of God. What is wanting cannot be numbered, and what is crooked cannot be made straight." If you be wise, you may reap benefit from all these things. They teach you to be more weaned from the world, to love it less, and to look forward to the second coming of Christ. I could show you at large, from the New Testament, how the first christians made this their steady object continually. They did not dream of any resting-place here. They did not fancy any moments, when they should find here all things as they could wish. They found the world a cruel stepmother: Persecution, and death itself they were exposed to from it; and they loved the appearing of Jesus. " Come, Lord Jesus, come quickly." Thus they groaned, and they longed for this; and they were supported by this hope.

Now, christians, this must be your wisdom. By prayer and watchfulness live for the next life, not for this. The evil of this world's crookedness will work its own cure, if you are led by it to look less at this world and more at the next. Guard, I pray you, against covetousness, and learn to be content with your condition. Without this you cannot feel the force of christian motives, and will be sure to have your lives embittered with the disappointments of the world. Recollect of how little consequence the world seemed to you, when you first began to attend to the care of your soul. It is of no more value now, though your eye be not so single and simple as it was then. And that you may be encouraged to all this, constantly bear in mind, that your salvation is of grace, not of works, and be, as the Scripture says, "waiting for the coming of our Lord Jesus Christ, who shall also confirm you to the end, that you may be blameless in the day of our Lord Jesus." God is faithful by whom you were called to the fellowship of his Son.

The crookedness you see and feel alters not your relation to God. You are his children by faith in Jesus. He will never leave you nor forsake you. "I commend you to God and the word of his grace; who is able to build you up, and grant you an inheritance among them that are sanctified." Be much in prayer, that you may be armed, taught, corrected, comforted, and led by the Spirit of God; and you shall find yourselves made more than conquerors through him that loved you. You have a noble prize, a blessed resurrection before you. A Saviour all-sufficient is provided, and a mansion is reserved for each of you in his kingdom. Enter into it now by faith; carry your cross daily, and, denying yourselves, and following Jesus, patiently endure the crookedness of the present scene, till your God make all things straight in eternity.

But what shall I say to you who are men of the world? I call you so, who have not laid to heart these things; who do not "consider the work of God" in all this. You place your bliss in the world. You have no idea of any other; and you think of being lucky or unlucky; and neither look at God's providence for your bodies, nor at his grace for your souls. If you are young, I pity you much. You are vainly hoping for that happiness which you can never get from outward things. The world is a cheat: You will find it so: The pleasures you love the most, will all disappoint you: Seek for happiness where it is to be found. Now is the time, while Jesus calls. "Seek the Lord while he may be found." Old Sinners! will you be as those trees, which the older they grow strike the deeper root into the earth? You are on the edge of the grave. Awake to righteousness, and lose no time to acquaint yourselves with God and to be at peace with him, so shall that good come to you, which you have sought in vain from the world, and its possessions. Let your treasure be no longer upon earth, where moth and rust doth corrupt, and where thieves break through and steal; But "in heaven, where neither moth nor rust doth corrupt, and where thieves do not break through nor steal." *Matt.* vi. 19, 20.

SERMON XVI.

THE SCRIPTURE DOCTRINE OF DIVINE AND HUMAN AGENCY IN THE WORK OF OUR SALVATION.

Philip. ii. 12, 13.

Work out your own salvation with fear and trembling: for it is God which worketh in you, both to will, and to do of his good pleasure.

The true meaning of this passage will be better understood by considering to whom the words were spoken. They were not spoken to men in an unconverted state, but to the pious Philippians, whom the Apostle regarded with peculiar pleasure, as real children of God. His words preceding the text are, " my beloved, as ye have always obeyed, not as in my presence only, but now much more in my absence." They had ever been obedient to the gospel of Christ, since they had "heard it, and had known the grace of God in truth." They had given this great proof of sincere conviction, by their conduct in the absence of the Apostle as well as in his presence. So that it was not merely a personal regard to the character and authority of the Apostle, but it was a heartfelt, rooted, and genuine regard to the word of God; it was the vital power of the truth itself, spiritually understood, which kept them true to the name and doctrine of Jesus. God had thus evidently wrought on their minds to will and to do, and therefore they ought to work out their own salvation with fear and trembling. And he observes afterwards, that they shone " as lights in the world, in the midst of a crooked and perverse nation."

From this view of the persons to whom the words are addressed, it appears to be an exhortation proper only for real christians, for those who shine as lights in the world. Indeed the Apostle evidently tells us so; " as ye have always obeyed, work out your own salvation." This can scarcely be properly said of an unconverted man, who has at present nothing to do with salvation, but is far from it. There are exhortations, indeed, proper for him, to be found in Scripture: Such as " repent and be converted, that your sins may be blotted out, repent and believe the gospel. Seek the Lord while he may be found*."

To real christians, then, the words are addressed. And they are reminded, that the power both to will and do that which is good is of God, and proceeds from his good pleasure. " For the condition of man after the fall of Adam is such, that he cannot turn and prepare himself by his own natural strength and

---

* And here I would remark, that it is of unspeakable prejudice to many, to take it for granted that they are true christians, and in the favour of God, and partakers of his grace, and under the influence of his Holy Spirit. Many seem to imagine they are so, because they are baptized and are called christians; and this notion is so very flattering, that they are always apt to call one uncharitable for endeavouring to strip them of it; and it is also one of the main advantages which they give to Satan to keep them in an unconverted state.

good works to faith and calling upon God.; wherefore we have no power to do good works pleasant and acceptable to God without the grace of God by Christ preventing us, that we may have a good will, and working with us, when we have that good will." So speaks the church in her tenth article. Her language is perfectly agreeable to the text, and helps to explain it. She teaches us, that the fallen state of nature is such, that it is not in us either to will or to do ; and therefore we need God's grace in Christ to *prevent*, that is, to go before us, that we may have a good will, and afterwards to work with us, when we have that good will. The truth of this statement is experimentally known by all truly godly souls. They feel that they cannot give themselves a good will, and even after it is given them by God's grace, they find not how to perform that which is good, without continual quickening aids from above. They know that they themselves are not masters of the times and seasons of grace, nor indeed of any thing belonging to the whole subject. God works all " of his own good pleasure." And since this is the case, they are exhorted, with zealous care, and devout reverence, and humble thankfulness to " work out their salvation" in all the branches of duty to which they are called. They are the subjects of divine operations, which require to be attended to with the most serious regard. How watchful should they be to improve the seasons of grace and the influences of the Spirit when afforded ! and with what fear and trembling should they answer the calls of God to their souls, in all duties! since it is in his quickening presence and support that they live. If they provoke him to depart from them, they can do nothing.

I think a humble and experienced christian, who feels how perfectly dependent he is on the Divine Physician, for his cure, will need no more to be said, to enable him to understand why he should work out his own salvation with fear and trembling, for this reason, that it is God which worketh in him to will and to do of his good pleasure. His own conscience is daily pointing out to him the duty and the wisdom of working out his salvation with pious awe, and humble reverence, and the sense he has of his entire dependence on God alone, will make him expect power from on high, that his labour may not be in vain.

But this whole interpretation proceeds on the supposition, which the context has shown us to be true, that the precept is addressed to believers. And before I proceed to exhort them particularly upon it, it will be proper to remove a false and dangerous conceit, which has commonly obtained among persons void of the grace of God, and to warn them accordingly.

The conceit is this: that men have a power, from natural strength, and resources, to work out their salvation; only they need some assistance from time to time, to enable them to complete it; so that salvation is wrought out, according to this notion, by God and man acting as partners, and fellow-labourers, each distinctly, and independently. It has been compared, by a Writer of great note, to the business of raising up a weight by two agents; where one of the agents is supposed to be incapable, by reason of weakness, to do the whole work for himself. This is the idea which many have of grace; that it is a sort of assistance vouchsafed to a weak, frail creature like man, who is able to perform a part, but not the whole. Hence the exhortation grounded on such doctrine is, do the best you can, and Christ will make out the rest for you. And those who attempt to support this doctrine by Scripture, think the text to be favourable to it; because it speaks both of God's working, and of man's working.

It does so, brethren; but not as joint partners, each doing a part independently of the other, like two men engaged in lifting up a stone together. "It is God that worketh in us both to will and to do;" and if I be inclined, and enabled to "work out my salvation," I am taught in the text, that it is not through any native strength. It is God that works in me, if I do work. Even the *will* to perform what is good is from him, and because it is so, I am directed and exhorted to labour with a pious awe and humility, as one sensible of my complete dependance on God, and ever careful of pleasing him on whom my all depends. Thus St. Paul says, after observing, that he "laboured more abundantly than they all," "not I, but the grace of God that was with me."

It is true, that men who are saved must work according to the will of God, and be faithful to divine grace, and endeavour to improve it. But then if the question be further asked; "Whence comes this faithfulness to grace; whence comes this sincere improvement of talents?" It must be said "Not I, but the grace of God."

Thus you see, how in every soul that is saved there is a work of God, and there is also a work of man. The fault of the notion I am opposing is this; that it allows to man what he has not since the Fall, a native power of willing, and doing what is good. You say, it may be, that this power of his is but weak, and needs strengthening by grace; and so you make out the joint concurrence of divine grace, and human strength, between them producing man's salvation, as two good causes distinctly and independently co-operating. But know, that however plausible this may look, it is not the doctrine of Scripture. This is not " the wisdom of God in a mystery." It is a common obvious notion, and what all mankind would hold, without any revelation at all. For I suppose all men have some consciousness, that they are weak, and need, somehow or other, a divine influence to help their weakness. But if you mean to be a christian, you are called on to confess not only that you are frail, but that you are naturally wicked; not merely that you are in danger, but that you are lost; not that you are too weak to bring yourselves out of an evil state, but that you are helpless. Nay you must be brought to see that you deserve to be left so for ever, because of the just displeasure of God against you for your sinfulness.

Does this offend your natural feeling? It does mine. But it is the more likely to be divine truth on that account. For as the " wisdom of this world is foolishness with God," the gospel of Christ, which is " the power of God unto salvation to every one that believeth," seems foolish to the natural man.

Let not men, however, pretend that they believe in Christ and receive grace, when they do not. Let them not say, " Lord, Lord, and yet do not the things which he says." Let them not think that it is enough to say, God works, and we must work also, for the necessity of both is fully allowed on all sides. But the question is, what is to be the dependance on the whole? On what is salvation founded; and on what does it all rest? The Scripture hath taught us, that " by grace we are saved through faith, and that not of ourselves, it is the gift of God; not of works, lest any one should boast."

There is an essential difference between this statement of the doctrine of grace, and the notions with which we may have been brought up. We were taught, perhaps, that the true doctrine was, that we must do our best, and Christ would make out the rest; that there is a real native strength in man to help and save himself; and I suppose, except where the real doctrine of divine grace has made its way, persons commonly hold this notion. And we know where the Scripture doctrine is clearly and warmly inculcated, there is much opposition and enmity. Let it not be said that these different views of the subject mean the same thing; for they do not so. And it is an unspeakable mischief to souls, for such notions to be generally believed, which " frustrate the grace of God."

And that which frustrates the grace of God must also frustrate the salvation of man. It is impossible, then, for you who have followed the plan of self-sufficiency, to gain true rest to your souls. I beseech you, see distinctly, what it is that you are called to learn that you may be guided into the way of salvation. I cannot directly exhort you, according to the text, to " work out your salvation, because God worketh in you to will and to do." For at present your willing, and your doing is your own, arises from mere nature, and comes not from the grace of God. You must not expect, that the operations of the Spirit of God will mix and combine with those of your nature. The old man and the new creature will not unite in the work of salvation. What you want is, to be stripped of your own righteousness, strength, and wisdom; to become poor, and low, and helpless, in your own eyes; and to give yourselves up to Christ as an entire and complete Saviour, that he may " work in you to will and to do." And as this is the distinct object to be aimed at, use all right means to come at the true knowledge of yourselves. A knowledge, alas! very uncommon in the world, but which yet is quite necessary, that you may be induced to embrace that method of salvation which is proposed to us in his word.

If you think you have a power to will and to do that which is good by nature, and of your own strength, try what you can do. Get to learn, by a course of experience, whether you can, indeed, love the Lord with all your heart, and your neighbour as yourself; whether, indeed, you can patiently bear afflictions, return good for evil, forgive injuries, and set your affections on things above, not on the things on the earth. Try to pray feelingly, and with sincere affection, to thank God heartily, and to offer and present yourselves a reasonable, holy, and lively sacrifice unto him. This is your bounden duty, and you must in practising it, not only do the outward good actions, which even a hypocrite may perform in many respects, but you must also bring the heart itself to correspond with the lips and the life, and be sincerely what you appear to be before men. Try to go through all these works without weariness even to your life's end.

It is right to exhort you to try and to endeavour to practise these things, because, as I said, they are the bounden duty of us all, whatever our present state may be. There may arise this good fruit from it, in your case, that by this means you may come to know what you can do, or rather what you cannot do. Numbers fancy themselves very capable of practising all their duties with ease, because they conceive not the strictness, spirituality, and extensiveness of the divine commands, and because of their carelessness, and insensibility. Let men earnestly strive, and they may find what they can do. And this may safely be said, as certain by experience, that all who have striven in good earnest to serve God, and sought unto him for light and direction, through his Son Jesus, have come to the point, to which I wish you to be brought. They have found themselves corrupt, and helpless, the "whole head sick and the whole heart faint." They have found the heart hard, and insensible; the will stiff, and froward; the passions violent, and untractable; the affections earthly, and sensual; the imagination—every imagination—evil, and that continually.

The first lesson, then, of true religion is to know ourselves, that we are corrupt, that we are helpless, that we are tied and bound with the chains of our sins. And I will venture to say, that he who is brought thus to know the plague of his own heart, will not easily find words strong enough to convey the sense he has of his native depravity. He will not, for instance, think David went too far, when he said, "I was shapen in iniquity, and in sin did my mother conceive me." Nor Jeremiah, when he said, "the heart is deceitful above all things, and desperately wicked." When you know these things, you will say with the same Prophet, "I know that it is not in man to direct himself."

Men only trifle with religion, till they come to some degree of self-knowledge, and see the fall by their own experience. Then of all the troubles you ever met with, you will find the burden of a guilty conscience, and the pollution of a depraved heart, to be by far the greatest. You will wonder, how you could before be so light-minded; so easy, and careless; so presumptuous, and insensible of danger. In short, when you are brought to know yourselves as you really are, you will be thoroughly convinced, however hard it be to convince you of it now, that all men are quite out of the way of salvation, while they are ignorant of their own hearts.

But for these things there needs, I own, a secret, but effectual work of God's Holy Spirit, for which you should pray continually. And if you do thus come to know yourselves, you will need no more arguments to convince you, that it is not you and Christ in conjunction who procure your salvation.

You will see, indeed, that you must work that which is good, and endeavour to perfect holiness in the fear of the Lord; but that it is not you, but the grace of God which is with you, that must make you successful. Among all the exhortations to holy duties, in Scripture, and they are many, there is not one which joins together man's doings and the doings or merits of Christ as conjoined partners. The church of England, also, teaches in her homilies, that "all the works and virtues of Saints are not to be coupled with the act of Christ in saving us."

But I wish you to seek and pray, till you find these things for yourselves. They are matter of experience. Such as you, are apt to complain that we do not make things of this sort plain to your understandings. How should mere words fully explain, what can only be distinctly apprehended by your own feelings? You must be the subjects of a work of grace, in order to understand it. Labour, pray, and seek, till you find for yourselves. If once you become humble, and learn to rest on Christ alone by faith, he will take you as subordinate workmen into his service. When you are heartily disposed to confess that you can do nothing, and find him working in you to will and to do, what is well-pleasing in his sight, then you will be fitted to do all things through Christ which strengtheneth you, and be capable of profiting by the exhortation in the text.

To you, who with the Philippians have obeyed the gospel, I would address a few words. Make use of these treasures of christian experience, which have been opened to you. Remember what you have received, and heard, and hold fast your profession. You may have learnt many things since the time of your conversion; corrected many mistakes; improved in the knowledge of many Scripture truths; and all this, even by the natural course of events. Then as you have grown in age and experience, you may have grown wiser, and more knowing in many things. But you never learnt any thing more valuable, or more directly entering into the heart of true happiness, than those first lessons which were taught you, when you through the Spirit learnt to repent and believe the gospel. Did not you seek God in extremity, in the anguish and bondage of your soul? Were you not made sensible that "the bed," you were upon, "was too short for you to stretch yourselves on it, and the covering too narrow for you to wrap yourselves in it?" Was it not music to your souls to hear, " come unto me all ye that are weary and heavy laden, and I will give you rest?" Were not the promises of the gospel most delightful? Can you conceive any thing on this side Heaven, so precious as Christ revealed in your souls; as the peace, joy, and love, thence derived, through the Holy Spirit? Have you found any thing, since, so suitable to an helpless creature; so calculated to inspire every holy temper; so abundantly powerful to give you that hope of a blessed immortality, which maketh not ashamed? Is not union with Christ the greatest of all blessings; and a believing intercourse with him productive of health to the soul; enabling it to bear, and to do the will of God, as well as to depart in peace, with an earnest of God's salvation?

I remind you of these things, brethren, that you may remember what your idea of bliss was, when you first obtained a comfortable sense of your acceptance with God through grace. If you have grieved the Spirit of God since; if you have grown negligent, or self-conceited, or worldly-minded, you have not now that taste of happiness, and that holy frame of heart you once had. Remember from whence you are fallen, and return to your first love; to the faith, humility, and simplicity of your first conversion. Seek in the same way as at first, and never lose sight of those elements of christianity. Kindle the fire of divine love again and again in your souls, by recurring to the first truths. Give yourselves up by faith to the God of your salvation, that he may " work in you both to will and to do."

When you find you cannot bring your will to a right frame, put HIM on doing it for you, " of his good pleasure," as he did at first. And when you have a GOOD WILL, but find, as you often may, through temptations, and the corruption of nature, that you cannot execute what the will desires, look to him to work with you. This is the method of persons truly experienced in religion. You never pray so fervently as when you find you are completely dependant on grace. Then is the time to " work out your salvation with fear and trembling." Remember who it is that softens, turns, and prepares and creates you anew in Christ Jesus, and that if he leave you to yourselves, you will be exposed to all the evils of a corrupt nature, and a tempting devil, and a wicked world. Provoke him not; but by humble, and watchful co-operation with his grace, labour to bring forth fruit, and adorn the doctrine of God your Saviour. For, " herein is your heavenly Father glorified, that you bring forth much fruit."

These christian principles, alone, will enable you to be thus fruitful; and it rests on you to show to the world that they are profitable for this purpose. You should appear indeed holy and useful characters. Let it be seen that you are men of peace and quietness; neither disturbing public life by seditious practices, nor private life by quarrels and slander. You are the sons of God, let his fair image appear in your life and conversation. While the world around you is crooked and perverse, do you shine as lights in it, hold forth the word of life. Show that you practically possess this word. Convince men that you have the Spirit of Jesus, and that the new birth is a real thing. And, O what a pleasure will it be to your Ministers, as St. Paul says, to rejoice in the day of Christ that they have not run in vain, nor laboured in vain.

SERMON XVII.

THE SEAL OF GOD'S FOUNDATION, OR PRIVILEGE AND DUTY CLEARLY STATED.

2 Tim. ii. 19.

Nevertheless, the Foundation of God standeth sure, having this seal, The Lord knoweth them that are his. And, let every one that nameth the name of Christ depart from iniquity.

In these words we have an epitome of God's government of the church of Christ, uniting two things which even persons serious in religion are too apt to separate from one another, I mean privilege and duty. The Scripture is as constant in joining, as men too commonly are in disjoining them. Hear another Scripture instance, similar to this of the text. " Work out your own salvation with fear and trembling;" here is duty: " for it is God that worketh in you to will and to do of his good pleasure;" here is privilege. What God *gives* to all his people, he *commands*; and what he commands, he gives. Salvation is wrought by him in all saints: yet *they* do it, though not they of themselves, but the grace of God that is in them. The good understanding, and the good inclination is from him: yet we are drawn to God, if drawn at all, with the cords of a man, that is, by such reasonable methods as win the assent; gently, yet invincibly; freely, yet effectually. The work of repentance, faith, and obedience, is our own, yet wrought by his Spirit to the glory of his grace. Hence we are the subjects of exhortation, and of command; of praise, and of blame; free agents, in the proper sense of the words, though the Lord alone, from first to last, carries on the work in our souls.

I am not disposed to strive about words to no profit; I advise professors of godliness to avoid those speculations that are too high for them. Much is said in Scripture against giving way to them. The passage from whence the text is taken is full against it. I cannot but exhort the common people again and again not to busy their heads with matters above their capacity. The self-conceit of shallow men, in this, has done much hurt, both to themselves and others. I purpose, in this discourse, to explain, with God's help, the seal which belongs to God's foundation. This seal has two inscriptions; and while I insist on them BOTH, some may perhaps call me inconsistent. Let them, however, remember, they cannot do this without calling the Scripture so; for both the inscriptions are in one verse. I fear many are very faulty in judging of things of which they are not at all competent judges. They are much more ready to criticise preachers, and undertake to explain doctrines, than to live christian lives by the faith of the Son of God. Some of my audience, I fear, are listening to hear what side I shall take in this controverted matter. If I follow not their side, they will be disgusted; or they may think I am true to neither.

Alas! alas! what poor christianity is this! What good can such men get to their souls. O Saviour! teach us to sit at thy feet; hearing thy words in simplicity; regardless of the praise of men; partial to no men, no sect; receiving the law from thy mouth; not leaning to our own understandings; but desirous above all things to be led simply and only by thee!

I shall, 1st, endeavour to explain what is meant in the text by God's foundation, having the seal with two inscriptions;—the nature of each inscription, in order, 2dly, to apply, more particularly, the instruction of this doctrine to our consciences and to practical use.

1st. With respect to the doctrine of the text, it is observable, that the Apostle had been guarding Timothy against " profane and vain babblings." There is no saying where men will stop, who once give into them : " they will increase unto more ungodliness, and their words will eat as doth a canker; of whom is Hymeneus and Philetus; who concerning the truth have erred, saying that the resurrection is past already; and overthrow the faith of some." The resurrection is one of the glorious truths of Christianity. What is it that comforts a real Christian amidst the cares and miseries of this vain life; the sorrows and burdens of sin and temptation; conflict and tribulation? Is it not this, that he shall one day enjoy his Saviour without a cloud, without any mixture of evil for ever? The body, now a capital seat of pain and weakness, shall be raised immortal and glorious, a fit residence for the happy soul for ever.

These men, in denying the resurrection of the

body, laboured, as far as in them lay, to overturn the christian hope. For "if in this life only we have hope in Christ," says the Apostle in a well-known chapter, when he is combating the same error, "we are of all men most miserable." He evidently makes, not any impulses, raptures, or present attainments, the source of christian patience, self-denial, and joy, " but Christ the hope of glory," to be hereafter revealed. Take away this, and nothing is left to make a christian superior to others; nay, he is " of all men most miserable."

Let all who seek eternal life observe this, that they may be pressing on for the prize of the high calling of God in Christ Jesus, walking by faith, and not by sight. False teachers may be expected, and none are so absurd, but they will find some converts. The devil, who sends them out to deceive mankind, provides them with hearers and approvers. And the Lord permits it, that men may be tried, and that they who are of the truth may be made manifest. The faith of some was overthrown in the early ages of the church. They lost true christianity; and, it is to be feared, their souls, by hearkening to these teachers. This is a distressing thought to a child of God. "These professors seemed once as likely to stand as others. They fell; others may fall; all may fall; I among the rest in the same manner. How uncertain, then, is the christian hope!"

Such thoughts might naturally arise in Timothy's mind, on hearing of the faith of some being overthrown. And such thoughts, on like occasions, naturally arise in our minds at this day. The Apostle meets these thoughts, and answers such objections thus: "Nevertheless the foundation of God standeth sure, having this seal, the Lord knoweth them that are his; and let every one that nameth the name of Christ depart from iniquity." As if he had said, "though some fall, all do not." God's foundation stands sure. His decree, his purpose, his scheme, call it what you please, of having a church that should remain for ever, to glorify his Son Jesus, is not in the least weakened by the fall of some, nay of many. Those who fell never had the seal, which marks his church. The Lord knew them not as his. They never were really his; though they might seem so for a time; they proved they were not his, by not departing from iniquity. They lived in wickedness. They never departed from it. God's elect are always a holy people. "Having predestinated us to be conformed to the image of his Son, and chosen us in him before the foundation of the world that we should be holy." It may not be always easy to pronounce who are holy and who are not. There is so much feigned holiness in the world, that, very often, it is only a work of time that can show who have the root of the matter in them and who have not. Yet the Lord's real people have it, and will have it for ever. So that with respect to some souls, at least, Christ has not died in vain; and of such it is said, "the Lord knoweth them that are his."

Of the first inscription, I despair of giving a truer or better account than that which our Church gives in the 17th Article. "Predestination to life" (our godly reformers say) "is the everlasting purpose of God, whereby (before the foundations of the world were laid) he hath constantly decreed by his counsel, secret to us, to deliver from curse and damnation, those whom he hath chosen in Christ out of mankind, and to bring them by Christ to everlasting salvation as vessels made to honour. Wherefore they which be endued with so excellent a benefit of God be called according to God's purpose, by his Spirit working in due season: they through grace obey the calling: they be justified freely: they be made Sons of God by adoption: they be made like the image of his only-begotten Son Jesus Christ: they walk religiously in good works, and at length by God's mercy they attain to everlasting felicity." Thus far the church. Thus it is that "the Lord knoweth them that are his." He ever has his eye on them for good, and has made an effectual provision that real benefit may result to them from the death of his Son. God's predestination and election of some souls to glory is so far from narrowing (as is often thought) the way to heaven, that remove it really, and the way to heaven is shut altogether. All others have just as good an ability for obtaining salvation by Christ as they would have had were there no election of grace. If the Lord bring some effectually to heaven, that, surely, is not excluding others. I am persuaded here is no real ground of difference in opinion, on this point, among those who love the Lord Jesus Christ in sincerity, and it is a pity that there should be any in words. Is it not allowed that God only by his Spirit inclines, persuades, draws, converts, enlightens, or convinces the souls of men? Is it not his work? Is not all the glory due to him? Who that knows any thing of real grace will dare to say, that he hath quickened his own soul? Had HE not chosen us, should we ever have chosen HIM? Alas! are we not all born in sin? And does not our evil nature even fight against the work of God's Spirit, instead of helping it? Men, all men may be saved, if they please. There wants the will only. But such is our natural enmity against God, that though the blood of his Son was freely spilt for ALL MEN without exception, not one soul would reap the benefit of it, if left to the will of the flesh. No one would return to God by true repentance, were it not for His blessed and adorable purpose of election, which, before the foundation of the world, determined that some souls should be benefited by his universal redemption, and led to repentance toward God, and to faith toward our Lord Jesus Christ. The gift of his son is as well a gift to others as to them, but by the special influence of the Holy Ghost the elect people of God are inclined to receive what the Lord freely gives.

In thus making the work of God the Son universal, and the work of God the holy Ghost particular, I speak with our Church Reformers, who understood our present subject much better than many, either Calvinists or Arminians, in our days. And if in speaking with the Church Reformers I seem, to some, to speak inconsistently, I am the more confirmed thereby that I state the doctrine aright, and that they who find fault err themselves in one extreme or other. One passage in the Church Catechism shows their peculiar view of the subject. "God the Son who hath redeemed me and *all mankind.*" Here is universal redemption. "God the

Holy Ghost who sanctifieth me and all the elect people of God." Here is electing grace.

For the full proof of the doctrine of election I might send you to the 8th and 9th chapters of St. Paul's Epistle to the Romans, and to the first chapter of his Epistle to the Ephesians. But I shall, at present, confine our attention to our Lord's own words, in *John* vi. He speaks there to the Jews, his enemies, and his open declaration of the mind of God, on this awful subject, much weighed with me to represent it to you, after this unerring pattern, though with fear lest the doctrine should be abused or misrepresented; for no doctrine of Scripture has been more so, by its friends as well as its enemies.

" All that the Father giveth me shall come to me," " and this is the will of him which hath sent me, that of all which he hath given me I should lose nothing, but should raise it up again at the last day." " No man can come to me, except my Father which hath sent me draw him." " No man can come to me except it were given unto him of my Father." Thus clear it is from our Lord's express testimony, that they who are saved, are chosen of God to salvation; so chosen however, that belief of the truth and sanctification of the soul must be manifested in all their conduct: Yet it is not any previous goodness of theirs that determines God to elect them. On this plan none would be saved; for all deserve to perish. It is the mere mercy of God, only, that saves any. He gave the elect into Christ's hands, that he might do all for them, and in them, and bring them at last to glory.

Some of God's people think that after they have

become his real children, they may lose his grace altogether. Here only is a real difference of opinion among them, and here much may be urged, from Scripture, on both sides. However, our Lord is positive that all the souls given him of his Father are safe in his hands, and shall be safe till the resurrection of the last day. He says, " my sheep hear my voice, and I know them, and they follow me: and I give unto them eternal life; and they shall never perish, neither shall any man pluck them out of my hand. My Father, which gave them me, is greater than all; and no man is able to pluck them out of my Father's hand." *John* x. 27, 28, 29.

Thus the " Lord knoweth them that are his." He ever determined, but secretly, to them, as well as others, that they should be saved. His own glory and their salvation are ensured, and the whole appears to be of grace. He finds them alienated from him, and children of wrath, by nature, even as others. He works on them by his Spirit, accompanying his law, and his gospel. They are persuaded freely, yet invincibly. I say not irresistibly; for the old man within them knows nothing else but resistance as long as they live. They are persuaded to repent, and believe the gospel. They are justified; adopted into God's family, and being made like to Christ, they live holy lives. His Spirit never leaves them till they are trained up for heaven, which at length, by God's mercy, they attain.

For once I have set forth the Scripture doctrine of election at large. It is intended by the Father of Mercies to afford strong comfort to his tempted, yet sincere children. Let them take the comfort from it that is intended, and may the Lord bless it to them. Let those who cannot receive the doctrine, be quiet and patient, at present, saying, " what I see not, teach thou me." This is more proper than to cavil and dispute.

But are any inclined to abuse the doctrine, and say, " I am one of God's elect, I may live in sin, and yet go to heaven;" let them know that they are wresting the Scripture to their own destruction. These would take one inscription without the other, though both ought to go together. The second is, " let every one that nameth the name of Christ, depart from iniquity." That is, let every one who professeth to look for salvation by Christ alone, see to it that he answer the character of his elect, that he be holy in all his life and conversation, and abstain from all sin, and hate and fight against it to the end of his life. This connection between election and holiness is very remarkable. They always go together in Scripture. One can scarcely recollect a passage which speaks of election, that does not also speak of holiness. One quotation shall serve instead of many. " He hath chosen us in him before the foundation of the world, that we should be holy and without blame before him in love." He does not choose men because they are holy; on this plan none would be saved, because all are unholy: but by virtue of his choice of them they are made holy. So far is his electing love from being an enemy to holiness, that it is the cause of all the holiness that is in the world. Take it away, and none will be left.

The Holy Ghost seems to have foreseen, that the

first inscription would be abused or misunderstood, and therefore we have here the second as distinctly expressed as the first. And it is at any man's peril to separate it from the first, or to represent the doctrine of election as against holiness. God's election is meant, in its use, as a doctrine to humble men, and cause them to trust to his grace alone, and not to themselves. It is not meant to allow men to live in sin. Indeed it is impossible that it should. If the Holy God chooses any man that he should be holy, (and that is the true election) his evidence that he is one of God's children must be holiness. He must live a good life, and continue so to do, if he mean ever to prove his election unto life, or to stand before God.

I wish this second inscription were more attended to by professors of godliness than it has been among us. Some spend all their zeal on points of doctrine, as if the first inscription could stand without the second. Others build too much upon inward sensations, or outward duties. And too many of both sorts are worldly, contentious, proud, vain-glorious, defective in brotherly love, selfish, negligent of a good life, not discharging aright the duties they owe to their families and other relations, reproaching one another, and not seeing themselves to be equally wrong. Let it then be observed, that to " depart from iniquity" is an infinitely surer mark of a child of God, than all the zeal about doctrine, and all the raptures in the world. A holy life proves a man chosen of God. The thing itself appears. Holiness must be wrought by the God of holiness. His election proves itself. The other things I mentioned may be wrought by Satan. He can give zeal, he can give joy, and high joy and zeal too, and he often has done it; but one fruit of holiness he cannot produce. See we a man live soberly, righteously, and godly, we see one of God's elect beyond doubt.

But you say, " mere moralists lead a good life, and yet hate the gospel." I believe not. No man that hates the glorious gospel of Christ loves either God or his neighbour; and the lives of men show this abundantly. Bring such persons to the tenth Commandment. They will pick and choose among the other commandments. One plumes himself on his honesty, and thinks that will do much for him with God, while he lives profanely and neglects the service of God. Another thinks a little regularity on the Lord's day will atone for his bad conduct the rest of the week. Thus men suppose their attention to some things will excuse their neglect of others. Here is no good life, though there may be much morality, much humanity, much decency. So long as men allow themselves in any one transgression in their practice, they are enemies of God, and will be treated as such. Such sort of christians, I say, pick and choose among the Commandments. " I will follow this; I will follow that. My breach of one will be excused by my attention to another."

Such phrases as this, *a good life*, have, I confess, been made too cheap among us. No man deserves the name of a good liver, but he who is one of God's elect, and a believer in Jesus. He only has respect to *all* the commands of God. For " he that keepeth the whole law and yet offendeth in one point is guilty of all." I would gladly have the professors of godliness to be better acquainted with the true *marks* of godliness. " How shall I know whether I be a child of God?" The answer to this question is not, " I feel such and such joys and elevations. I had at such a time such manifestations." Alas! nothing more delusive, nothing more liable to deceive men. But this is the proper answer. " I find, as to my faith, that I can trust in Jesus Christ in low as well as high frames, in adversity as well as prosperity; that though I know myself carnal, sold under sin, and a miserable hell-deserving sinner, yet he has satisfied for all my sins; I trust in his righteousness, and I thankfully receive eternal life, which is freely given me of God in him. As to my practice, though very far short of what it ought to be, I labour more and more to be conformed to Christ, I find a sincere love of God and my neighbour, drawing me not merely to say high things concerning love, but to love indeed and in truth, and to live soberly, righteously, and godly."

He who can say these things of his faith and practice, is a christian. He names not the name of Christ in vain. Christ lives in him by faith. Hence he knows his election of God. And if through temptation, or for chastisement, he do not know it for a time, it is nevertheless certain in itself: nay, if he went mourning all his days in much perplexity, his salvation is sure. Whereas those who live not a sober, righteous, and godly life, though their confidence and joy mount up to heaven, will only have the more dreadful fall at length into hell. The true operations of the Holy Ghost are not meant to puff us up with joy and pleasure; (there is pleasure and joy, indeed, in Christ in this world) but to make us lead holy lives. Perfect joy, and true happiness is for the next life; patience for this.

I shall close this account of the seal of God's foundation with a few suitable reflections :—1. Let me beseech those who seek God, to study after christian knowledge. It is too much neglected by many. The want of it makes them self-conceited, and easily imposed on by false pretenders to religion. One necessary part of true knowledge is a right idea of duty and privilege. Let it be remembered, that whatever is *commanded* is also *given* to all God's people. They are *commanded* to persevere, and he *gives* perseverance. He gives repentance and faith, and they are commanded as duties. He gives a new heart, and he commands us to make to ourselves a new heart. Ignorant men suppose that *both* these cannot be true. Hence have arisen the religious disputes among good men. Too narrow in their views, one supposes that if God gives all, we need not work; the other, that if we are to work, God does not give all. But both conclusions are false.

I have in this discourse chiefly attended to matters of knowledge, for the purpose of explaining, from God's own word, my general manner of preaching, which to some appears inconsistent. I derive satisfaction from the supposed inconsistency: For I am supported by Scripture; and in one verse, the verse of the text, you have that view both of duty and privilege, which I constantly inculcate. Zeal and fire without knowledge will not stand. True knowledge influencing the heart will stand to eternity.

2. Here is comfort for those who walk sincerely and humbly with God. Seeing so many professors of religion fall, they are apt to fear it may be their case also. That the foundation of God standeth sure, is the advantage which their knowledge of God's election may give them. Though none have any right to the comfort of it but those who are at present walking right with God, yet such may be confident that the Lord will take care of their persevering in his holy ways. I cannot better express this comfort than in the words of the 17th Article, which deserve to be written on the heart. " The godly consideration of predestination and our election in Christ is full of comfort to godly persons, and such as feel in themselves the work of the Spirit of Christ mortifying the works of the flesh and their earthly members, and drawing up their mind to high and heavenly things, as well because it doth greatly establish and confirm their faith of eternal salvation to be enjoyed through Christ, as because it doth fervently kindle their love towards God." This is the comfort of the godly; I pray God it may abound among us. Then follows the rebuke of careless people. Election is a delicate thing, and no man is fit to think of it but one who is serious, contrite in spirit, and low in his own eyes. Oh! it will make such a one happy in Christ, thankful, and more holy and more humble than ever. But " for curious and carnal persons, lacking the Spirit of Christ, to have continually before their eyes the sentence of God's predestination, is a most dangerous downfal, whereby the devil doth thrust them either into desperation, or into wretchlessness of most unclean living."

A word to the wise in general, and I have done. Remember, the way to salvation is only by Christ, through repentance and faith in him. You are inexcusable, if you obey not the gospel call. Predestination takes not away man's free agency. They understand not the subject who think it does. God's promises in Christ are calls to your souls to come to God by him, and his commandments are the rule of life. The church guards this matter, and I leave the caution with you. " Furthermore we must receive God's promises in such wise as they be generally set forth in holy Scripture, and in our doings that will of God is to be followed which we have expressly declared unto us in the word of God."

SERMON XVIII.

AN AFFECTIONATE ADMONITION TO SEAMEN.

Acts xxvii. 20.

And when neither sun nor stars in many days appeared, and no small tempest lay on us, all hope that we should be saved was then taken away.

These words represent to us in a very simple and affecting manner, the distress of a company of seamen, in a storm of long continuance. I apprehend there may be some of my audience who can, with that sympathy which experience alone gives, feel for the sufferers. Those of you, I mean, who know how terrible the sea is, when tempestuous; what it is to have been tossed up and down on that ungovernable element, threatened with ruin every moment by the mountainous waves. Reduced to such extremities; involved in profound darkness; uncertain every moment what the next will produce; and beholding first one, and then another part of a frail habitation failing; who can paint the horror, distraction, and despair of such a scene, but those persons whose experience and knowledge of maritime affairs enable them!

I shall not attempt it, being neither able to do justice to the tremendous scene, nor inclined to enter upon it, if I were able: for I have chosen these words to speak from, not with a view for your entertainment, but for our profit. My design is to take occasion to speak to mariners some things that belong to their spiritual interests; and yet at the same time to say what may not be unworthy the attention of all my audience. May it please the Most High to pour down his Spirit upon us, and give us the hearing ear, the seeing eye, and the understanding heart, that we may pass through the ocean of life with Christ Jesus for our pilot, and under his guidance at length reach the shore of a blessed immortality.

How happy must it be for a man to be possessed of such a treasure in his heart, as to be enabled to meet the various troubles of life, serene, undaunted, and composed, from a well-grounded prospect of endless happiness. However the wicked and the careless may scorn a truly religious character, while they themselves are in ease and prosperity; yet when they come to experience scenes of distress, such as that which the text describes; when all hope of temporal salvation is taken away, they cannot but wish they were in the situation of the godly man, whose hope is laid up sure in heaven. His portion the winds and waves cannot destroy, though they may be the means of freeing him from the prison of the body, and ushering him into the possession of his heavenly home!

Such was the case of St. Paul; that poor, despised follower of a crucified Jesus; that prisoner in the ship, who was led to his trial as a mover of sedition, and one who turned the world upside down, as a pestilent fellow, who was not fit to live. Such terms of reproach have constantly been the lot of the wisest and most upright of the followers of Jesus, in all ages. They " are not of the world," but testify, with their master, that " the works thereof are evil;" therefore " the world hateth them," as it did him.

Yet what wicked, insensible sinner, who admits only the truth of a future state, but must see, how much more enviable was the condition of Paul thus circumstanced, thus covered with infamy, now that death threatened all the company, than the condition of the rest of the ship's crew. Involved in the horrors of a menacing tempest, they had no prospects of a happy eternity to cheer their hearts in this trying hour; but were either hardened in brutal insensibility, or trembled at the view of the torment without end, because they had lived without God in the world. Paul can say to this ship's crew, " the God whose I am and whom I serve." I am not my own, but his. To him have I given up myself; in storm, or calm; in sunshine, or darkness; in life, or death. I am safe. Underneath me are the everlasting arms. " I know whom I have believed, and am persuaded he is able to keep that" soul " which I have committed to him against the last day."

How desirable is such an assurance of salvation! especially in trying and critical seasons. How can the man who thinks seriously of the value of his soul be happy on such occasions without being at peace with God? If men were deeply impressed with a sense of the value of their souls, they could not bear the idea of the near approach of eternity without it. That any can deride, as whimsical, this privilege of the saints, which the voice of Scripture and the experience of all earnest seekers after God demonstrate to be attainable, and content themselves with a hope founded upon no certain grounds, must arise from that carelessness of spirit which keeps them from musing, at all, upon the dreadful state of dying unreconciled to God.

You who may shortly be called hence by Providence, to the mighty waters, reflect how possible it is that you may be brought into imminent danger of your lives. Is not then a knowledge of certain peace with God, in this life, desirable? Blessed be God, it may be had. Jesus still lives, and will for ever live. Seek to be acquainted with his real gospel, that which Paul preached. The constant attendant of this gospel has ever been the reproach of the wicked, from without; the consolations of God's holy Spirit from within. Content not yourselves with the form, the outside of religion. Consider how much happier it is to be able with Paul to say, " I am God's, and my God will protect me," though you be despised by the men of this world, than to share with those who are respected, and courted upon earth, though they live without God in the world. The same Jesus will be your's, and manifest to you the same blissful consolations, if you seek him.

If we look at the rest of the company in this ship, whose voyage and wreck is here described, we see a true picture of natural men, unconverted, and deplorably regardless of every admonition to take care of their souls; men not to be moved by the most imminent peril to call upon God. On the contrary, see how the mariners act! " Under colour as though they would have cast anchors out of the foreship, they let down the boat into the sea, with an intent to flee out of the ship." What perfidy and cruelty is here! To leave the soldiers and prisoners, who were their charge, to perish in the storm! Paul, indeed, discovered the base design, and prevented it. But we have another instance of hardened wickedness, which works with more deadly marks of desperate enmity against all goodness. It is the wickedness of the soldiers, I mean, who were for killing the prisoners, lest any should flee and make their escape. The humanity of their commander prevented it indeed; but that men, in such imminent peril of their lives themselves, should be capable of meditating such barbarity, would be surprising indeed, did not the fallen state of human nature, confirmed by the testimony of history in all ages, prove that nothing is too base and wicked for unconverted men to perpetrate.

Let me now look nearer home, and ask you, O mariners! are there not too many of you as void, as these men were, of the fear of God? As ungrateful to him for past preservations, as insensible of his kind providence, and living as much without real religion, and regard for your immortal souls?

Having opened the story of my text sufficiently for our present purpose, I shall consider, a little, the happiness of the really religious mariner, and the misery and folly of the too many irreligious ones among us, and labour to give some practical exhortations.

What can be conceived so desirable as for a man to have that within him which shall give him an inexhaustible fund of comfort and satisfaction, in all seasons, on all occasions, and in all possible circumstances? Born as we are, with appetites and desires; weak and frail in ourselves, as all allow; corrupt and evil, as the real christian knows; we must have some suitable good that may satisfy the desires, and be a strength and a stay to the soul. We need a sanctifying principle to direct the will and affections into the ways of true felicity. We must have this, or we are miserable. Now what is this good, and how is it to be obtained? Riches, pleasures, honours, cannot give it. An infinite source they are of misery and vexation of spirit, when they are not obtained; and when obtained, are ever found vain, delusory, and unsuitable to the wants of an immortal spirit.

The enjoyment of the favour of God alone can fill the soul, and give it that all-comprehending, all-sufficient good. And this enjoyment of God's favour is not to be obtained by any way but that of God's own providing. For us fallen, corrupted creatures there is but one method of obtaining and enjoying God's favour. Self-condemned we must come to him through Christ the surety, the peace, the reconciler between God and man. He who has come to God in this manner, and found Christ the pearl of great price—that man is holy and happy. He carries the earnest of heaven within him; the living hope of everlasting glory. In all troubles he can go to God, and unburthen himself before him of all his cares and fears; and the Lord is to him a certain refuge in every time of trouble. His times are in God's hands; in his heart are God's ways; the Spirit of God is his guide, and counsellor and sanctifier; neither the world, nor life, nor death, nor hell can rob him of his treasure. He is " kept by the power of God through faith unto salvation." How happy is he! How sweet to him is it to meditate alone on God his portion! How sure and sound is the provision made for his soul and body, for all his concerns in time and eternity!

If such a treasure as this be infinitely desirable to all men, is it not particularly so to those whose situation in life exposes them to frequent perils and dangers? Such as that of the mariner, who experiences serious scenes of distress, and is in every voyage exposed, in some respects, more than other persons, to the danger of death; in some voyages very sensibly and eminently so. How happy before he sails, to be able to say with a heart breathing with the love of God as a father; "I know that the events of this voyage, be they what they will, shall work together for my good, and therefore I can cast all my care on him who careth for me." It is a treasure, surely, to be desired by all mariners to have Christ in their hearts, for with him they have all things. It is not in the power of winds and waves to rob them of it.

Oh! mariners, how few are possessed of this treasure. Are any of this occupation longing after it, seeking it, conscious of their want of it, concerned at the thought of venturing upon a treacherous element, that may give them a watery grave, without feeling any well-grounded prospects of eternal felicity? If you "will inquire, inquire;" come and ask of God. He will, by his word, lead you to Christ. There is, indeed, such a treasure as I have spoken of to be had in this life, through him, of which many pretended christians have no idea. He who has it, has "Christ in him the hope of glory." He has external good morals, but proceeding from a principle of internal purity of heart.

But, surely, you will give me leave to complain, and pity, and lament the unhappy case, the sad moral and spiritual condition of too many mariners! Alas, in what open immorality do too many of them live! It is too possible, and too common for regular moralists to have no inward religion, no more love of Christ in the heart than immoral persons. But unquestionably those who live in avowed immorality are utterly destitute of every good thing; they are at open war with God, and so dying must feel his vengeance for ever and ever, " where the worm dieth not and the fire is not quenched."

In this season of spiritual concern, which it has pleased the Most High to raise among us, of late years, when not a few, I trust, are turning from sin to the Lord, surely it is to be wished, by every benevolent mind, that you also, O mariners, may partake. You, also, are invited to share in this sweet, heavenly influence; to taste and see, with others, how gracious the Lord is, in pardoning and renewing ungodly men. And why will not you come unto Christ that you may have life? You have heard what love he has shown to sinners, in bearing such torments for them. Surely he deserves your esteem and regard, He deserves your heart to be given up to him in love.

To bring you to this, is the design of the religion of Christ which I preach; let men call it by what reproachful names they please. Its grand purpose is to bring men to enjoy that salvation which Jesus has purchased with his blood, and give up their hearts in love to a Saviour thus kind, thus bountiful to them. How reasonable and happy a service is this! How base and ungrateful to live in avowed neglect of such a Saviour, without a spark of regard to him in their hearts, with no thankful meditation on his kindness, without any hearty testimonies of respect to him in common conversation and conduct.

O mariners, do not pretend to christianity, to any sense of honour, generosity, or gratitude, if you live thus without regard to Christ. Do not pretend to any goodness of heart, if Christ's love has never yet melted your breasts. Every oath and curse is a spitting on his face; every act of lewdness is a nailing of his hands; every wanton breach of the sabbath a scourging of his body; and a constant course of carelessness about an hereafter in your conduct is the same thing as saying, " O Jesus, thou needest not have died to obtain eternal redemption for us. We will have our portion in this life. We desire to have nothing to do, either with thee, or the heaven thou hast purchased." As men, as rational, accountable creatures, you ought to be moved with fear of hell, with desire of real happiness, with sense of favours received.

I address you with an affectionate concern for your souls, and beseech you to bear with me while I mention a few instances of wickedness, which I wish I could say were not too commonly practised among you. Weigh and consider them well. There is no hope of your hearty repentance and amendment if you never be brought to serious consideration. How, and why is this, that one cannot come within the sound of your voices, in the haven of this town, but one's ear is struck with the constant repetition of oaths and curses? This horrible language is particularly heard when you are in a hurry, or under the influence of anger for some little cross, or untoward accident. Surely you will not think of excusing this by the force of habit? Consider, that if you had any reverence for God in your hearts, you durst not affront him so basely. Why do not you pray earnestly, and strive earnestly against it? The continuance of such a vile, ungrateful practice, which you cannot pretend to be of any sort of service to you, evidently shows that you are living in open war against God, and that dying thus you must feel his wrath for ever. Alas! what shall I say? Is God who has been so kind in preserving you, hitherto, in so many perils, deserving of this vile usage from you? Is Satan so very good a master, and are the wages of eternal destruction, which he gives to all his slaves, so very pleasant, that you should serve him with such zeal? If you had any feeling of your baseness, you would weep and howl for your horrid blasphemies, and cry out. "O thou much injured Jesus! wash out my oaths with thy blood, and teach me to use my tongue, for the future, to thy praise, and not to thy dishonour."

I am afraid there are too many, not only among mariners, but others also, in this profane libidinous age, who have no idea of any great guilt, or perhaps, any guilt at all, in fornication and whoredom. Hence they can live in sin without remorse or fear. But if Scripture is to be regarded at all, fornication as well as adultery are sins that incur the wrath of God. For it is written "marriage is honourable, and the bed undefiled; but whoremongers and adulterers God will judge." Light as whoremongers may make of this offence, the last chapter in the Bible ranks them with " dogs, and murderers, and idolaters, and liars," who shall be shut out of heaven. Make a conscience, then, I beseech you, of this sin, and carry past transgressions to the throne of grace, to be washed from them in the blood of Christ, and taught to live soberly, as well as righteously, and godly in this present world.

I am afraid too many mariners, also, make little conscience of observing either private or public worship, even when they have opportunity. There is not a day but gives you opportunities of praying in secret, and surely you are answerable to God for every day's neglect of this duty. As to public worship, surely, when you have opportunity, you should not let a trifle hinder you from attending it. Oh, if you had hearts at all sensible of the kindness of God in preserving you from so many dangers, and were impressed with any lively ideas of the providence of God, which you of all men have the greatest opportunities and occasions of being impressed with, you would gladly wait upon God in his house. You would pay your vows in the sight of all his people, with thankful acknowledgments of past deliverances, and listen to the sound of the blessed gospel of Christ, which alone can make you wise unto salvation.

Let me ask you also, O mariners, how have you fulfilled those resolutions which you made of amending your ways, when you were in distress. You seemed, in a storm, to be near approaching to eternity. Then, perhaps, you cried to God, and promised how good you would be for the future, if he spared you. But did you not return immediately, when danger was over, to your old sins? Think of the aggravated baseness of this ingratitude.

In truth, it is no wonder you kept not those resolutions; not only because they were extorted from you by fear, but also because there is a reason why no resolutions whatever, made by a man in his own strength, have any power to turn him to God. The new creature in Christ is not the product of man's resolving. Those who are, indeed, born again, are, as the Scripture tells us, " born not of the will of man, but of God." Read the third chapter of St. John's Gospel carefully with prayer, and be well assured from thence, that if ever you be, indeed, saved from your sins, and made good and holy, you must be born again. Whether you have led moral or immoral lives, in time past, this change is necessary to all who would enter the kingdom of heaven. Shake off that levity and carelessness of spirit, I beseech you, too common among persons of your profession, and begin to inquire what you shall do to be saved, with the earnestness becoming men, who are sensible they have immortal souls, which must one day appear before God in judgment.

Would you carry with you, in your hearts, to the seas, a God in Christ, a reconciled and a loving father to you? Oh, be supremely concerned to seek his face. Consider, you are sinners by nature and in practice. It is no light thing that can take away your iniquities, and reconcile you to God. The sole Physician of Souls who can give you both repentance and remission of sins is he who is exalted for that end, to be a Prince and a Saviour. Implore him to look upon you, to create in you new and contrite hearts, that " worthily lamenting your sins, and acknowledging your wretchedness, you may obtain remission," perfect remission from the God of all mercy, through his well-beloved Son. If any of you are sensible that you have hitherto lived in sin and wickedness, and would gladly be guided into the way of salvation, I declare unto you, That JESUS IS THE WAY. Through him there is plenteous redemption. Yes: he whom you have pierced with your sins, is good and gracious, and of great mercy unto all them that call upon him. All things are now ready. Pardon is ready; sanctification is ready; the consolations of God's Holy Spirit are ready. They wait your acceptance. What you want is faith in Christ, to lay hold of him for holiness and happiness. The Lord draw you by his power; and whoever is willing to be saved from his sins, and taught to live righteously, soberly, and godly, let him come to Christ, and take of the water of life freely.

Thus far, O mariners, I have endeavoured to exhort you. Some of you may be sailing hence very shortly, and perhaps you may never more have an opportunity of hearing the glad tidings of salvation. You will be answerable to God for the neglect of what I have said, if you do neglect it. Some of you may shortly be involved in imminent peril of your lives. If so, may you then think of what I have, this day, said to you, if not before.

I add no more but this: Sin and wickedness will entail God's everlasting curse upon those who die in it: If you would escape it, seek to God by Jesus Christ to obtain pardon, and holiness of heart and life.

SERMON XIX.

PARABLE OF THE RICH MAN AND LAZARUS, CONSIDERED.

Luke xvi. 22, 23.

And it came to pass, that the beggar died, and was carried by the angels into Abraham's bosom. The rich man also died, and was buried; and in hell he lifted up his eyes, being in torments, and seeth Abraham afar off, and Lazarus in his bosom.

The parable of the rich man and Lazarus is one of those strong paintings, which can scarce fail to arrest the attention, and captivate the imagination of all to whom it is presented. But, with the blessing of God, I hope this day's consideration of it may do more; may be the means of penetrating the heart, and persuading men to seek after the blessings of the heavenly country.

May each of us view ourselves as strangers here! May we sit loose to the earth, and behold eternity before us! When we view the rich, and the poor; our neighbours, our relations, and ourselves; may we remember that an eternal state of bliss or misery lies before us! This eye to eternity enables a person to form a due estimate of the goodness of characters, and the happiness of stations. Forget Abraham's Bosom, and you would deem the poor, despised Saint, an unhappy object. Forget hell-torments, and you would think a proud, rich man, the happy person.—But will you go with me to look at "that within the vail?"—"Saviour! let thy Spirit touch our hearts, and lighten our darkness, and dispose us to hearken!"

The grand moral, as it may be called, of the whole parable, appears to be this—He who places his happiness in this world's goods of any kind, however successful he may have been in his pursuits, will find in the life to come unspeakable disappointment and confusion: but he who in obedience to the word of God receives the gospel of Jesus Christ, and cleaves to his God with determined faith, however poor and miserable he may appear in the present life, will in the life to come find unspeakable, everlasting joy, and satisfaction—the drift of the preceding chapter all tends to establish the same doctrine.

But let us not be diverted from our subject. " Come forth, O rich man! clothed in purple, and fine linen; faring sumptuously every day. How do many envy thy equipage, and ease; thy prosperity, and success! What numbers pay court to thy greatness!" Since man fell from God, how natural is it for him to admire riches! For however common it be for us to affect to despise them, yet is there something in them which commands respect from men. On the contrary, the beggar, laid at the rich man's gate full of sores; who is in so wretched a state, that he is desirous of the crumbs which fall from the rich man's table; while the dogs lick his sores—such a poor object as this—though it may excite pity, excites also contempt in the proud, selfish, corrupted taste of man.

Do not excuse yourself too hastily. No man is naturally without this corrupt propensity. Solomon certainly spoke truth, when he said, " the poor is separated from his neighbour; but the rich hath many friends." Neither can we be effectually divested of this corrupt partiality, but by connecting both worlds, and viewing the whole of the state of each. Look forward, then, brethren. Our Lord has drawn the circumstances of both in vast extremes in this life; that even still the advantage may appear very far on the side of the truly righteous.

" And it came to pass that the beggar died, and was carried by the angels into Abraham's bosom." The angels are " ministering spirits sent forth to minister for them that shall be heirs of salvation." They encamp about the righteous man in the present life, and deliver him from evil. After death they conduct him into happiness. They disdain not, thus, to attend on the squalid beggar, whom the meanest servants of the proud rich man despised. We have no account of the poor man's burial; mean enough it probably was, and unnoticed in the world.

But " the rich man died," and it is said that he " was buried," with grandeur and pomp, no doubt, and in a way that was much noticed in the world. But follow him into the other world, and then judge, which on the whole was the happier man. " In hell he lift up his eyes, being in torments, and seeth Abraham afar off, and Lazarus in his bosom, and he cried and said, Father Abraham have mercy on me, and send Lazarus, that he may dip the tip of his finger in water, and cool my tongue; for I am tormented in this flame. But Abraham said, Son, remember that thou in thy lifetime receivedst thy good things, and likewise Lazarus evil things; but now he is comforted, and thou art tormented." In these words the grand instruction of the parable is couched. Therefore we must here endeavour to set forth the principles of the rich man, and of the beggar, and also to guard the parable against the abuse too often made of it.

I should not be at all surprized, if some poor people that hear me, should be pleasing themselves with censuring and reviling the rich, and make very little doubt but their own sufferings here will contribute to their happiness hereafter. They call the rich proud and insolent; not considering that pride may be as strong in rags as in purple. If, then, any poor persons here think that they shall be happy hereafter, merely because they are miserable in this life, they deceive themselves exceedingly, and mistake the intent of the parable.

Again: Others of the richer sort may be pluming themselves upon this, that they shall be excused from the sufferings of the rich man hereafter, because they now behave with humanity, and kindness to the needy, and live in the practice of temperance and sobriety. They may do this and many good things besides, and yet have their treasure in this world, and not be " rich towards God."

I shall not stay to argue these cases of the rich and poor; in both which it is hard to say how much self-deceit may be practised. But as the establishment of truth is the best refutation of error, let us endeavour, according to the real drift of the parable, to set forth the true characters of the rich man, and of the beggar. And here let the 13th verse of the chapter—all the foregoing part of which belongs to the same subject of laying up treasures in heaven and not on earth—be a key to open the characters. "No servant can serve two masters: for either he will hate the one and love the other, or else he will hold to the one and despise the other: ye cannot serve God and mammon." The Pharisees, it seems understood the drift of his discourse. They "were covetous, and heard all these things, and derided him."

Now all neutral characters being set aside, *two* characters only remain, and *two* only will appear at the day of judgment. Insignificant indeed are all distinctions of another kind, compared with these; converted, or unconverted; lovers of God, or lovers of mammon; heirs of heaven, or heirs of hell. Do not suppose that the rich man's riches sent him to hell, or that the poor man's poverty sent him to heaven. If poor people allow themselves, at all, to view the parable in this flattering light, they view it in such a light as will deceive their souls. It is possible enough for a rich man to be, in heart, affected as Lazarus was; and a person as poor as Lazarus, may be as proud as the proudest of the rich. The true reasons why the rich man is set forth as the unhappy character, are to be drawn from the entangling nature of riches, and from the consideration of the superiority of heavenly things above earthly, best illustrated by such vast extremes of situation as the parable describes.

What was then the character of the poor man? You may know the foundation he stands on, by his being taken up "into Abraham's bosom" after death. He must have walked "in the steps of the faith of Abraham," the father of the faithful: He must with him have seen heavenly things afar off; being persuaded of them, and embracing them. The fourth chapter of the Epistle to the Romans illustrates this matter at large. There the relation of all believers to Abraham is set forth. They believe with him, and their faith in Jesus is imputed to them for righteousness. Lazarus, then, was determined for God and heavenly things. There was his treasure and portion. He looked not at things seen, but at things *not* seen. Hence he adorned his profession by patience, humility, submission to the will of God, and every other fruit of the Spirit which his state allowed him an opportunity of exhibiting. Hence after death he was not ashamed of his hope. Abraham is described, particularly, as owning him. All heaven owned him.

But the rich man had his treasure on earth. He had no faith in Christ at all. He regarded not heavenly things. He is described as rejoicing in his riches only. A man's particular taste and temper may incline him to employ his riches to the purposes of cruelty and oppression; or of luxury, and riot; or both. But the radical evil is this; that his *heart* is in his riches, and his happiness expected from them. This seems to have been the fault of the rich man. Therefore he is now "in hell." In his lifetime he received his good things, and Lazarus evil things. The first chose his portion here;

the latter, in patient faith, looked for it hereafter. Hence the first is tormented in hell; the latter is comforted in heaven. God gives him at length that for which he looked, while he patiently bore the evils of life.

O ye rich! O ye poor! envy not one another, nor endeavour to extol your own particular rank at the expence of the other's. The grand inquiry of all should be, what are the good things you have in view; earthly or heavenly? If you be ever so poor and miserable in this life; yet if earthly things be what you are thirsting for, as much as the rich, and the successful, poor Lazarus's comfort belongs not to you. Your " good things " in view are the same as the rich man's, and so dying your fate will be like his.

To be brought by your own evil conduct to a state whence there is no release, is dreadful. And yet this is the state of the prisoners in hell, as it is described in the parable, " besides all this, between us and you there is a great gulf fixed; so that they which would pass from hence to you cannot; neither can they pass to us that would come from thence." The Saints of the Lord are despised on earth, so that even this which is the Scripture name of a real christian, is treated with scorn. It is a sad sign of the low state of religion, when the very profession of it is disgraceful. But see the difference in the world to come. To teach us to look forward to that is the grand business of the parable. The rich man who, in his lifetime, would have scorned poor Lazarus, and have looked on him as scarcely fit to tread the same ground with himself, now would be glad of his assistance, glad of his company. But he cannot obtain it. A gulf separates between them. Lazarus is gone to enjoy life eternal. The rich man is gone to everlasting punishment, and "in hell lifts up his eyes, being in torments."

If rich men think that surely this will not be their condition, let them not be "high-minded, but fear." Presumption is too plain a mark of danger. Had the rich man of our parable been afraid for himself while alive, he had not been in so great danger of ruining his soul. It is not that riches ruin the soul: But they give so much occasion to pride, and scornfulness; and encumber the possessor with so many cares, that this may safely be said, that the rich man who does not watch and pray, lest he enter into temptation, is in it already, is asleep in his sins, and hastening to follow the rich man of the parable both in his crimes and in his punishment.

The rich man finding that all prayer was vain for himself, recollects that he had five brethren still alive; who like himself were lovers of riches more than of God; and had no more apprehensions than he had entertained of a judgment to come. "I pray thee therefore, father, that thou wouldst send him to my father's house: for I have five brethren, that he may testify unto them, lest they also come into this place of torment." Unwilling he was that they should be as miserable as himself; or else afraid that they should upbraid him as having contributed to harden them in wickedness. Could one, indeed, take a view of the regions of torment, perhaps, one of the most afflicting scenes would be, that of relations accusing one another of being the cause of misery to each other. "I would have hearkened to the voice of God, speaking in his gospel, under such a sermon; in reading such a chapter; at such an afflictive season; nay in my last sickness; but you, O father, mother, husband, wife, brother, or sister, were against it, and assisted me to get quit of my convictions. And now this is the end of all your cruel tenderness." Oh, relations, that love one another tenderly, in this, at least, imitate the rich man in hell. You may now, in this life, with success, seek to further one another in hearing and attending to the gospel of your salvation.

"Abraham saith unto him, they have Moses and the prophets, let them hear them." The rich man thinks that a miracle would rouse their sleepy minds. "If one went unto them from the dead, they will repent." He talks like one who never had known, as indeed he never had, what the turning of a sinful soul to God means. There are great and valuable purposes in miracles; but the converting of sinners is not their province. That belongs to the Holy Ghost. It is his office to quicken the dead, and to enlighten the dark soul; and he doth both by the WORD, called here "Moses and the prophets." The word is a lantern to the feet and a light to the paths. St. James says, "of his own will begat he us with the word of truth." And Abraham closes the whole discourse, by assuring the rich man, that such a miracle would be vain. The Scriptures are sufficient, as means, to persuade and to convince. If unbelievers and ungodly men think otherwise, they are assured the fault will be charged to their hearts, not heads. They may think themselves sincere; but their hearts deceive them. The rejection of the word of God argues a desperate corruption of heart, not to be cured by any other means whatever. "If they hear not Moses and the prophets, neither would they be persuaded though one rose from the dead."

Now that we have taken a brief survey of the transactions in the unseen world, which our Lord has favoured us with, should we not apply them to ourselves? Do thou also, good Saviour! by thy Spirit apply them in a suitable manner to all our souls!

1. It is obvious here to lament the stupidity and unconcern with which so many can read or hear the amazing, and inconceivably awful things of eternity, revealed in the word of God. They can hear of a place of rest, and eternal joy in Abraham's bosom, and yet feel scarcely an emotion of desire to be there. Nay some will even openly confess they would rather live here awhile longer, than go to heaven. They can hear of hell; a place of never-ending torment, represented by a burning flame, without the allowance of a drop of water to cool the tongue, and yet be quite unconcerned. I wish this scene, so often displayed, may not be exhibited again this day. I wish wicked men may not go out of this house, as fearless of judgment as they came into it. What can be the reason of this dreadful stupidity; even in men otherwise of great discernment, and keen sensibility? It is the Fall that occasions it; "there is none that understandeth, there is none that seeketh after God."

You find yourselves naturally disposed to be more

afraid of men than of God: More haunted with the fear of losing a little money, than your soul: More allured by the prospect of earthly, than heavenly riches. Now if you would, indeed, be put into the way of deliverance, you must feel and know the disorder. You must lament, not only the sin of some particular crimes, but the sin of your nature itself. Surely it is ineffably absurd for men's passions to be affected in so disproportioned a manner; and a proof, indeed, of the corruption of nature, since the same fault is natural to all men. Desire, then, to feel the evil that is in you, that you may at length be properly affected with the doctrine of such a parable as this; and ask seriously, "how shall I be admitted into Abraham's bosom?" If you desire this, observe,

2. You must be content, in this life, to receive "evil things;" and believing the promise of eternal life, embrace that as your happiness and portion, on the credit of the word of God, which proposes it for your acceptance, and by virtue of the offering of the precious blood of Jesus. The 4th chapter of the Epistle to the Romans, and the 11th of that to the Hebrews, thus teach us to "follow the steps of the faith of Abraham."

But this grand remedy obtained by BELIEVING IN JESUS CHRIST, how foolish does it appear in the eye of nature! Nevertheless, receive it, if you would be happy here in expectation, and supremely happy hereafter in enjoyment. For "Christ is the end of the law for righteousness to every one that believeth." "Neither is there salvation in any other." We may apply for happiness to many things besides, but all will fail. Worldly pleasure is a phantom deceiving in the very grasp: Riches either make themselves wings and fly away, or if they stay, they give often more pain than pleasure, and always disappoint on a death-bed. Family comforts are all frail, and fading: Honour is an empty shadow. Our own righteousness is that which many, under the name of virtue, think to be a real good. But it is all pride and hypocrisy at the bottom, and if the cheat be not detected before death, after death it will appear to the poor soul's eternal confusion.— What is, then, the real good? That which the Apostle calls, " Christ in you the hope of glory!" That will give peace in life, and death; and carry you with poor Lazarus into Abraham's bosom. Seek this Saviour, if ye be at all sensible of your need, and you shall find the only true happiness of man.

3. But some may say, they cannot understand the Scriptures, learned men differ so much in their explanation of them. In answer to this, I beg leave to remind you of the close of our parable; that if wicked men will not be persuaded by the Scriptures, neither would they be persuaded, though one rose from the dead. We set before you Jesus Christ as the sum and glory of the Scriptures; the only foundation of a sinner's hope; the only righteousness for him to appear in before God. It is not a pleasing sight to see so many persons quite unconcerned, whether this doctrine, or any other doctrine be true; and easy without any certain plan before them, though hell and heaven are in prospect. But remember that our Lord, by the mouth of Abraham, sets his seal to the sufficiency of the Scriptures to teach men aright. There needs no working of

miracles now; which brings to my mind what some persons very ignorantly object to Ministers of the Gospel, "Work miracles, and then we will believe what you say." "Would you indeed? Assuredly you would not: if you will not hear what we tell you out of Moses and the prophets; if God's word set before you gains not your assent." While you put this word from you, and judge yourselves unworthy of eternal life, neither would you be persuaded, though one rose from the dead, and told you how unspeakably miserable all those are who have died without an interest in Christ, as all their righteousness. In truth, the fault lies in your heart, not in your head. Pray for Divine illumination, as the Scripture itself directs you, otherwise you do not use it in the way that it directs you to use it. Be concerned for your souls, and seek, that you may find. All who have used this method will bear witness to the sufficiency of the Scriptures to make a man wise unto salvation, through faith in Christ Jesus.

Lastly, let believers be patient under the scorn and contempt, the afflictions and evils of this frail life. Let them be diligently employed in the Lord's work, looking forward to the things not seen: "they shall obtain joy and gladness, and sorrow and mourning shall flee away." Who so wretched as Lazarus outwardly? Yet who more happy within? Christ in the heart is heaven in the heart, however disagreeable outward things may be to the flesh. Hold on your way, strong in the grace of the Lord: for, "the ransomed of the Lord shall at length return to Zion with songs, and everlasting joy upon their heads."

SERMON XX.

DUTY OF DRAWING NIGH TO GOD, AND RESISTING THE DEVIL.

James iv. 7, 8.

Resist the devil, and he will flee from you: Draw nigh to God, and he will draw nigh to you.

The Scriptures continually represent to us, that there are two opposite interests and kingdoms in the world; that of God, and that of the devil; which never can be reconciled: The one advancing goodness, happiness, and truth; the other aiming only at the production of wickedness, misery, and error.

The whole world in which we live having fallen from God, by the first transgression, lies dead in trespasses and sins, and we are all children of wrath by nature: insomuch that Satan is called in one place " the god of this world," in another the " prince of the power of the air, the spirit that now worketh in the children of disobedience." And "for this purpose the Son of God was manifested, that he might destroy the works of the devil." For this he lived; he died; he rose again; ascended into heaven; now intercedes for us at the right hand of God; and sheds forth the sweet and strong influence of his own Spirit on the Church. His intention and desire is, to have every member conformed to himself; separated from this evil world; and partaker of his divine nature, with eternal glory.

The devil's kingdom and cause is the very contrary of all this. As Christ dwells and walks in his people by a real, powerful union, so the devil dwells and walks in his people, that is, in all the unconverted who remain in a state of nature. We are not so much affected with this thought, as we ought; else how would it stir up every one seriously to reflect, " I am either under the ruling influence of God, or of Satan."

Let men's fruits prove to their consciences how it is with them. There are no middle characters, for we " cannot serve God and mammon." Just as goodness, or wickedness; heavenly things, or earthly, have the predominancy in our hearts, so are we the servants of God, or the servants of the devil. Indeed, the servants of God have flesh as well as spirit; but they do " not walk after the flesh." Their practice is heavenly; because, " greater is he that is in you than he that is in the world." " Ye are of God, little children, and have overcome them."

The text gives us a very weighty exhortation, formed upon this doctrine. " Resist the devil, and he will flee from you: draw nigh to God, and he will draw nigh to you." It may be conceived as addressed to the converted, or to the unconverted. For as men begin, so must they continue to walk with God: and the rules, for recovery after backsliding, are the same as for first conversion. I shall therefore handle the subject in a way adapted to both. Nor need we be solicitous to know exactly in all cases, when we are tempted by Satan: for he *worketh in* the " children of disobedience," and to the " children of God" he has access by the flesh.

As then " he that committeth sin is of the devil," to *resist him* and to resist evil is the same thing, in effect.

We are invited to " draw nigh to God; to cultivate acquaintance with him, in the gospel way, by all means; and are assured, in that case, " he will draw nigh to us ;" will show himself gracious, will bless us. And because Satan will fight against us, especially if he see us draw nigh to God, we are commanded to *resist* him; and mighty though he be, and we poor worms, we are assured, he shall flee from us. Though he may tempt again; fleeing from us only for a season, as from our Lord; yet he shall flee from us again. For HE is strong that executeth his word. Glorious, precious encouragements these! to come near to the best of beings, and be enabled to resist the worst.—Son of God! bless what we have now before us! Oh! that we may prove both parts to be true, by our own experience, Oh! that we may be thoroughly persuaded to obey, in faith, thy directions, and bring thee eternal honour by our success.—And here I would, 1st, consider the motives which should induce us to draw nigh to God, and to resist the devil—and, 2d, give some instances of this practice.

The motives I shall mention are four. Let the first be drawn from the opposite character of God and the devil. It is a certain truth, that God is the most glorious and best of beings; whose goodness and compassion are as infinite as his power and wisdom. Nothing but good ever proceeded, or will proceed from him. Creation and providence are daily multiplying innumerable instances of the excellence of his law, and the beauty of his holiness, as set forth in the Bible. Were there no other proof, these would demonstrate the perfect character of the Supreme Being; that he "loveth righteousness and hateth iniquity." And the foul falsehood of those who despise the Bible, is fully proved by this circumstance: that to a man all such persons make light account of HIM. The Bible manifests the glorious character of God its author, by being always on the side of true goodness. No man can show his hatred of the Scriptures, but he is sure to show a hatred of true goodness at the same time. There is, there is such a being as the devil; the enemy of God; "the spirit" that worketh in the children of disobedience! What do all his temptations lead to; especially those of them which would draw the soul from Scripture truth? Do they not lead to one thing; to make men careless how they live, and to indulge sin? On the other side, christians, and all who know any thing of a divine work on their hearts, can bear witness, that holy Scripture tends to one thing; to real godliness; *practical* goodness, and virtue; not of this and that sort only, but of every kind.

I will suppose a man solicited, in his soul, two ways—no uncommon case—I would scorn to represent things different from what they are. There is no such thing as any man's falling, all at once, into the full belief, and determined reception of the gospel. I say, a creature corrupt as man is, may be solicited, by Satan on one side, to continue easy in sin, and live as others do who are careless of hereafter. He may also be drawn, by the Spirit of God, to the

arduous and self-denying path of faith in Jesus.—
I value not the religion of those who dream of the
latter without the former; of peace and holiness
without temptation and conflict. It suits not the
Scripture doctrines, nor the present state of things.—
But here is the thought, the motive before us, which
ought to persuade us to " draw nigh to God, and
to resist the devil," that God calls us, by Scripture
doctrines, to nothing but what we are sure is right
and good. Whereas, however varnished the cause
of Satan may be with smooth words, *he* calls us only
to what is evil and wicked.

Confess, ye who have hearkened to the devil, however you may have endeavoured to disguise the truth
to yourselves, it is nothing but your dislike of real
goodness at the bottom, and your unwillingness to
part with what is evil, that causes you to remain unbelievers. It is not that you want POWER, but you
want WILL. Your fault lies in your want of inclination. And hence you are without excuse.

If there is a God, the Bible doctrines are true,
and must make those happy who follow them; because real goodness is all that they lead to. No
infidel can disprove; nay, hardly deny this. What
ail, then, men's hearts, that they " do not come to
the light," but this? that " their deeds are evil, and
they hate to be reproved." And what a sad proof
it is of man's natural corruption! that man should
so readily yield to the devil's suggestions, when
they all lead to evil, and should be so backward to
come to God, as if he had no goodness in him! Is
he not all goodness? and whereas his law requires
satisfaction, has he not given in the work of redemption the highest proof of his goodness? And

now that the road is open to guilty man, and he calls, " draw nigh to me, and I will draw nigh to you," can it be any thing else than wickedness of heart, that keeps us back from him? What does he want of us, but to receive him freely as our Lord and Saviour? Is he not worthy of our hearts? Is happiness possible on any other plan? Be stirred up, brethren, by this motive, to turn to God; to come close to him by Christ; and to get a real acquaintance with him. God is good. What harm can goodness do you? Must it not in the nature of things promote your happiness? What folly! to talk of delaying, or of going too far. Can men go too far in that which is good?

I wish men to see, what they are very unwilling to see, that by delaying to turn to God, with their whole hearts, they betray that they love what is evil. The vile way of excusing themselves, and calling their wickedness by soft names, will not excuse them. The devil should be RESISTED, and he will FLEE. But he should be resisted resolutely, as an enemy to truth and goodness, and without allowing him any quarter, or he is not resisted, to purpose, at all! " Thou art evil, Satan, and leadest only to evil!" Thus short and strong should be the language with which we resist him. And it will be seen how this roaring lion will flee like a coward, according to the text, while the poor helpless worm, drawing nigh to God, shall find HIM draw near, in his infinite goodness. " The haters of the Lord shall be found liars," and " with honey out of the stony rock" shall he satisfy the desire of them that seek him.

I desire this plain argument may be weighed. If it can be truly said that what we exhort you to, when we invite you to turn to God by Christ, leads men to wickedness; to insincerity; to any one evil under the sun; and not rather to all practical goodness; then hearken no more to us. But if the truth be as we have stated the matter, you certainly hearken to Satan, not to God, while you delay one day to repent and to believe the gospel. Truth, wisdom, and happiness must as surely be found on the side of goodness, as light and heat are in the sun. Therefore, because God is good, hear him; because the devil is evil, resist him.

A second motive need only just be mentioned. The Lord of all power and goodness surely can, and will make all those eternally happy, who " draw nigh" unto him. The devil can only make us miserable, as he himself is. Reflect, then, ye who have felt your hearts stirred up to seek for happiness in the gospel-way, that the devil envies every poor soul, that would flee from his hard service, into the liberty of the children of God. He loves not that any should " recover themselves" from his snare, " who are taken captive by him at his will." To himself nothing but despair is left; and we should have been justly dealt with, had God left us so to perish. Thanks to God! there is a remedy in Christ, full and perfect, for all the evils of our fallen nature, and we shall find it such when once we heartily embrace it.

Satan may be expected particularly to discourage us when we set ourselves to seek the Lord. The god of this world will labour to pour blindness around us, when the light has begun to draw us. RESIST him, ye seeking, ye tempted souls, thus: ." Thou

Satan art HELL; and canst only lead me to partake of thy endless torments. Begone: I hear thee not." Then turning to God, say, " O Lord! thou hast begun to show to thy waiting creature, happiness in Christ, the Son of thy love. Thou hast promised to draw nigh to those who draw nigh to thee. Surely thy presence, love, peace, forgiveness, joy in the Holy Ghost, and conformity to the spotless image of thy Son, must be happiness. Even here it is happiness. How infinitely more so must it be after death, to all eternity! Here would I hold, and hang, and seek, and wait, longing for that REST which remains to thy people."

Oh! that we had more of this heart-work. For you will suppose I do not think that the bare uttering of a few words is any thing. I express what I conceive right in a form of words, in order to be understood. But to RESIST Satan indeed, and " draw nigh to God" indeed, in the faith of these two short promises, " God will draw nigh to me," " Satan will flee from me," is an experiment worth making. And Scripture-truth would prove itself indeed, did we thus put its glorious Author to the test. But coldness, worldliness, and mere doctrinal formality, keep many in deadness, without the power of godliness. —" O Lord, awaken us, to prove thy words; that we may find thee true, and Satan false; and we shall praise thee."

The third motive I shall mention should stir up the generous indignation of every soul, that would not be imposed on. It is this. In God there is all truth; in Satan there is all deceit. Those who have had some experience of godliness know this. They know that God's corrections, grievous though they be for the present, are wholesome; they come from the best of friends. Satan's most alluring baits of temptation come from a deadly enemy. Shall man then be so foolish as, knowingly, with his eyes open, to yield to his enemy; to be scandalously befooled by the vilest of beings, who means to lead him to the lake that burneth with fire and brimstone? In worldly things it is not thus. There is a charm in plain truth and sincerity, that affects the heart, however unadorned its dress and rough its manner: and deceit and falsehood are hated, though gilded even with Cicero's eloquence. Why is it not so in divine things? "Come unto me," says Christ, " all that labour and are heavy laden, and I will give you rest." " All they that forsake thee shall perish." " He that believeth on me hath everlasting life. He that believeth not shall not see life, but the wrath of God abideth on him." These are the plain truths of God. Heaven will witness to eternity the pleasing fulfilment of the one; and hell to eternity the awful fulfilment of the other. " Draw nigh then to God, and he will draw nigh to you."

The God who made you deserves to be trusted. He has told us of an evil spirit, our enemy, whose very essence is lying and falsehood. This deceiver says, "sin, and no harm shall come." Oh! that men should hearken to falsehood. Yet all do, who go on carelessly in sin. Be stirred up, then, with indignation, on the side of truth, "to resist the devil," and be serious to come close to God, to feel his truth.

Let the fourth motive be this. Jesus will " bring forth judgment unto victory. He shall not fail nor be discouraged." Satan may rage as he pleases, it is an unavailing war. The gentle lamb of God is victorious over him. Draw near and close to Christ; put your whole selves upon him, and his whole weight of interest, merit, and might is yours. Oh! seek to be closely acquainted with him: and it shall be seen, in HIS STRENGTH, how strong you, who are poor worms, shall be. Judge not by what you feel, in temptation, but by the promises. God will draw nigh: Satan shall flee. Let certainty of victory encourage you to rely upon God.

Let us now consider a few instances in which the directory of the text may be practised. I shall mention three cases similar to those in which our Lord was tempted, by Satan, in the wilderness. A Christian has fellowship with Christ, in all things; therefore in temptation. HE was tempted in all points like as we are. He is able, through sympathizing experience, to succour them that are tempted. He can be touched with a feeling of our infirmities. Precious encouragements these! It is an honour to suffer with the Lord of Glory!—to reign with him and be glorified together hereafter, is glorious indeed!

One temptation was, to the love of the world. He showed him " all the kingdoms of the world, and the glory of them," and promised to bestow them upon him, if he would fall down and worship him. " Get thee hence, Satan; for it is written, thou shalt worship the Lord thy God." This is the answer and the victory. The world has objects suited to the taste of the natural man. We are blind to the beauty of God, and therefore we employ our faculties, ever since the Fall, on sensible objects, in such a manner, as to give them that place in our affections which belongs to God. Hence the love of money, of power, of praise, of grandeur, of pleasure. The beginner in religion; the experienced saint; the whole church, especially in days like ours, days of ease and prosperity, need to resist the devil strongly here, with " it is written, thou shalt serve the Lord only."

When it is become needful to part with " the right hand" or " right eye;" when carnal lusts or worldly friends, with " the god of this world" at their head, are drawing the soul from God and his Christ; then is the time, indeed, to prove both parts of the text to be true. Exercise faith upon them; and by steadfast trusting try their force and power. If you will still cleave to God, and constantly make supplication to him; praying always and not fainting, for the discovery of his glory in Christ, and the participation of the divine nature; you will find him draw nigh to you, in mercy and loving-kindness. This will give you pleasures worth the name; which the world can neither give nor take away.

You may expect to be violently opposed by the devil in this undertaking. It may be suggested to you, that a strict course of self-denial will be intolerably grievous; and worldly pleasures may be represented to your senses in the most enchanting forms. But RESIST Satan. Trust God's account of things. Wait, in patience, for the event. Be determined not to yield an hour; and Satan must flee, and victory must be yours, if God be true, if there be indeed a living God.

A second temptation of our Lord's was, to presumption: to throw himself down a pinnacle of the temple, because it is written, "he shall give his angels charge over thee." He answered, "it is written, thou shalt not tempt the Lord thy God." Thus many are tempted, and overcome, by the suggestion, that God is so very merciful, as to save them without making so much ado about religion. Thus his holiness is not seen; nor his justice regarded; nor his threatenings believed. Oh! how Satan deceives the nations with this thought! "keep only from gross crimes, and all will be well." Men do not consider, that heaven itself could be no heaven, but to the holy. Talk of being saved, and living careless in sin! You might as well talk of being in the fire and not being burnt. Salvation must consist in being brought into a holy state, and that in this life.

Oh ye, who have begun any thing of serious thought for your souls, resist this flattering suggestion, or it will ruin you. Though this is not to be done in your own strength, but in Christ altogether, you must cease from the love of all sin; you must heartily approve and follow all holiness; or you must perish for ever.

Let all religious persons beware of sinning, that grace may abound. Christ Jesus died, not that you should be saved, going on in a careless, easy way, without mortifying your lusts. No: "he bare our sins in his own body on the tree; that we being dead to sin should live unto righteousness." In the hour of temptation draw nigh to him for strength, and he surely will draw nigh to you, and you shall be more than conqueror through him who loved you. But he never meant to have you excused from the pain, and trouble, and labour of mortifying all evil lusts and tempers.

Only, what he commands he gives, and works in

us by his Spirit, if we truly trust in him for it. RESIST Satan, therefore, and give him no quarter, so shall " he flee from you."

I have no hope of any man's salvation, who remains presuming upon the mercy of God, while he thinks only of going on in his sins. Not one sin; not the most darling lust, which seems necessary to your very happiness; not the most favourite gratification of the flesh, must hold its place in you, if you ever get to heaven. They must all be given up, however unwilling you may be to have it so. Were it possible for you to live all your days in obedience to all the divine commands, except one, and yet to live knowingly in the breach of that one, it would prove you rebels and hypocrites, and seal your eternal damnation. " What must we do then?" Turn to God wholly. Is it reasonable, think you, that he should violate the laws of his government to please you? " Draw near to him, and resist Satan." Though you have already justly forfeited all, yet in Christ there is plenteous redemption, righteousness, and strength. You are without excuse if you refuse. There wants only your hearty consent, and Christ will do all things for you.

The remaining temptations of our Lord, in which his followers have fellowship with him—and all temptations, it may be, are reducible to these three— is to unbelief, impatience, and despair. " Command these stones to be made bread." " It is written man shall not live by bread alone; but by every word of God." This comes in, with peculiar strength of comfort, to all who earnestly seek the Lord; determined to know HIM only for happiness. But HE draws not nigh; they are in a dry desert, and in the spirit of heaviness; hard thoughts of God; dreadful, and strong inward corruptions; violent, and long, and sore temptations, with darkness, and Atheism, distress them. " Resist the devil, steadfast in faith" as our Lord did in the wilderness. THE WORD OF GOD, brethren, can make you live; and you do live by it, though without sensible comfort, at present.

I do not mean to argue hence, that you should be slothful in the business of your salvation; but that you should be still and patient in temper, till he draw nigh in comfort. No set time is promised. HIS time is the best. All unbelieving, impatient, and hard thoughts of God should be resisted with steady faith in his character and promises, as set forth in the Bible. You may be growing and thriving now, in divine life, though you think not. He is purging you, that you may bring forth more fruit. Learn to give up your will to God in bearing the cross, and suffer the word of exhortation. Instead of poring continually on your miseries, up and be doing the Lord's work, in a way of duty, and in dependance on his strength. He will meet you in his own way, though not in yours. He has promised so to do. "Tarry then the Lord's leisure, be strong, and he shall establish your heart; all ye that put your trust in the Lord."

SERMON XXI.

A PRICE IN THE HAND OF A FOOL TO GET WISDOM.

Prov. xvii. 16.

Wherefore is there a price in the hand of a fool to get wisdom, seeing he hath no heart to it?

A FOOL, in Solomon's Proverbs, constantly means a wicked man, and wisdom with him is but another term for godliness. The text intimates, that a wicked man has " a price put into his hand to get wisdom;" so that had he a heart for it, he might become godly. So much cannot be said for the condition of fallen angels. In the just judgment of God they, after having fallen by sin, remain exposed to the consequences of their rebellion for ever. But for sinful mankind there is a remedy—that which is the constant theme of all true preaching—the mediation of Jesus Christ the righteous. A price is put into our hands to get wisdom. The means are before us; and it is said, " seek and ye shall find."

May not there be times, think you, when evil spirits feel the keenest envy on this account, and may not this fill them with rage and malice against men? " *They* may be saved, *we* are shut up in despair." On this account Satan may tempt men with the more eagerness, and labour to blind their minds, lest " the light of the glorious gospel of Christ should shine unto them." And alas! the folly of men gives him but too great advantages. There is a " price to get wisdom in the hands of a fool;" but he has no heart to it. He relishes it not; he might find much comfort here, as well as solid bliss hereafter; but he chooses to remain as he is; foolish, and therefore miserable.

I shall endeavour to show this in several steps, of the proceedings of fools. Some, perhaps, go through them all in order; some only through a part; but in all of them I would meet the consciences of some or other of my hearers, with a view to lay open to them the folly of wickedness, to rouse them to a sense of danger, and lead them on to seek true wisdom with all the heart.

The first and grossest sense in which the text evinces itself, is in the conduct of a thoughtless rake, or drunkard, or debauchee. Even *his* worldly friends, especially the aged and prudent, can tell him, that he has a " price in his hands to get wisdom," and foolishly throws it away. I mean, they can show him his want of human prudence. How easily might he obtain friends, and earn his bread, and enjoy the good things of this life with a fair character, and with temperance and sobriety! He has had many opportunities; but he throws them all away. He will not learn wisdom by experience. He involves himself in debt and penury by foolish extravagance. He injures a good constitution by excesses. He lays himself open to the frauds of knaves, and by bad company exposes himself to many miseries continually.

I wish the place we lived in did not afford too many proofs of this; for surely idle, vain and dissipated young men abound among us, even in respectable families. And I wish their parents could stand clear in their own consciences of having neglected to teach them the fear of God, which alone can effectually secure men from these evils. If young men see the old to be immoderately saving, and hear no other lecture from them, but "get money, and save money," they may fancy that their parents have done this sufficiently already, and may be tempted to the other extreme of extravagance and idleness.

But if it be so, young men! you are not excused. What was good in their advice you should follow, and you have the word of God before you for a guide. Yes, the word of God, which you leave to your SISTERS to attend to. Do you suppose that religion belongs to women only—that men have no souls, and will not rise again at the last day? The careless lives of young men among us might tempt one to suppose they thought so. One hears from time to time of the other sex being awakened to solid concern for their souls; and truly the evidences of true conversion and its fruits do appear among some of them; but with young men, especially of the richer sort, is it not far otherwise? How seldom are they seen in public worship, and how constantly do they profane the Lord's day! When do they ever read the Scriptures? Yet they have learnt to read, and considering the use they make of the talent, it had been better for many of them if they had not. Inflammatory publications, that teach sedition and self-conceit, suit their taste better than the word of God. They set up to correct both King and Government, when it appears, by their conduct, they are unfit to govern a private family. Nay, they have not learnt to govern their own lusts and passions, and, what is worse, have no desire to learn. Oh! unhappy youths! Who thus mispend your time in reading seditious pamphlets, novels or plays, or whatever tends to inflame your passions. I would mourn over you; I would engage you to mourn over yourselves. Take the text and apply it. None have more cause. " Why is a price put into your hands to get wisdom, seeing you have no heart to it?" You might have been growing in Scripture knowledge; but you are foolish, both for this life and the next. Why will you go on in a way to please Satan? Why will you die, while the Lord exhorts you to turn and live?

But some of these reform their manners, and grow more prudent. The instructions they have received in the arts of getting money, as if this was all the business of human life, are not lost on them. They begin to see it a foolish thing to do nothing but spend money. They, at length, apply themselves to labour to gain some. After a few years experience they grow more cautious, and he who at eighteen was quite a spendthrift, becomes at thirty a miser, eager and keen after every opportunity of enriching himself. This is no uncommon case. Such may be more agreeable to their aged friends; but alas! from God they are just as distant as ever. The price that was put into their hands to get wisdom, they still have no heart to. Formerly pleasure, and now business, takes them up all the day long. Indeed some fill up their time between both; at any rate prayer, self-examination, the word of God, and all serious attention to his word, are still set aside.

I speak to your case. Can you read what our Saviour so solemnly declared, " ye must be born again," and yet expect to enter into the kingdom of heaven without the new birth? Can you be fit for heaven, who have no worship of God in your houses, nor in your closets; who think it quite sufficient to come to this house once a week, and hear a single sermon, and attend to nothing of religion the whole week besides; but place your happiness in amassing riches? What would you do in heaven? You would soon be weary of its employments.

I could mention many things, which become a servant of God; the honouring of his holy name and word; the propagation of his gospel; the support, and encouragement of his ministers; the bringing up of children in the nurture and admonition of the Lord. All these things are quite neglected. You live to yourselves, just as if there were no God to govern the world. Being quite strangers to his grace, and having no idea of any pleasure in communion with him, you certainly have not one of those marks which belong to a christian, set forth in the word of God. Your heart is dead to God, buried in the world, and taken up with business. Anxious after this world's profits, you look at those who are richer than yourselves, and intend, by and by, to become as rich as they. For you measure happiness by sums of money, and with you, the man of ten thousand pounds is twice as happy as the man of five thousand. If you read the Scriptures, and attended to what passes within you, in a due manner, you would see, that the nature of man is corrupt altogether. " There is none that understandeth, there is none that seeketh after God."

With you it has been thus ever since you were born. And now that you are become wise for this world, you are as yet as far from God, as when you were careless.

I have attended you in your progress from thoughtlessness to prudence, and it does not appear, though you think more of your worldly affairs, that you have any more concern for your soul. Oh! what signifies it to you, that the gospel doctrines of salvation, by the grace of the Lord Jesus Christ, and the new birth unto righteousness, have been preached among you? You remain still with the curse of all your sins upon you, and the power of them unbroken. Do not you see that there are those among us, both of the poorer and richer sort, who are truly religious? And do not you see, amidst the chaff of false profession, that a number of them are evidently real christians? They were not born so; they lived, some of them, for years, as you have done, lovers of the world. There was a time when they had no more notion of converting grace than you have.

They were brought to feel their depravity; their damnable state by nature: They felt the burden of sin; they heard with eagerness of the Saviour; they sought him, and they found him. In him they obtained peace, and forgiveness; by his Spirit their heart has been set free to know, to love, and to obey God. Him they now behold as a father; and Jesus is not seen at a distance, merely as a terrible Judge, but he is their Saviour, Husband, Shepherd, Brother. All these pleasing names he has in Scripture, and they are not mere names: Believers find him to answer these characters to them in experience. And they do not look forward to death with terror as you do. They look beyond it with comfort. They have mansions above, where they hope to rest. They would not live here always; this world, even in its most pleasing forms, is no home for them. They have a taste much above its best things, since the Holy Ghost made them his temple, and gave them fellowship with the Father and the Son. Under his influence they are training up for heaven, learning patience, meekness, charity, letting their light shine before men by good works, and waiting for the blessed hope above.

Now, do you ask these persons, how they were brought into this state? You have every opportunity and advantage to know it. I may safely say, the truth, as it is in Jesus, is preached plainly, and you may see it exemplified in the lives of those who truly believe. If you saw some of your mercantile acquaintance make much profit in a branch of business with which you were unacquainted, you would endeavour to learn how they managed, that you might succeed in the same way. Perhaps you would find some difficulty to learn their method. Men are jealous of their profits, and such is the scanty nature of this world's gain, that one man's profits must be crossed, if others were let into his secrets. It is not so in the kingdom of heaven. As "yet there is room." You are called on by my mouth: "We pray you in Christ's stead, be ye reconciled to God" through Jesus. The conversion of others makes not your conversion more difficult. And if you would open your hearts freely, and ask, I will venture to say, there is not a true believer, who would not, with pleasure, assist your inquiries. All of them would tell you how they found themselves, when convinced of guilt, and how they sought after God, and obtained peace of conscience. And their conversion might be of use to you.

I would to God there were more of a disposition to encourage such discourse among ourselves, instead of that corrupt, and, at best, worldly conversation which prevails. But the persons I am speaking to, have no heart for these things.

Yet some of you may go a step farther, and learn a little of Christian doctrine. By hearing, attending prayer, and going through certain forms of religion which you once neglected, you may persuade yourselves, that your state now is good; especially if attended with a moral, blameless conduct. But if you rest here, you are Pharisees, just as St. Paul was before his conversion; proud of your own righteousness; quite unacquainted with the pollution of your own spirits; resting on your own goodness, and strangers to Christ's righteousness. In this state you are fond of the praise of men; exalt yourselves above others, and are unwilling to bear the cross of Christ, and his reproach in the world. There is a price in your hands, and still you have no heart to it. Christ calls you to come to him; but you cannot come to him, except you part with the pleasure which you have in your own righteousness, and in the admiration of the world; till you give up your idolatrous dependance on your own works. All this Babel must come down: You must be humbled, before Christ the hope of glory can dwell in you.

We have seen the fool, of the text, first thoughtless, and giddy even for this world; then reformed, and prudent; taking care of worldly interests; bu still, though there be a price in his hand to get wisdom for heaven, having no heart to it. Even when, in the third place, we saw him religious, in a certain way, he rests on external acts, and a round of duties; he is not at all disposed to come to Christ; he leans on self, and the wickedness of his own heart is quite hidden from him. Have patience, brethren, while I consider him, in the last place, still nearer to the kingdom of heaven, yet not coming into it. The review of these things may, under God, help some here present to see their own state, and what it is that God calls them to. And if but one soul reap any such instruction, I shall think it a rich requital for the displeasure of others, and infinitely more valuable than all the applause given to a correct and polished discourse, that does not reach the heart.

The " price in his hand to get wisdom," through what Austin calls the " severe mercy of God," comes now nearer. His heart is touched; his conscience is more steadily affected; he begins to feel the evil of his doings; and through increasing light, he learns the emptiness of the outward religion in which he gloried. His want of delight in God shows him he is not fit to die, because heaven would be no delight to him as he is. He finds he has not purity of heart; and from the knowledge he obtains of christian doctrines, of salvation by grace, and the new birth unto righteousness; he suspects, and justly too, that he is not right. The Spirit of God is striving with this man; would humble him; would beat him off from his false pleasures, his conformity to the world, his good opinion of himself, his love of ease and reputation among men, and show him, that he ought to deny himself, take up his cross daily, and follow Christ.

This, then, is "the price now in thine hand to get wisdom:" thus does Christ speak to thee. " Oh, that there were such an heart in thee, to hear my voice, which calls weary sinners to come to me for rest. Thou hangest upon the world which crucified me; thou expectest happiness from it, and it has not happiness to give thee. Why art thou afraid, what this, or that man should say, or think of thee, if thou wert to follow me entirely? Why not willing to be despised as I was? Why still keep back thy heart from me; still clinging to thy idols, now against thy conscience? Why not come and venture on me by faith, and receive me as the husband of thy soul? Am I not able to promote thee; to give thee infinitely better than any thing thou art called on to part with? I upbraid thee, but with pity; I rebuke thee, but in love; I strive with thee; I give thee sting after sting, and present thy guilt before thee, from time to time, that thou may'st not rest in thy folly, which I see thou art striving to do; wanting to persuade thyself that all is well as thou art."

Now, is there a man in the congregation, whom this may suit? Perhaps there may be a number, who for years have carried the burden of a filthy heart, and a disquieted conscience, having the " price to get wisdom in their hands," and yet still having no heart to it.

By such cases it is made to appear, brethren, that salvation is of the Lord. He only can engage the heart, and cause it to draw near to him. But he has various ways of doing it. Some he drives more with terror; others he draws more with love. He suits tempers and circumstances, and acts with infinite variety of wisdom in his methods of bringing sinners to Christ and to true rest. And while we are apt to attend little to this work of God, He is going on in convincing and converting souls, and gathering into his church such as shall be saved. While we are taken up, some with the affairs of nations, and the tumults of countries; some with merchandise; some with pleasures, he is steadily doing good to souls, and rescuing them from the tyranny of Satan, by the effectual grace of his Son Jesus. Jesus is interceding continually, and rejoicing to see of the travail of his soul. The Holy Spirit is quickening, enlightening, and sanctifying their hearts.

Oh, that we attended more to this; studied God's word more; our own hearts more; and brought these concerns more to our own case, which are so profitable, so important! How little would then appear to us the grand, the noisy, the busy pursuits of the world! Do you say, you have not brought the matter to a point? I have gone as far as my text directs, and if there is here a soul in this state, and he be brought to feel it, it may prove a wholesome lesson of instruction. May he learn to prize the means of salvation, and to profit by them. Having a price in his hands to get wisdom, may he diligently improve it, and may his heart be bent upon knowing the only true God, and Jesus Christ, whom he has sent, which is life eternal.

SERMON XXII.

THE TEMPORAL ADVANTAGES OF GODLINESS.

———

1 Tim. iv. 8.

Godliness is profitable unto all things, having promise of the life that now is, and of that which is to come.

The Apostle's own remark, which immediately follows the words of the text, naturally leads us to conclude that they teach a truth of immense importance. "This is a faithful saying," says he, " and worthy of all acceptation." Let us then view and consider, with God's assistance, this sentiment dictated by the Holy Ghost, which he holds out to us as of eminent worth.

What godliness itself is, I stay not now to consider at large. To describe it is the constant business of the Gospel-Ministry. Suffice it to say, that where the heart is brought to depend on the Lord Jesus Christ alone for all things, *there* the love of God and our neighbour will be implanted, there, and there only. This is faith working by love. This is the godliness of Scripture. There may be, and have been many other things said to be GODLINESS, or parts of it: but christian godliness is that which I have mentioned, and which alone is worth the name. It is acquired by believing in Christ. For there is no way to God, and goodness, but by him.

Oh! that young persons would seek after godliness, as the one thing needful. Weakened by a corrupted nature, and tempted by a subtile devil, and an enchanting world, how are you liable, O young persons of both sexes, to be seduced and flattered to your destruction! How prone to yield to the insinuations of those who call godliness melancholy! Alas! if you be not acquainted with godliness, you will never know true satisfaction of mind, even in this world.

Mighty Saviour of Sinners! be pleased to shine through the gloom that sin hath spread upon our minds; overcome our prejudices; make known the real pleasantness of thy ways; let our hearts feel the joy, the gratitude, and the love which the manifestation of thy grace, by thy Spirit, can create; and, Oh! give us to know experimentally, that "godliness is profitable unto all things, having promise of the life that now is, and of that which is to come."

I would beg, indeed, the attention of all, but in a particular manner of young persons, while I endeavour to set forth some of the advantages of godliness. Great they must be even in this life! Consider what our Lord says, Luke xviii; "Verily I say unto you, there is no man that hath left house, or parents, or brethren, or wife, or children, for the kingdom of God's sake, who shall not receive manifold more in this present time, and in the world to come life everlasting," We see from hence, that in godliness there is a self-denial, which in the nature of things is unpleasant to the flesh; but yet in proportion as self is denied, that is, as godliness

is really followed, manifold more pleasure, even in
this present time, is obtained than lost; besides the
inconceivable surplus of eternity.

Believe it, then, on the credit of our Lord, that
godliness has the advantage even in this life. All
godly persons know this to be true, so far as they
are godly. It is to the imperfection of their godliness that the troubles, for the most part, which
they undergo in this life, are to be ascribed. If
then you find you do not enjoy such and such advantages as we shall describe, yet if you really
believe in Christ, you may possess them, by living
up to your privileges better than you hitherto have
done. All that you can conclude from your present
situation is, that you need to grow in godliness;
since your experience of the love of God, little as
it may have been, proves to you its superior pleasures. You know enough to believe, that "the
grace of your God is exceeding abundant with faith
and love in Christ Jesus," and that in godliness
only is to be had true pleasure and satisfaction.

The first advantage of godliness, which is received
in this life, is the " peace of God which passeth all
understanding, keeping the heart and mind through
Christ Jesus." I choose to express this in Scripture language. It is also the language of our Church,
with which she concludes her morning service. To
describe this peace of God, and what a blessing it
is in itself, I shall not attempt. Even those who
enjoy the most of it cannot describe it; because
though it " keep their hearts and minds through
Christ Jesus," and they are " filled with all peace
and joy in believing" by the God of their hope,

yet the same word of God which thus asserts the reality of the peaceable and joyful feelings of the believer, describes them as "passing all understanding." Though they are not contrary to, yet they are above human reason. And no wonder, considering the incomprehensible greatness of the Author of them. "I," saith God, "create the fruit of the lips; peace, peace to him that is far off, and to him that is near, saith the Lord, and I will heal him."—Indeed if God be for us, who or what can be against us? "He that spared not his own Son, but delivered him up for us all, how shall he not with him, also, freely give us all things?" What an advantage then of godliness is this, that it brings divine peace along with it. What is the evil of evils that infests the world? Is it not the loss of the favour of God? All the other evils that sin hath caused are not worthy to be compared with this, that it separates between God and us. But the godly soul, reconciled to God in Christ, "who is our peace," has the sense of this peace imparted to him, and is made to "abound in hope by the power of the Holy Ghost."

With what cheerfulness and joy may he bear many temporal evils that flesh is heir to; who enjoys the sense of peace with God. To God as his refuge he can flee in all times of distress, and find unspeakable consolation in pouring out his heart before him, "who is the strength of his heart and his portion for ever."

I wish godly souls walked more closely with God than they do; were more watchful unto prayer; more simple in spiritual desires, and more steady in dependance on the Lord Jesus than they are! The full assurance of faith and hope described in Scripture, and David's experience of the forgiveness of his sins, or God's peace, spoken of in the 23d Psalm, would not be so uncommon as it is among professors of religion. Probably too many who are not without spiritual desires cannot, as they wish, bear witness to the truth of this first advantage of godliness, "the peace of God." They may thank for this the love of the present evil world. The little reality of godliness there is amidst much profession is owing to this. For be it remembered, that it is not the profession of godliness, but godliness itself that has the promises belonging to it: so that still it is true, that godliness does bring with it all the advantages that the word of God describes.

Reflect, then, you who have known in a little degree, it may be, the divine peace of godliness, and have lost it again, upon the cause of this. Your conscience bears witness to the excellency of godliness. "Oh! if I had had more of it, I should have had more peace; and if I had not left the Lord, he would not have left me." Will you, then, return to God more heartily than ever? Again you shall have God's peace. It is not, that you are to work out a righteousness of your own to justify you. There is no peace to a troubled conscience, but torment, in that way. Renounce self and come to Christ, that is repentance, that is faith. Cleave steadfastly to Christ as all your salvation and all your desire, that is holiness. Expect from Christ, both in this life, and the next, all your comfort and happiness, renouncing all other pretenders that would rival him, and surely you will find, as it is written, "thou wilt keep him in perfect peace, whose mind is stayed on thee, because he trusteth in thee." Yes: show us a man or woman whose mind is stayed on Christ in the gospel way, and there, there is true peace. Be that man or woman in much worldly adversity, in rags, they are even now—setting aside the happiness of the next life—they are now by far the happiest persons on earth. Ungodly men have no conception of the bliss of communion with God; how he fills and satisfies the believing soul. And then to see all one's concerns kindly ordered aright, by the care of infinite power, wisdom, and love; to be freed from all guilty fears and heart-devouring cares by the dear Redeemer and Intercessor—how great is this! I trust, there are persons here, who know in some real degree, what these things mean. You can witness that " godliness has promise of the life that now is, as well as of that which is to come." But perhaps the most instructive view of this part of our subject may be, to show the want of peace attendant on ungodliness.

Say, ye careless sinners, amidst all your prosperity and jollity, are you happy? No. There is an uneasy void in your soul; you want something to fill it. You try first one thing and then another. Nothing satisfies the soul. The "peace of God" can do this for you. This is to be obtained by coming to him, as lost wretches, through the blood of the Lamb; and nothing else can do it. But besides this uneasy void, there is the sense of guilt, and the slavish fear of divine displeasure, often embittering the soul. From this you find no refuge, but the temporary one of flying from thought. Still you are gnawed by an evil conscience.

Even those decent, but unconverted men, who by formality and external morality have procured to themselves a false peace, are not happy in it. They have nothing of that enjoyment, which results from the application of the blood of sprinkling, which speaketh peace. They know nothing of joying in God through our Lord Jesus Christ. Their hope being built on self, is liable to be shaken continually. Not so the true christian's. His hope is set on the Lord; and Christ is the same yesterday, to-day, and for ever. Besides, if ever the self-righteous man obtain true peace, all this false peace must be destroyed, else he dies self-deceived, and his end is so much the more miserable. Oh, fellow christians, know ye God's peace? Examine what you build on for eternity. One foundation only is authorized for a sinner to rest on, that is Christ Jesus. You who are stayed on this shall have perfect peace, and be kept in it, for it is written, "Thou shalt keep him in perfect peace, whose mind is stayed on thee." I have dwelt long on this first advantage of godliness. The rest flow from it.

While the creature lives at a distance from the Creator, as all men do by nature, the state of the soul is like that of the earth at its first creation, "without form and void, and darkness upon the face of the deep." But when the Spirit of God has quickened the soul, and the Lord has caused his face to shine upon her, through Jesus, in peace and love, as above described, then the movements of man begin to be as they should be. Order rises out of confusion, and the appetites begin to be subject to reason, the moment that reason itself begins to be subject to God. Philosophy may say fine things of the subjection of the appetites to reason; but whoever saw it in practice? In the true scholars of Christ, alone, is this brought about. Man being, then, recovered to his right state of willing subjection to his Creator, by faith in Christ Jesus, the other advantages of godliness follow according to this beginning.

The godly man, through the mighty influence of the Spirit of Christ, now ruling in him, learns the due regulation of his tempers. Receives he an injury? He can pass it by with meekness. Is he reviled and abused? He practises Solomon's method: "a soft answer turneth away wrath!" Do his temporal affairs turn out unsuccessfully? He can bear it with patience, till an agreeable change befal him. If it please his God still to afflict him, his God supplies him still with patience and inward consolations. No temporal things are of such importance to him, that the frame of his soul should be quite disordered on their account. He is seeking a better country, even an heavenly; he cannot be deprived of that. Such are some of the tempers of a godly man. I should add also his humility and lowliness of mind, by which he prefers others to himself.

I might dwell upon other branches of the christian temper: but perhaps you may say, who practises according to all this? There is in the godly an old man, we know, as well as a new. "The flesh lusteth against the spirit, so that they cannot do the things that they would." But still so far as men are godly, so far they practise as I have described, though it must be confessed, the tempers of some require far more grace to humble and subdue them, than those of others. However, christian principles alone can produce these amiable fruits: and in all converts they do, though in some an hundred fold, in some sixty, in some thirty. To which I add, he that lays any stress on any supposed conversion, which was not followed with some measure of real change in his tempers and practice, let that man know he has deceived himself. If he had actually passed from death unto life, the alteration of his conduct for the better, and indeed of the whole frame of his soul, in some real degree, must have ensued. Such unsanctified pretenders to religion should rather submit to begin religion afresh; and as vile, blind, lost sinners, seek Christ afresh, lest they perish in their hypocrisy and delusion.

See, now, what advantages godliness has in this life, from this article. What misery and torment do pride and envy cause in the world! Need a man be more miserable than impatience of spirit will make him? What dreadful feuds, what long-protracted calamities, have desolated the earth, for want of mutual meekness and benevolence? Oh! brethren, it is not misery, it is happiness itself we exhort you to seek after, when we exhort you to receive the gospel of Jesus Christ into your souls. For the godly man, so far as his tempers are regulated by it, is clear of these evils. He loves peace, and his peaceableness of disposition prevents him.

from either causing the woes of contention to himself or others. Oh, if there were more godliness on earth, this gloomy earth of ours, *gloomy* because of sin, would brighten into heaven. The fair fruits of heaven, love, mercy, and kindness would gladden the face of nature, and it would appear with far greater evidence than it now can do, because godly men are so rare to be found, that " godliness is profitable to all things, having promise of the life that now is," as well as " of that which is to come."

If there be one earthly blessing more valuable than another, it is health. I will not say how far it may please the Most High to try, even godly men, with much sickness. But as their day is, their strength shall be, if it be thus; and all things shall work together for their good. But surely the godly man has far the advantage of the ungodly, in this respect. Need I say what thousands have perished in the bloom of life, through drunkenness and lewdness! What shattered constitutions too many vicious men carry, perhaps, to the verge of old age!—Miserable souls! This world's enjoyments they looked for alone; and what can men enjoy without health? Wretched contrivers! to manage for yourselves in such a way, as to lose both worlds, and to bring upon yourselves the pains of both.

But the godly man is temperate in diet, sleep, and in the whole regimen. I might add also he is laborious. And what fine advantages for health result from labour and temperance united? Hence, is he enabled to redeem much time; to go through the work which God hath set him, with cheerfulness; and to be useful to his fellow-creatures. I might add, he is more free than others from that dejection of spirit, and all the melancholy with which this world abounds. Do not, O young persons! trust profane people when they tell you, that if you seek after the new birth unto righteousness, it will make you melancholy. Look about you, and see who are more cheerful than the godly. Among what sort of people are the gloomy-minded to be found? Is it not very commonly among persons well known to be void of godliness? Oh, then, cast in your lot among God's people, if you would know what true pleasure is.

If you attend to matter of fact, you will see no manner of foundation in another censure of wicked men, that the following of religion makes men neglect their worldly business. Look around, and see it to be far otherwise. Who follow their business with more regularity, and usefulness to their families, and society in general, than the godly? Nay one might appeal to wicked men on this head. With whom would you sooner choose to do business than with men who are conscientious in religion?

I wish christianity were better known amongst us. Certain it is, the more it is known, the more amiable it appears. The better it is practised, the more good results from it, even of a temporal nature. What, is it no advantage to a family, to a town, to the regular and succesful pursuit of business, that men are temperate, chaste, sober, and not busy bodies in other men's matters? But such is the godly man; and those parts of the land where godliness prevails, there temporal advantages, in abundance, are the result. What think you? When the godly man devotes that leisure time, from business, to public means of grace, or to private meditation and prayer, which ungodly men devote to places of gaiety, or gaming, whether of the two is the most likely to thrive, even in this world? Nay, indeed, it seems to be confessed that godliness has its advantages for this life, while wicked men with a sneer observe, that they take care of the main chance as well as other people. This is a confession, that the declaration in the text is fulfilled, " godliness has promise of the life that now is, as well as of that which is to come." The christian owns it to the glory of his God; and yet these worldly things are not his God, his portion, his chief joy. His real riches, seen now by faith, are laid up sure in heaven; by patience waited for, in the way of self-denial; oft enjoyed here by anticipation, and fully hereafter, " when Christ shall appear;" for then shall he " appear with him in glory."

It is a great comfort to a person to have some suitable entertainment, with which innocently and profitably to amuse his spirits, and employ his leisure time. Who has this advantage like the godly? Men of pleasure are improperly named. Their excess of amusement renders amusement itself a burden. And yet they cannot bear to be alone, nor to think alone. But the christian has a God to go to, in his hours of privacy; the promises of the Bible wherewith to regale his mind; the comforts of the Holy Ghost wherewith to cheer his spirits, when his God sees needful; the strength of the Almighty to support him, when his flesh and his heart fail; and the expectation of Jesus's second coming to complete his salvation, as real, as certain, as it is that God is true.—Want you entertainment, to refresh the mind withal, when weary; to sweeten the temper withal, when likely to be soured by adversity? Oh, young men! make Christ your friend, while you may. How many have regretted, even in this life, their following the ways of sin! But none ever repented his following of Christ.

What a damp does it strike on the hearts of those, who live for this world only, to think, " this house, this estate, this prosperous trade, these agreeable connections, will one day forsake me." What a sting is there in death! What a damp does it cast on all earthly joys! But the christian looks beyond death with pleasure; beyond death lies his complete happiness. Here is an advantage: it cannot be said how great it is. " In the world to come he shall have everlasting life; but the wicked shall go away into everlasting punishment."

I have, in this discourse, confined my regard to the *temporal* advantages of godliness. Oh, young persons! look here to Christ. He is the way of pleasure, here as well as hereafter. Oh, that you might effectually believe in him, and prove by experience the truth of what has been said.

SERMON XXIII.

THE USE AND ABUSE OF HEARING SERMONS.

1 Cor. iii. 5, 6, 7.

Who then is Paul, and who is Apollos, but Ministers by whom ye believed, even as the Lord gave to every man? I have planted, Apollos watered; but God gave the increase. So then, neither is he that planteth any thing, neither he that watereth; but God that giveth the increase.

A very great, but common evil, had infected the Church of Corinth. The people were grown very wise in their own conceits; heard their pastors with a critical and curious spirit; were "puffed up for one against another;" and hence had among them envying, and strife, and divisions.

It affords no small ground of patience to faithful pastors, in every age, to find, that if they be treated contemptuously and ungratefully by their people, it is what St. Paul himself met with. And yet he could say, "though ye have ten thousand instructors in Christ, yet have ye not many fathers; for in Christ Jesus I have begotten you through the gospel." To the same purpose, in the chapter next to that of the text, he addresses the Corinthians, who it is evident had encouraged a number of other pastors, to the prejudice of the Apostle.

St. Paul strikes at the root of this factious, proud, and uncharitable spirit, by showing that it was utterly contrary to the spirit of the gospel. Christ alone is the foundation of all hope, of all glorying, of all confidence. Even wisdom of words made use of, instead of christian simplicity, with a design to win men to the gospel, may have an opposite effect. The Apostle preached the gospel, not with wisdom of words, lest the cross of Christ should be made of none effect. " The world by wisdom know not God." The gospel is a dispensation, which to the carnal mind, to man in a natural state, appears weak and foolish. However, it is God's method, and divinely calculated to bring to nothing the pride of men, and to teach us to glory alone in the Lord: In so much that the Apostle was determined to know nothing among them, save Jesus Christ and him crucified. In this doctrine there is divine wisdom, indeed, to enlighten, and to heal the sons of men.

The Apostle describes, in the second chapter, the nature, and importance of a spiritual understanding, and shows that we not only need the written WORD of revelation, but also the Spirit's light to behold its glory, and to understand it in a due manner, for the salvation of our souls. If, then, this spirit of faction reigns, it is because men, in that respect, are " carnal and walk as men." They set up one man, or one sect, and party, and they undervalue another, and suppose that the blessing of God peculiarly belongs to one, and is quite removed from another, even though the same gospel of salvation be preached. And it often happens that this spirit is nourished against their first teachers, under whom they learnt all that they know. For whenever the divine simplicity is lost, and men grow worldly, and vain, and formal, they are apt to ascribe the fault to their pastors, however faithful, laborious, and exemplary they may be, though it evidently lie at the door of their own neglect and unwatchfulness. Then succeeds the love of novelty. They become fond of new teachers, by whose means they learn to depreciate the Ministers under whom they first learned to believe. They easily conceive every fresh Preacher to be more holy, more zealous, and more upright than the first.

So it seems to have been the case at Corinth. Lamentable proof of the depravity of our nature! even in those who have known something of real godliness. Such ungrateful treatment even from persons sincerely religious, has been experienced by the best pastors. The Apostle Paul felt much of this, and the first four chapters of this Epistle constantly allude to it. But let us see how he argues against it in the text.

"Who are Paul and Apollos," can they give grace? Does the Holy Spirit so join himself to their ministry, that they can dispose of his influences at their pleasure to the people? Alas, so far from it, they cannot even dispense the least comforting, enlightening, or sanctifying grace to their own souls; but must receive from the Lord, in the same way, as others. Who are they but ministers by whom ye believed? God made use of them as messengers to convey his grace to your souls. Through their preaching of the word, God opened your hearts, and enabled you to believe in Jesus, "even as the

Lord gave to every man." For the Lord alone by his Spirit's influence, both with pastors and people, does the work. If Paul planted and Apollos watered the Church of Corinth, it is God that gave the increase. They who fancy, that any particular man, or sect, is so divine, as to bring the special blessing of God along with them to souls, to the disparagement of all others, they are guilty of idolatry. They set up a graven image, in effect, to worship, and break the spirit of the second commandment.

When image worship was practised among our fathers, and wherever it was practised, the worshippers supposed a divine power and influence necessarily to attend the image itself. So is it in this superstitious attachment to ministers, and sects in religion. " Neither is he that planteth any thing, neither he that watereth: but God that giveth the increase." It is HE, only, who fills, and gladdens, and sanctifies the soul, by his grace in Christ Jesus.

" We know all this," it may be said. Do you so? There are two ways of knowing a thing; one is a careless assenting to an assertion upon any subject, without knowing it; the other is a *practical* knowledge. If this last were so common, would professors of godliness—many of them—be so addicted to sects and parties, and have such strong attachments to some, and such unreasonable dislike to others, setting forth the same truths? Many evils are connected with this spirit. I shall endeavour, in what follows, to make a few observations on the subject, all tending to show the right frame and spirit of persons who attend on the ministry of the word.

1. Care should be taken that men do not learn to despise all Ministers. It is true, they are nothing in themselves, and if any excel, there is nothing to boast of. " For who maketh thee to differ?" They should neither glory themselves, nor should others glory in them. Yet, if they be faithful Ministers, they shall every man receive his own reward, according to his own labour. They have a "treasure in earthen vessels; that the excellency of the power may be of God, and not of them." But though they are not to be idolized, as we have seen, yet they must not be despised; because if they be, the message they deliver from God cannot fail to be despised also. If they be Ministers by whom men believe, it is our duty and wisdom to give an earnest attention to their message from the Lord; "for he that despiseth, despiseth not man but God," whose message it is.

2. The great thing to be attended to, is the doctrine itself, that is delivered. If a man preach not Christ, you cannot expect the influence of the Holy Spirit to accompany his words. But the true gospel itself has, in every age, been accompanied with the divine blessing on men's souls. Nothing but the gospel itself is " the power of God to salvation." Whatever other things be delivered, or however pleasing to flesh and blood, they profit not, for no man ever became holy but by the way of God's own appointment.

If the Word, in order to profit us, must be believed, it must be understood. " Faith cometh by hearing." The ordinary method of God, in the conversion of sinners, is by the preaching of the Word, so much so in all ages, that wherever and whenever preaching comes into contempt, profaneness and ignorance of all true religion is sure to be the consequence, together with all sorts of vice and wickedness. Even an angel sent to Cornelius did not preach the gospel to him. He directed him to send for Peter for that purpose, " who shall tell thee words whereby thou and all thy house shall be saved." God would have "men of like passions with others," to preach his Son Jesus Christ, and the method of reconciliation through his blood, to their brother worms. Gracious condescension! God himself became man for us, and by man he still designs to instruct us. If we do not, then, attend to the doctrine preached, how are we to believe it? Nor let it be said that among us, men in general do understand the doctrine of salvation. Far from it. The knowledge itself is far from being obvious. Plain, indeed, it is, and simple; but through the pride of our nature not readily understood. Worldly and carnal lusts blind the judgment, and pride lifts men up far above it. How many are there among us, who do not understand any one peculiarly christian doctrine aright, even after having heard it for years! Even professors of godliness, many of them, were they more established in christian knowledge, would never be so easy a prey as they are to deceivers. Whoever knows himself, at all, will find, in the blindness of our fallen nature, how backward we are to understand.

3. After having shown that the ministerial character ought to be respected, and that the doctrine should be attended to, it may be proper to warn and admonish you, brethren, to be looking above

for divine influences. Make a covenant with your eyes and your tongues, while in this house, to avoid every distracting object. Be serious, as men who are come here to inquire of God. The profoundest reverence is due, while we pray to him, and worship him in the name of his son Jesus.—But I am led by my subject to speak to you more particularly concerning preaching.

If Ministers are they by whom men learn to believe, as the Lord gave to every man; if he only give the increase, should we not wait for the Lord's "loving-kindness in the midst of his temple?" Should we not pray, " Lord, teach me thy statutes: give me understanding, and I shall live?" Many reap no profit from the Word. They come to gratify curiosity. The newest preachers are to them the best. They compare one with another. They are quite mortified, if their favourite preacher be not there; and he continues a favourite only for a time. See you not the evil of all this? What scandalous falls are made! What instability, unsteadiness, ignorance! What self-conceit, and contempt of one another! What great neglect of family duties! What slander and backbiting!

The way to get profit, is to be humble, and serious, and to hearken what the Lord shall say concerning us. And when we are rebuked, not to be angry, because our pride is hurt, but to be thankful to God for correction, and to set ourselves seriously to amend what is amiss. It is very absurd to be inquiring whether the Minister mean such and such things for such a person, or such a set of men. The question is, whether his doctrine be true, and whether conscience points out to you that you are guilty in that point. There may be persons, besides you, guilty of the same, and other parties of men, besides yours, may be in the same error; but if you have heard what needs correcting, can you be a christian, and yet, like profane people, be inquiring whether this was not personally meant for me? Are you to show resentment for that which calls for your gratitude? Instead of all this, let me beg you to be looking above for divine influences. Even a Preacher, with the poorest gifts, may be as useful to your soul as one of the greatest eloquence, provided the true doctrine of Christ be faithfully preached by him. For the blessing is from the Lord.

And we are to examine what our frame is. We often are ready to quarrel with the Preacher, when we have real cause to find fault with our own state of mind. You may see in reading the Word itself, at some times, how flat and insipid the same portion of Scripture is to your mind, which at other times seemed to overpower you with its sweetness. So much difference arises from the frame of men's minds! Besides, if God shine not into the heart by his Holy Spirit, the Word itself is but a dead letter to the mind. All truly taught of God find this by experience. The difference of their views at different times, when yet they have been as attentive at one time as another, proves experimentally to men, that it is of God if they feel, and love, and taste divine truth.

I mention these things, that you may learn, feelingly, to pray much for quickening influences from above, for that same Holy Spirit which was promised to be with the church in all ages. Let many of us consider, what a quantity of sermons have been heard in a course of years, and to how little purpose!

You went to hear the Word, like common business. You looked for nothing from God, and he gave you nothing. Consider, it is by the ministry of the Word that souls are to be trained for heaven. Expect to learn something; pray that the Spirit of God may make what you hear profitable. Let this be your constant method, for it is the way in which humble souls thrive and grow.

I have only one duty more to mention, in regard to what religious people owe to their Ministers, and shall then close with an address to careless sinners. And I could wish, that what I am going to mention may not be passed over as words of course, or as a strain of affected modesty and humility; but that you would weigh it as its importance deserves, and as it seriously concerns myself; as well as other Ministers of God's word. It is a simple, plain thing I am going to mention, soon expressed. I express it in St. Paul's words, "BRETHREN, PRAY FOR US." In another place, where he recommends prayer for all saints, he adds, "and for me, that utterance may be given to me, that I may open my mouth boldly to make known the mystery of the gospel." He did not mean, merely, that he might deliver the system of christian doctrines. He knew them thoroughly. He felt a need of divine illumination, that he might experience the power of christian truths; that he might speak of them with comfort, authority, cheerfulness, affection, and with that boldness which is always joined with true humility. This quality in a true Preacher of the gospel is the farthest possible from what we call impudence, or self-conceit, since it arises from an experimental assurance of the truth, reality, excellency, and importance of the things which he delivers. St. John calls it "an unction from the Holy One." It is generally the case, that wherever this is granted from above, there the gospel is preached with success. He who ministers is comfortable in his own soul, and the Lord makes the Word to be quick and powerful to the souls of others. This is what I wish to know, as abundantly as God shall please. It richly recompenses for all the reproach and contempt of the profane, as well as for all the discouragements arising from inward conflict and temptation, and the melancholy prospect of so much evil in the world, and so little prospect of doing good.

Our situation is very different from that of players. They speak things pleasing and delightful to the corrupt taste of men. The whole nature of man as alienated from God, vicious and worldly, falls in with their lectures. And they are looked on as comforters, who furnish the pleasure which carnal minds delight in. Poisonous pleasure no doubt, and leading the soul that loves it to an eternal separation from God! But with us every thing is just the contrary. The truths we have to deliver are contrary to nature; not easily received as true; much less deeply relished, and delighted in, by those who hear us! We are censured as harsh, gloomy, and uncharitable. We often give offence, where what we mean is not only true, but dictated by charity itself. Can we persevere in a faithful and zealous course, amidst the scorn of many, and the indifference of still more; having, ourselves also, the same passions by nature as other men; unless possessed of a divine light and unction, emboldening, and drawing us forward, with the consciousness of divine approbation, and the sense of the love of God in Christ, shed abroad in our hearts by the Holy Ghost, given to us? You see the importance of the thing which I desire of you. I surely need not be ashamed to crave that of you, which so wise and holy a person as the Apostle begged of those Christians to whom he wrote. How much your own benefit, as well as ours, is concerned in it, I need not explain.

And all this follows very naturally from the subject of the text. It can scarcely be too often repeated, that God alone does the work. It is his gospel, ministered by his Holy Spirit, which converts the soul. He alone gives the increase. Ministers are his instruments, by whom men believe, and all this is, " as the Lord gives to every man." By praying therefore for us, and that not formally, but in faith, and with perseverance, and affection, you honour the Lord, you evince your hearty belief that the doctrine of the text is true, and you put yourselves into the way of the Lord's blessing to your own souls. For you are not called on to teach us what, or how we are to preach, no more than we are called on to teach you how, or in what way you are to manage your temporal callings. Let every man learn to do his duty, in that state of life unto which it has pleased God to call him. But you are called on to pray for us, both for your own good and ours, and for the glory of God. And if you find no benefit from the Word, and are barren and unfruitful; before you undertake to lay the blame on us, it will be your wisdom to charge your consciences with the question, very seriously, whether you have, indeed, prayed for us at the throne of grace, from time to time. For whether you treat us with indifference and contempt, or idolize us superstitiously; either way, you affront God. You are not looking to him for that increase, which he only can give, and you do wrong to your own souls. Suffer, I beseech you, brethren, the word of exhortation, and may he " that giveth seed to the sower, and bread to the eater, endue his Ministers with righteousness, and make his chosen people joyful!"

What new topic of argument, or entreaty, or exhortation, or rebuke, can I, in the last place, take up to you, who hear as though you heard not; who are unaffected with what you hear from Sabbath to Sabbath; who wish every sermon, either to be very short, or, if longer, to be entertaining to your vicious inclinations. Your own consciences tell you, that you look for no such quickening influence from above, to attend the Word, as the text speaks of. Your hear a sermon like a story, or a political essay; with easy minds, and worldly affections; and neither see any thing of God in it, nor desire to see it. It is the will of God that men should look to him, even all the ends of the earth, that they may be saved. The Lord is very earnest in calling on men to take counsel together; to come near, and examine the evidences of divine truth, in the word of God; to take notice of the proofs of Christian doctrine; and to understand their own concernment in the subject; to listen to the divine message of reconciliation by Jesus Christ, proposed to their souls; and to remember that when we pray you in Christ's stead to be reconciled to God, it is as though God did beseech you by us. The proofs of divine truth are not hard to be found. The very fulfilment of Scripture prophecies is so striking, so powerful, and so demonstrative, that it seems scarcely possible for a serious mind to stand against any one of them; much less against them all in conjunction. That one in the 45th chapter of Isaiah, on which I have had my eye, in what I have just been saying; namely, the calling of Cyrus by his name, a long time before he was born; and distinctly describing what he should do to the Jews, in delivering them from captivity, surely none but God could deliver. The same may be said of innumerable other prophecies. Well may the Lord say, " I have not spoken in secret, in a dark place of the earth." The frauds and tricks of heathen oracles are very different from this plain dealing. But men like you, who will not examine, and read, and search, and inquire, cannot understand such things. With you a sneer, or sophism, of some infidel, stands for Gospel, and because you love not the holiness of divine truth, and because it condemns your way of life, you fly from God, and will not learn any thing that is good. Remember, however, the danger is all your own. If you be wrong—and the whole course of things shows you are wrong—you perish everlastingly. What do I exhort you to? Not to take things merely on our words; but to search the Scriptures, and their proofs; to commune with your own hearts; and seriously to consider, what will bring a man peace at the last.

SERMON XXIV.

PARABLE OF THE RICH MAN, WHOSE GROUND BROUGHT FORTH PLENTIFULLY, CONSIDERED.

Luke xii, 16—22.

And he spake a parable unto them, saying, The ground of a certain rich man brought forth plentifully: And he thought within himself, saying, What shall I do, because I have no room where to bestow my fruits? And he said, This will I do: I will pull down my barns, and build greater; and there will I bestow all my fruits and my goods. And I will say to my soul, Soul, thou hast much goods laid up for many years; take thine ease, eat, drink, and be merry. But God said unto him, Thou fool, this night thy soul shall be required of thee: then whose shall those things be, which thou hast provided? So is he that layeth up treasure for himself, and is not rich toward God.

THAT men should learn to set their affections on things above, and not on things on the earth, is the evident and obvious use of this plain parable. May the Spirit of Christ who spoke it, be with you and me in considering it: may he enliven and quicken our souls with true views of the heavenly riches, and take off that deceitful glare of beauty and pleasure, which sin has cast upon earthly riches, that we may choose our portion with our Maker and Saviour in heaven, and walk with him here by faith, in the strong hope of eternal glory, with the world and its vanities under our feet! May it please God so to bless his own word, that those who are now contriving for happiness, with the fool of this parable, may be deterred by the awful view of his fate, and be persuaded indeed to seek for the true riches!—We will consider the parable in an orderly manner, and then deduce, as God shall help us, a general application.

"The ground of a certain rich man brought forth plentifully."—Nothing can, with certainty, be concluded of a man's real state, before God, from the dispensations of Providence. Wicked men may have abundant success and prosperity, while the righteous are very much afflicted. But how often is the prosperity of the former a curse to their souls, by filling them with pride and self-conceit! How often also are the afflictions of the latter made a blessing to them, by humbling their hearts, and spiritualizing their affections! The man in the parable before us had no regard for God, no spirit of thankfulness to him for favours already received; yet does the Lord heap more upon him. He causes his ground to bring forth plentifully. Sometimes there is reason to believe that the Lord gives success to wicked men, as a reward for some actions useful to society, and good in a lower worldly sense, which they perform. Instances of this we have in the Old Testament. That of Jehu is remarkable. " Because thou hast done well in executing that which is right in mine eyes, and hast done unto the house of Ahab according to all that was in mine heart, thy children of the fourth generation shall sit on the throne of Israel."—Yet it is said he took no heed to walk in the law of the Lord God of Israel with all his heart:

for he departed not from the sins of Jeroboam, that is, from the idolatry of the two calves*. Thus God gave this worldly man a worldly reward for the good actions which he did with a worldly spirit. So also our Lord speaks of those who give alms with an ostentatious view, to be seen of men : " they have," says he, " their reward." They sought to be esteemed generous men, and they were so esteemed by the world.

Those who expect, besides this, the salvation of their souls in another world, as the reward of their deeds, will find themselves disappointed. The works of good men have in them the view of glorifying God; and while they obtain salvation only on account of their Saviour, their good works shall be proportionably rewarded also in another life, because they are spiritual works, and grow from a heavenly spirit. But it is fitting that the materially good actions of wicked men should meet with an earthly reward, which you may suppose to be the case of the man in the parable. For there is nothing in the whole course of the parable that should make it necessary for us to charge him with want of generosity to the needy, or with any injustice in the manner of acquiring his wealth. He might be both honest and generous in the common sense of those words, and yet be an earthly-minded fool in God's account, as too many are.

" And he thought within himself, saying, what shall I do, because I have no room where to bestow my fruits?" Here he lays open the true springs of his character. He makes his very heaven to consist

* 2 Kings x.

in his worldly possessions. These are his gods: he has no sense of gratitude to the true God; no desire of pleasing him with his wealth; but only himself. How to dispose of it in such a way as may most promote his own pleasure, this is his governing care! Methinks, one may see here, also, a lively representation of the cares and anxieties which grow upon men, as riches increase. While they were poor, they could easily reckon up their possessions. Having but little of the world, little thought about it served them, comparatively speaking. But after their possessions increased, then, " what shall I do with this and with that affair?" employed their minds. Cares grew upon them exceedingly: envy and pride, ambition and covetousness started up, and in their turns tormented their souls. So evidently does it appear, that these temporal things can give no happiness; and what Solomon says of learning may be said also of riches, " in much *wealth* there is much grief, and he that increaseth *riches*, increaseth sorrow."

" And he said, this will I do: I will pull down my barns, and build greater; and there will I bestow all my fruits and my goods. And I will say unto my soul, Soul, thou hast much goods laid up for many years; take thine ease, eat, drink, and be merry." Here one may observe, that as a man's heart is, so is he accounted in the sight of God. Many have proceeded in their thoughts, and counsels, and conduct, exactly as this man did, who yet never uttered his words. Nay, many persons will own that nothing in this world is to be depended on; that life is short; and that our grand business ought to be, to prepare for another; who yet, with full purpose of heart, act as this fool did; though through the unmeasurable deceitfulness of their hearts, they persuade themselves that they do not so. But the *spirit* of this man's conduct is the thing that is to be attended to. He took measures to secure his substance, and to enjoy it comfortably. He feasted himself beforehand with the thought of the many years of enjoyment which lay before him.—There are two capital and ruinous deviations from true wisdom here, for either of which he deserved the name of a fool.

1. That he made earthly indulgences his heaven. " Take thine ease, eat, drink, and be merry." He had no idea of any pleasures of a better nature than these low carnal ones. Let him have his fill of them, angels and saints may take to themselves the enjoyments of spiritual pleasures; of the love of God. He envies them not; for he has no idea of any higher gratifications than those that are earthly. Nor does it at all make the character more heavenly, if the man should, in his taste and desires, aim at something more refined and elegant than the bare animal pleasures of eating and drinking. However elegant the amusement be, yet if it is merely earthly, if the man's heart be here, he is earthly, and comes as much under the denomination of the fool in the parable, as the most sordid glutton in the world.

2. The other capital mistake was the reckoning of many years to come, as certain. This bewitching forgetfulness of death, this always putting off the thoughts of it, as a day removed to a prodigious distance, is too natural to us all. Man by the Fall lost the true measure of time and eternity. He schemes for the former, as if it was eternal; he

neglects the latter, as if it was never to come at all. Though we see deaths heaped upon deaths around us; one dying before he comes to the age of manhood; another just after he has attained what has cost him years of toil and pains to procure; one dying while he lives, wasting years of a tedious and insipid existence, in pain and weakness; another cut off in an instant; yet still we reckon upon many years to come as certain. Thus the devil deludes the fallen sons of men, and even when the infirmities of age begin to admonish us very sensibly of our mortality, yet so long as we can see any older than ourselves, we dream of attaining their age. Nay those who live to an uncommon age still think they may live to another year.

"But God said unto him, Thou fool, this night thy soul shall be required of thee: then whose shall those things be which thou hast provided?" Not thine any longer. Thine they never were in fact. They belonged to me, God may say, and I now take them from thee, and give them to whomsoever I please. They are henceforth and for ever no more to thee, than if thou never hadst had them at all. Thy soul is this night required of thee. Thou art called to answer before me for the abuse of my talents and gifts which I bestowed on thee; and thou mayest expect the everlasting punishment which thy sins, unpardoned as they are, do merit at mine hands. What horror! what amazement! How may such a soul condemn its folly and presumption! But this is not the case of some particular extraordinary sinners only.

"So is every one that láyeth up treasure for himself, and is not rich toward God."—These words describe, very particularly, the heart of the character before us, and require therefore to be particularly considered. It has been the fault of our modern divinity to extend the consideration of sin no farther than to some outward crimes, and not to specify, as the Scripture does, the heart, in which is seated the principle of indwelling sin. Yet was it by the Tenth Commandment, " thou shalt not covet," that the Apostle Paul was convinced of sin; felt himself slain by the law; and was therefore necessitated to look out for a better righteousness than his own, to be justified by; since his nature constantly sinned even by lusting, and sin deserved death; sin of heart, as well as of practice. Hence men learn true humility; hence, and hence only; for by the heart-felt knowledge of this body of sin and death within us, it is, that they are brought to cry out, " O wretched man that I am, who shall deliver me from the body of this death!" And till they know this experimentally, they can never say, " I thank God, through Jesus Christ our Lord." And till this repentance, and this faith be taught, which can only be through the view of indwelling sin, no holiness, no humility, no love of God, in the least degree, is attained. The man lies under the wrath of God, with the guilt of all his sins upon him; and all the pride, and strength of them too in his heart, though he may have outwardly reformed his manners.

I would preach, then, original sin, with reference to our subject, or I do it not full justice. For indeed where men have no idea of a root of sin within them, where they confine the notion of guilt to gross vices, the decent and regular part of an audience, whose lives have never been stained with great enormities, come off uncondemned, and honourably acquitted. But surely this is not the Scripture way, by which " every mouth must be stopped, and all the world be found guilty before God."

Some that hear me this day may be saying in their hearts, " To spend our money, indeed, on vain trifles; or to live merely for the sake of eating and drinking, and to do no sort of good with what we have, we look on as wrong, and are as ready as any one to condemn. But this is not our case. We live in a manner suitable to our circumstances. What we have acquired, we have acquired honestly, and reputably. We are not deficient in generosity to those who deal with us, and the poor will own the advantages they reap from us. We hope therefore that we are not to be classed with the fool in the parable."—O God, who searchest the hearts! be pleased, by thy good Spirit, to speak to such souls in mercy and pity, that they may well understand, while there is time to remedy their case, that they are the persons who " lay up treasure for themselves, and are not rich toward God." We admit that you make a sensible use of your temporal goods; that you are not defective in liberality, or in generosity; and that you will not be condemned for enjoying, in a subordinate sense, the good things of this life. But where is your heart, all this time? As men's hearts are, so they are in the sight of God—and it is to be feared, indeed, that you are utter strangers to the true riches, because your desires and affections too evidently centre in this world. Now would it not be well for you to examine, what is that which has the possession of your souls? What it is you long after as your chief good, and supreme delight?

Mankind are not forbidden to make use of this world's goods, according to that Scripture rule, "using this world as not abusing it." But as men "cannot serve God and mammon;" as either the riches of this world or of the next have possession of their hearts; should you find that your affections are cold, and dead with regard to the things of eternity, then you "lay up treasure for yourself, and are not rich toward God:" though it may be confessed, you are more sober and prudent in the manner of enjoying this world, than gluttons and spendthrifts; and at the same time do more good to human society than they. Were it not for the blindness of self-love, it might seem amazing that men cannot see, that their being exempt from drunkenness and other acts of intemperance, though good and right, so far as it goes, can never of itself prove them to be walking the right way to heaven. For are not many sober, temperate people, as averse to praying; as dead to God; as little moved with heavenly hopes, and objects, as the vilest and most profligate spendthrifts? If conscience were awake, it would show this to be the case with too many. Alas! how hard it is to show men to themselves. And yet if they do not condemn themselves, they will never be led to the Lord's way of justifying a sinner. If they see not the evil and vileness of heart sins, and the depth of their fallen state, they can never rise to a new life of righteousness.

He, then, who hath his treasure on earth, looks to his own possessions with supreme complacency. Whenever he comforts his mind, it is not with any spiritual pleasures here, or with the hopes of any to be attained hereafter. He delights in the thought of indulgences of time and sense, which he has it in his power to enjoy. Death he removes from his view, and thought. It is a dagger to all his happiness, whenever it comes powerfully across his imagination; and he flies from it with horror and trepidation. "What is it to me," God may say to him, "if thou hast chosen more discreetly than some others, the way of enjoying earthly pleasures. Thou livest to thyself as much as others. Thou regardest my glory, as little as do others."

Surely, brethren, here is nothing said against this fool for hard-heartedness to the poor; nothing for his gluttony, lewdness, or intemperance. No: They have false, nay ruinous views of this parable, who deem so; because all that such persons obtain from the view of it, is to please themselves with the thought that they are better than others. They escape that conviction of sin, which leads to repentance, and thus go on the way to destruction, unacquainted with their need of a Saviour, and his infinite value. May God grant such men a better light to see themselves by!

Consider. You lay up "treasure for yourselves," because that which has your heart, is this earth, not heaven. Here you could love to remain for ever; had you all worldly things agreeable to your wishes, without the least desire to enjoy the vision of God! A true christian has a sublimer taste: he cannot rest contented without heavenly pleasures. Earth has nothing supremely suitable to him. But this taste, this light, is from heaven. It excites the affections of the new nature, and your utter want of it proves you yet not born of God.

Let us now attend a little to the latter part of the

description "not rich toward God." He whose treasures are on earth only, is of course "not rich toward God." What is it to be "rich toward God?" In setting forth this we shall at the same time, and in the same words, set forth the true christian spirit, and also what the fool in the parable wanted. He wanted, then, an interest in what St. Paul calls "the unsearchable riches of Christ." He knew nothing of them; nothing of his need of them; of the poverty and misery of his nature, and natural state without them; nothing of justification by his righteousness; nothing of the spirit of adoption, and the hope of eternal life which God bestows on all his children; nothing at all of the light, the spirit, the love, the humility, the joy of those, "who walk not after the flesh, but after the Spirit." What it is to be "rich toward God," can never be scripturally explained, but by "the unsearchable riches of Christ." No man can have any riches toward God, but through Christ. God bestows all through him. A man must feel himself poor and lost indeed, and in the view of his death and poverty apply to the Father, through the Son, for life and riches. "I counsel thee," says Jesus, "to buy of me gold tried in the fire, that thou mayest be rich." Thenceforward the man ceases to have any treasure in himself. Whatever the lustings of an evil nature may say and speak to the contrary, he who has, by faith, received Christ for all his treasure, allows them not, obeys them not, so as to fulfil them. His practice evinces that he lives not to this world; not to its pomps and pleasures; its riches and honours; not to himself; his own glory and praise, either before God or men. "I gladly," says he, "suffer the loss of all things, that I may win Christ." I make him all my treasure. My "life is hid with Christ in God." When he, who is now my life, shall appear, I shall appear with him in glory. In the mean time, I would be stedfast and unmovable in the faith and hope of the gospel. As God has made me willing to be saved by grace, and to give Jesus all the glory, the Saviour I have thus accepted will never leave me, nor forsake me. I may well triumph over sin, the devil, death and hell, while I can trust in such a deliverer. I may well bear with patience worldly losses, having in store an immortal inheritance reserved in heaven for me. I may well sit very loose to earthly gratifications, and look on all the enjoyments of time and sense, in a mean light compared with the superior pleasures I expect in a future life, the earnest of which I even here receive. I may well be liberal to the needy, out of my substance, from grateful love to my God, and abound alway in the work of the Lord, since none of my labour shall be in vain in the Lord. When I come to my Father's house, I shall find every work of love to have a weighty reward through the immense liberality of my God. What work, what exertion of my talents, while I am on earth, can be so pleasing, so useful as this? "He that soweth to the flesh, shall of the flesh reap corruption: He that soweth to the Spirit, shall of the Spirit reap life everlasting." I would not then be weary in well-doing: All other kinds of doing, however splendid in the world, will at the last day be found either mere nothings, or painted pageantry to dress the soul for the fire of hell; but the works of love to God shall receive an eternal recompense of reward.

Such is the spirit of him who is "rich toward God." And it is his privilege to use this language, and to live up to these vigorous views. Many real christians live, indeed, below this: but it cannot be too often repeated, that they should not be content to live short of this. Thou who layest up treasures for thyself, though otherwise generous and liberal; honest and equitable; decent and regular, yet soarest in thy desires no higher than earthly enjoyments: Thou knowest, or shouldst know, that in the true riches, in this living spirit towards God thou hast no lot or part.

Let me now address thee more closely. Thou art called "fool," because void of heavenly wisdom: But let me not miss my aim. Ye who answer in your character to this whole description, do not put it off from you, because you are poor in circumstances. You may have the same spirit and views as rich people. And those who are really rich may, through grace, be poor in spirit, and rich toward God. In truth: though the snares of riches are exceeding great, and it is said "not many mighty, not many noble are called," which observation too sadly evinces, yet still there are immense numbers of poor as well as rich who are the fools of the text. I mean not to speak according to the *circumstances*, but to the *hearts* of men. Look to your hearts: oh! weigh their inmost motions. Are things with you as in the parable, or are they not? Are you ruminating as the fool did? "By and by I shall compass this, or that point. Such a disagreeable and tedious affair will be brought to an issue. I shall have my children well settled in the world. I shall make such a profitable adventure, and then I shall be happy. Then I shall live comfortably, and enjoy myself in the world." You have, before this time, had such thoughts, and, it may be, have accomplished many points, which you thought, when once secured, would place you on the true point of happiness. But yet you are as far from happiness as ever. It is not in the power of these earthly things to give you what you want in order to be happy. Feel you not that it is so?

But this is not all: Even while you are ruminating, scheming, and planning, death, even sudden death, may seize you, and for ever divorce you from all concerns with this world. Nothing can then remain with you, but an interest in Christ. That, however, you have not, you cannot have, in your present state. Your inordinate love of the world has hitherto prevented this. Oh! think within yourself, how awfully true were our Lord's words, "ye must be born again: except ye be born again, ye cannot see the kingdom of God." Your natural state, in which, like other men, you were born, is a state of sin, of distance, and alienation from God; of rebellion against him, and idolatrous serving of the creature. You have, all along, too sadly proved both your evil natural state, and your still remaining in that state, by your seeking for happiness from the world, and not from God: and therefore, if death find you this night, if it find you now, it finds you rebellious, and with all your sins unpardoned upon you. Nothing but an interest in Christ can answer law and justice: "thou shalt answer for me, O Lord, my God; in thee have I put my trust," says the real christian. But this he could not say, were he not made sensible of his lost state. He confessed his guilt; transferred it to his precious Surety; left his cause there by faith; and had in consequence peace in believing, and became fit for death, whether it come suddenly, or gradually. He shall be admitted into regions of everlasting joy. "It is God that justifieth, who is he that condemneth? It is Christ that died, yea rather that is risen again, who is even at the right hand of God, who also maketh intercession for us." This is his plea; not his repentance, no nor his faith, nor any thing of his own. His plea is CHRIST, through whom he has obtained the power both to repent and believe. His plea is CHRIST, who has satisfied the law in his room, and brought in everlasting righteousness. In the Lord he is justified, and in him shall glory eternally.

But you "who lay up treasure for yourselves, and are not rich toward God," are so far from being in this state, that his law and justice stand in full force against you, and he may at any moment send his messenger Death to convey you into the land of weeping and torment; of everlasting destruction from the presence of the Lord and the glory of his power. Oh! I feel an evident want of power to do justice to this subject. It is a terrible stupidity, that any have heard these things; can hear them continually, and read them very plainly in the Bible, and yet be solicitous only about this world, and as careless of death and judgment as if they were not at all obnoxious to them. Already they are under the curse, as every soul of man is by nature: but the execution of the sentence is delayed. They are under a reprieve, and there is a way of obtaining the King's pardon too, and oh! that they would follow it.

Awake, then, ye proud, ye scornful, ye high-minded worldlings, who are yet my poor fellow-creatures, with whom I would sympathize, as feeling with you the common miseries of fallen, human nature—awake from your dream of sloth and carnal indulgence. View your real condition, and ask, " what shall we do to be saved?" Come as condemned malefactors to God. Thank him for his patience with you in not casting you off, and beseech him to show you Christ Jesus, and give you a vital, an heartfelt interest in his blood. No soul can get to heaven but by this self-humbling way! "Thou wast slain, and hast redeemed us to God by thy blood," all that go to heaven will say. " God resisteth the proud, but giveth grace to the humble." And who are ye, that heaven's laws and ways must be dispensed with for you? Oh, that I could see real evidences of softness of heart, and humility of soul; of awakened, and earnest desires after another world; as real, and as strong as too many of you carry marks of hardness of heart; of pride; of the love of this world. Oh! be humbled. Suffer God to humble you. It is good to be humbled. To this man God will look, " even to him that is of a poor and contrite spirit, and that trembleth at his word." Christ will be precious to you, as he is unto all them that believe. You will esteem him as the pearl of great price, as the treasure hid in a field that will make you rich indeed. You will possess a portion of which death itself cannot deprive you. For when every earthly comfort fails, he will be the strength of your life, and your portion for ever.

SERMON XXV.

DIFFICULTIES ATTENDING THE SALVATION OF THE RIGHTEOUS, AND CERTAINTY OF THE DESTRUCTION OF SINNERS.

---

1 Peter iv. 18.

And if the righteous scarcely be saved, where shall the ungodly and the sinner appear?

The Apostle was speaking of the punishments to be inflicted on the house of God, on those that obey the gospel of God. They, even they had many evils which needed to be chastised, and the persecutions which they suffered as christians, though they proceeded from the malice of the devil, and of wicked men, his instruments, were yet, under divine direction, scourges for their sins. Such inflictions were meant to teach them that submission to the divine will, and that conformity to their living Head, (who was made perfect through sufferings) which was necessary for their perfect enjoyment of his heavenly kingdom. The Apostle is hence led to make a very serious reflection. "If judgment first begin at us, what shall the end be of them that obey not the gospel of God?" and in the text, " if the righteous scarcely be saved, where shall the ungodly and the sinner appear?" He then directs christians to patient suffering, since their sufferings are "according to the will of God," and to rest assured, that their faithful Creator will take care of their souls, which they "commit to him in well-doing."

But such an assurance, and such consolation to animate men to patience and well-doing cannot be delivered to " the ungodly and the sinner." Where shall he appear? What shall be the end of him? are questions which lead the mind to the most awful apprehensions of divine vengeance.

Such is the general view of our subject. That it may, under God, speak to the consciences, both of the righteous and the wicked, and give practical direction to each, it will be proper to illustrate more distinctly the proposition of the text, which is, that " the righteous are scarcely saved."

That I may guard the meaning of this aright, let it be observed, that St. Peter does not mean, that it is a matter of doubt and uncertainty, whether they ever shall be saved or not. Heaven and earth shall pass away; but the divine word, which assures us of the salvation of the righteous, shall not pass away. There is not any thing in nature more certain. All Scripture in its plan, in its doctrines, and in the decrees of God, and in all the means for fulfilling those decrees, ensures the everlasting felicity of the just. But the meaning of their being "scarcely saved" is, that in the manner in which their salvation is to be effected, there will be much difficulty. And if we look at their experience, and their apprehensions, with the variety of their trials, and consider the great opposition made to their salvation from the devil, the world, and their sorest enemy, their own sinful nature, it will appear a very hard thing indeed for them to escape destruction. Yet the difficulties are not like those which attend human and worldly affairs. These are often so great as never to be surmounted; a man may sincerely exert himself with all his might, and yet miscarry. But it is not so in religion. Whoever strives sincerely to enter in at the strait gate, is sure to succeed. He will, however, be made sensible how strait the gate is, and how narrow the way.

Here is, then, a strong ground of consolation to all who seek God through Christ. Amidst all difficulties, success is certain, and there is no difficulty of access to God; for it is laid open to us through the satisfaction of his Son. Neither is there any difficulty of pacifying his holy displeasure at our sins; for Jesus has finished that work completely, and made full reconciliation for our iniquity. Nor do these difficulties arise from any pleasure that the Lord hath in punishing; for " he willeth not the death of a sinner, but rather that he be converted and live." Nor do they arise from hence, that God is backward to their prayer; for he is gracious and merciful, and as his Scripture name is LOVE, we may be confident that he is easy to be entreated.

From what circumstances, then, do you think the difficulties of salvation can arise? Thou, O careless and presumptuous sinner, art apt to flatter thyself, that if God be so merciful, thou wilt very easily be saved. Whereas I could wish thee to be seriously thinking, what it is that makes the work of salvation so difficult. It is the misery and ruin of souls, that subjects, which enter into the heart of real religion, are not seriously attended to. We cannot prevail with men to think closely on them at all. There is an impudence of thinking and talking which they have attained to, at this time, beyond the example of former ages. " That nothing can be more easy than to be saved; that God *must* be merciful to his creatures; that it would be very hard if he were not; that so far is it from being true that the righteous are scarcely saved, that the wicked are scarcely damned; that it is a very easy thing to please and serve God aright; that there are no difficulties in religion and the paths of virtue." Such is the language of men whose lives are a constant affront to the Almighty; who are living in all lewdness, excess, and profaneness. Indeed the more wicked men are in their conduct, the more do they show of this insolent spirit. The bad effects of it on practice are apparent; they are evidently encouraged from hence to live in sin.

But, careless persons! however confident you may be of the easiness of salvation, be assured that the word of God is against you. The text flatly contradicts it; so does all Scripture. The strait gate, and the narrow way, are serious proofs to the contrary. The complaints, the conflicts, and trials of good men, which appear in the accounts which they give of themselves in Scripture, such as David in his Psalms, and Paul in his Epistles, demonstrate, that they, who are surely true judges of the matter, found that the "righteous scarcely are saved." And at this day, take any truly serious person in the world, who fears God, and works righteousness, and he will own, that it is with difficulty every day that he proceeds. How arrogant, then, must it be, for

such as you who know nothing by experience, and
whose lives every day speak against you, to talk of
the easiness of religion. But impudence and ignorance, as they are fit companions to each other, so
are they commonly joined together. What I charitably wish you, for your good, is, to learn that
you are out of the way altogether, and have need
to be alarmed to flee from the wrath to come.

And, surely, the whole course of nature shows
that St. Peter's proposition is true. If sin is so slight
a thing, and it be so easy, in all respects, to place
man on a right footing with his Maker, it is inconceivable that there should be so much suffering in
this world as there is. You see continually, that by
wrong conduct, even in this life, troubles great, and
sore, and of long continuance, are brought on men.
The whole administration of Divine Providence
is perpetually showing that even the " righteous
scarcely are saved." They evidently are chastised,
and suffer much ; and the wrong things which they
have done bring upon them trouble, and often for
a long time. How can men make so free with God,
and think he minds not how they sin against him,
when they see, in the consequences, how sharply he
punishes for sin ? And if their notions will not hold
good, but are contradicted by experience, in this
life, have they not reason to believe they will find
themselves equally disappointed in another?

Enough has been said to show, that the ungodly
are sadly wrong in their conclusions, and I was wish-
ing to lead them, by a serious course of thoughts, to
conceive how it is, that the salvation of the righteous
should be so difficult. But, after all, till men begin to

think seriously, it is not to be expected that they will form a just idea of it. They will, if careless, be apt to presume, and to fancy that it must be a very easy thing to be saved. If they be struck, and pierced in conscience, at times, then they are apt to despair altogether; because they have no right notion of any strength but their own, such as they have by nature. Now I have shown that the difficulties, whatever they be, may certainly be surmounted; despair makes no part of this subject. To conceive, then, that the righteous shall *scarcely* be saved, and yet to see that they shall *certainly* be saved, requires an understanding plainly enlightened from above.

In truth, the difficulty arises entirely from that which we are most apt to overlook, from the state of sin which we naturally are in. Let our real circumstances be feelingly understood, and men will see at once, that it is a very hard thing for them to be saved. We are in a state altogether wrong by nature. Here is a creature made by God, and endued with faculties above the brutes, capable in his formation of loving and knowing God, and formed with powers both of mind and body for serving him, and of being completely happy in serving him, and behold! his understanding is darkened, and his will is corrupt, and his affections are obstinately bent against his Maker. He is turned wholly from God, and given up to please himself, in seeking happiness altogether from the world. What a monstrous state is this! How evil, and hateful, and miserable such a condition! It is not the less so for being common. This very circumstance, at the same time that it gives an opportunity for men to increase one another's vices, and tempt one another to sin exceedingly, diminishes in their minds the horror of the situation. " I am only in the same state as my neighbours," is a thought which gives a deceitful peace to many.

It hath pleased God to provide a redemption for fallen men, by Jesus Christ. But if you think that God may save you easily, without any more ado, by overlooking all your sins at once, without providing either a satisfaction to his justice, or making you a new creature, you deceive yourself, and show you know not God aright, nor yourselves aright. Nor do you know, indeed, what is meant by being saved, nor what it is to be happy.

In all other things God Almighty speaks and it is done: HE commands, and it stands fast. Difficulties are nothing with him, and even to make a thousand worlds ten thousand times larger than this we live in, costs him no trouble. But in recovering men from the guilt and power of sin, in which salvation properly consists, and in the way of happiness, to speak after the manner of men, a large circuit of infinitely wise contrivance is necessary. Salvation, be it known to us, cost the richest blood that ever flowed in human veins, the blood of GOD made man. He who is " over all, God blessed, for ever," condescends to become man " under the law," and to satisfy the law by his own sufferings. For mercy is not the only perfection of the Godhead, though unconverted men will not think of any other. His justice, his purity, his hatred of sin; his power, his wisdom, must also be discovered in the way of saving sinners. That it must be so, is sufficiently evident from this, that it is so in fact ordered and contrived. And what greater proof would you desire, that it was proper and becoming that salvation should be made thus difficult, than this, that so it hath seemed good in the eyes of infinite wisdom. To us it is sufficient to see, that our sinful state by nature is the proper cause why men are thus " scarcely saved." For were it not for sin, there would be no difficulty at all in the whole subject.

Let us pause a moment on this, and reflect what a cursed thing sin is, which has put the infinite God to such an expense of contrivance for our salvation. He who understands thus much aright, will see that which will make him hate, and dread, and abhor, and forsake sin, as the curse of curses; sin, I say, which so many practise in sport, and conceive no harm in at all.

But this is not all: besides satisfaction for sin, recovery to holiness is necessary. What could an impure creature do in heaven? suppose it were possible, though it be not so, that he could be admitted into heaven: He would be weary of his condition presently; he would soon find himself in hell; for he carries hell within him. Can a *place* give happiness? Bethink yourselves, ye who talk of the easiness of being saved by God's mercy: Is it proper, or is it possible, all things considered, that God should make out another sort of happiness for his creatures, by which they should perfectly enjoy themselves, without loving and obeying their Maker? Pride, envy, malice, fleshly and worldly lusts, discontent, and self-well, are *now* their own tormentors. He in whom these things reign, must be miserable, here on earth, in the nature of things; and so he would be if he were in heaven. I rather think he would be more miserable there, than here. For *here* he stupifies himself often, and prevents himself from seeing what his real state is. But *there* the light of heaven would make him exquisitely feel his misery.

What sinners should learn from hence is, that they "must be born again," be changed in their whole character, in their desires, and dispositions, or happiness is impossible. I would to God, that they felt this great truth to the very bottom of their souls; they would then seek for bliss in good earnest, and seek it of God, through the grace of Jesus Christ. Now it is needful, not only that God should give his Son to redeem us, that we may find salvation, but also, that we may indeed apprehend and enjoy salvation. It is needful, that we feelingly understand this doctrine of redemption by Christ through the operation of the Holy Spirit, together with our own sinfulness and misery, that we may learn to repent, to believe, and to love God. A clock may be made to move regularly, and point to the hour, without communicating either understanding or feeling to the machine. But men are not to be wrought on as clock-work; they are creatures endowed with reason, and if they be brought to move freely in the real way of salvation or happiness, their judgment must be convinced, that they may choose the right way. They are not to be compelled or driven into it. Indeed they cannot be so driven. If men do not choose what is right, and absolutely prefer it from conviction, in the nature of things, they can never follow what is right.

This notion, then, of the easiness of being saved,

for such a corrupt creature as man, is immensely absurd. Here is a creature choosing, loving, delighting in evil; hating, abhorring, directly contrary to God, that is, to real goodness. When a man, taught of God by his Holy Spirit, feels the truth and importance of the doctrine of salvation by Jesus Christ, he feels all is wrong in him; every thing must be made new.

Have you considered what a thing this is; for you to be quite transformed, brought to love what you before hated, and to hate what you before loved? Consider, O sinner, how disgustful all religion is to you: how weary you are of prayer, the Scriptures, godly conversation, serious meditation, and heavenly contemplations, and how difficult to you the denial of all the worldly pleasures, which make your happiness! a miserable happiness indeed; but you have no idea of any other. Thus you may learn how it comes to pass that the righteous scarcely are saved, and how hard it is for a man to part with himself, to control his very nature, to mortify the whole course of his desires.

In those who truly believe, this is brought about by the powerful operations of the Spirit of God. But you are much deceived, if you think that it can be accomplished without feeling violent opposition. Are our desires so easily to be mortified? If they were, they could scarce be called desires. And how true does all this appear from experience. Even where God's salvation has long been preached, as in this place, how have I been mortified to find persons betray the completest ignorance of the whole affair! How common is this ignorance! Nay many, in some measure, enlightened, turn back to folly, or embrace an airy cloud for the substantial gospel; and even with those who are truly changed by divine grace, how slowly, how painfully, often, does the work proceed! Indeed the most serious minds, after years of christian labour, will own how unready still they are to that which is good.

The subject may seem disagreeable, but it is highly useful, and when rightly understood is productive of the very best consequences. Let no serious soul be discouraged. Having fled to Christ for salvation, under a consciousness of thy lost condition, I will call thee a christian believer, whether thou canst allow thyself to be one, or not. If it grieves thee to find sin so obstinate, so determined, as it were, to keep its hold, then thou mayest understand what the great Apostle did, who so feelingly describes the christian conflict in *Romans* vii. Thou art " scarcely saved," but thou art saved, continually. Hold fast thy confidence in Christ, and the rejoicing of thy hope firm to the end. After the conclusion of that precious description I have mentioned, the Apostle does not say, there is *no corruption*, but he says, " there is *no condemnation* to them that are in Christ Jesus, who walk not after the flesh, but after the Spirit." It is thy privilege in this life, that " sin shall not have *dominion*" over thee: In heaven it will be thy privilege, that it shall have no *being* in thee. And why is there " no condemnation?" Because " it is God that justifieth, who is he that condemneth? it is Christ that died, yea rather that is risen again." Blessed be God for Jesus Christ.

Let the sense of thy difficulties, which will remain

while thou art in the body, humble thee, keep thee watchful, cause thee to prize thy liberty which thou hast in Christ Jesus, teach thee to forgive daily, as thou art daily forgiven, keep thee from scorning thy fellow creatures, and also from foolishly admiring any man, as if he were an angel, or almost an angel, and dispose thee (though with St. Paul in this life thou groanest, being burdened) to " rejoice in hope of the glory of God." For even amidst all these difficulties, it is thy privilege to maintain a peace, and a joy, and a comfort in God, through Christ, which renders, even here, thy lot by far the best of any on earth. And if thou look not at things which are seen, and temporal, but at things which are not seen, and eternal, thou wilt find thy light afflictions working for thee a far more exceeding and eternal weight of glory.

But " if the righteous scarcely be saved, where shall the ungodly and the sinner appear?" Let me conclude with a brief application of this alarming thought to the ungodly. When first a Christian, by sound conviction, was made sensible what an evil state he was in, what an idea had he of the difficulty of salvation! How helpless, how dark, how vile in his own eyes! But that God, who is nigh to the contrite in spirit, taught him experimentally, that what he feared the most, was the best for him; that what he dreaded, was his real bliss; and though it went sore against his nature to be led into paths he had not known, yet he found, under crosses and afflictions, the most powerful comforts, far surpassing carnal mirth, and the pleasures of sin. Yet he is *scarcely* saved all along. What a state then must thou be in, O ungodly and sinner! He has all the promises of the Divine Word to comfort him; thou hast all the threatenings of God set in terrible array against thee. If he who loves the Lord Jesus supremely (loving him whom he hath not seen above all he ever saw) daily feels difficulty, trial, weakness, the incursions of Satan, and in-dwelling sin, what must thy state be, who art altogether the bond-slave of sin? If he, whose chief delight is to please God, is yet exhorted to commit himself to his faithful Creator by patient continuance in well-doing, suffering here frequent chastisement for his sins; what horrors await thee—horrors of divine vengeance—whose life bespeaks thee at enmity with God? If he who watches and prays daily, and keeps his heart with all diligence, yet in many things offends, and will look on it as a marvellous mercy, that he be saved after all; what hope can there be of thy salvation, who takest no pains, utterest no prayers, watchest against no evil, nay, runnest into every sort of temptation, and withholdest from thyself no pleasure of any kind, but followest a multitude to do evil? There is no hope at all, while thou neglectest conversion.

A time will come, O ungodly men! it hastens apace, when you will have to appear before the judgment-seat of Christ, and where will you appear but at his left hand, to hear "Depart, ye cursed." Yes, if you remain as you are, nothing is more sure, than that this will be your case. The same word of God which declares that he will appear "to be admired in all them that believe" at that day, declares also that he will "take vengeance on them that know not God, and obey not the gospel of his Son, who shall be punished with everlasting destruction."

If smooth words and flattering speeches could take away the terrors of this judgment-day, there might seem some reason in men's making use of them. But if the only use they can be of, is to harden men's hearts, and to lull them asleep in presumptuous security, it is a base imposition which a reasonable creature passes on himself, when he hearkens to such delusions, and calls such attempts charitable.

Some of you may be disposed to censure the truths laid down in this plain discourse, as severe and uncharitable; but they are truths that will, one day, be seen and felt, far beyond your present conception, or mine. Ought we not therefore to lay them carefully to heart, while we may profit by them? In hell they will be seen too late. Let me, then, by way of conclusion, endeavour to impress upon your minds a serious reflection which our subject strongly suggests. If the light afflictions of the righteous, which are but for a moment, work out for them a far more exceeding and eternal weight of glory; the pleasures of sin, which are also transient, and but for a season, are working out for the ungodly and the sinner a far more exceeding and eternal weight of punishment, "where their worm dieth not, and their fire is not quenched."

SERMON XXVI.

BENEFITS DERIVED TO BELIEVERS FROM THE RESURRECTION OF CHRIST.

Coloss. iii. 1—8.

If ye then be risen with Christ, seek those things which are above, where Christ sitteth on the right hand of God. Set your affection on things above, not on things on the earth. For ye are dead, and your life is hid with Christ in God. When Christ, who is our life, shall appear, then shall ye also appear with him in glory. Mortify therefore your members which are upon the earth; fornication, uncleanness, inordinate affection, evil concupiscence, and covetousness, which is idolatry: for which things sake the wrath of God cometh on the children of disobedience: In the which ye also walked some time, when ye lived in them.

THE words which I have now read to you contain the portion of Scripture, appointed by our Church, for the Epistle on Easter-Day. And, perhaps, there is not a portion of the word of God more suitably adapted to the occasion of that festival; so deeply and so powerfully does it represent to us the right use and proper improvement of our Lord's resurrection. This great event is of vast importance, as a matter of fact, since the truth of christianity depends upon it. The benefits and privileges also resulting from it to the christian, are of an essential kind. On these I would particularly dwell at this time, and suggest to you such considerations as enter into what St. Paul calls the POWER of Jesus's resurrection.

A risen Saviour is the object of the believer's hope, the pledge of his justification consummated, the signal of a justly incensed God fully satisfied, and really propitious. The believer cries, " it is God that justifieth, who is he that condemneth? It is Christ that died, yea rather that is RISEN AGAIN. Knowing that he dieth no more, death hath no more dominion over him." United with Christ by faith, it is his privilege, and his boast to be risen with his Saviour from sin unto righteousness, " dead indeed unto sin, but alive unto God through Jesus Christ our Lord." Meagre and low indeed are those comments which overlook the benefits of Jesus's resurrection, and make it consist in a mere historical fact, that affords rational motives for obedience. Fallen man needs not motives only, but a new heart, new power, and strength to obey. Not a man in this congregation, who has learnt that most necessary science, the knowledge of himself, but can see that if this were all that Christ has done for him; to give him laws, and rational motives to induce his obedience to those laws, and to put him into a capacity of saving himself by his sincere obedience, it would answer to him no good end at all. A fallen being can never perform the condition of sincere obedience, any more than the dead can walk by a power of their own. No: Christ is offered to the penitent sinner as a complete and entire Saviour. The believer is in him not only freely pardoned, but has actually a divine nature communicated to him, whereby he is enabled to obey, being quickened and made alive to God by the same power that raised Jesus from the dead. And heaven, the end of what awaits him, is not the purchase of his own works, but of the works of Christ Jesus. A salvation like this is suitable to the state of fallen beings: less than this would not be a remedy adequate to their wants.

I shall not wonder if self-righteous men despise what I have said of it. In this they will act consistently with their false views of God and themselves. Yet I would wish them to spend a thought on the danger of their case, and consider that should they be found in an error at the last, their ruin will be inevitable. They yet stand on mercy's ground. The Saviour of sinners is ready to receive them, whenever their stubborn spirits can bend to live like needy beggars on the bounty of the Almighty. They may consult, if they please, the sixth chapter of the Epistle to the Romans, from whence the short view I have given of the benefits of Jesus's resurrection, is extracted in connection with the general scope of Scripture.

The blessings resulting to the believer from our Lord's resurrection being thus generally stated, I now proceed to consider the passage of the text, in which the rational inferences from this doctrine are laid down. My design is to open the several parts of it in order, and to intersperse useful matter of application and advice, as I go along. May the Spirit of God be with you and me in this.

" If ye be risen with Christ,"—what an " IF " is this!—I cannot but pause; for eternity, a happy or a miserable eternity, is suspended on this " IF," to each one of us. Are you " risen with Christ?" Know you what it means? Have you experienced this resurrection? Has the baptismal ceremony remained to this day a mere ceremony? Or have you been, indeed, " buried with Jesus unto death, and like as Christ was raised from the dead by the glory of the Father, so do ye also walk in newness of life?" Are you "quickened who were dead in trespasses and sins?" I ask each one to consider for himself. Are you risen with Jesus through the faith of the operation of God, who hath raised him from the dead? Hath God indeed " quickened you together with him, having forgiven you all trespasses?" Talk not here of cant terms, and mystic phrases. It becomes you, as professing Christians, to answer these questions every one for himself. They are the questions of Scripture, in the very language of Scripture. You expose either your pitiable ignorance of Scripture, or your enmity against the Holy Ghost himself, by deriding his terms. The Colossian Christians were thus " quickened with Christ," were thus forgiven all their trespasses. Look at the chapter before that of my text. I suppose Christianity is not altered from what it was in their days, however the *idea* of Christianity may be altered. Evade not then, I beseech you, the question: Are *you* risen with Christ?

The plain meaning of the question is this: Since you were born in sin, and children of wrath, have you ever found pardon and deliverance from the curse through Jesus, and are you with him risen to a new state, new nature, and new life? I would not distress mourning penitents, seeking for deliverance.

If you can heartily say, " I see Jesus alone to be the way to heaven; I am looking to him only; I feel and own my own dead and condemned state, and am seeking for deliverance in the way spoken of in the text, though I cannot receive or experience it as I could wish:" You are in a happy way. Seek on; faint not; you shall find. But if you rest contented with your external duties, and moral honesty, and conclude all is well, you are in a state that, if continued in, will issue in your destruction. You have no union with Christ, and if you die out of Christ, you will die in your sins. And out of Christ you must die, if you continue despisers of the power of his resurrection.

Bethink yourselves. Were you not born in sin? Is not the necessity of the new birth laid down in Scripture in positive terms? Where has been your knowledge of it? Where you seeking after it? When did you begin to see your need of it? When was the time that you thought meanly of your state? The complete ignorance of many, in all these particulars, and still more their contempt and carelessness, demonstrate them as yet to be dead in their sins, with this property also of dead men, that they have no feeling of their condition. God help you to know yourselves.

" If you be risen with Christ, seek those things which are above, where Christ sitteth on the right hand of God." The connection of these words demonstrates, that the being " risen with Christ," can mean nothing less than the actual change of state, before described, produced by the same power of God that raised Christ from the dead. For men thus changed, to be exhorted to " seek those things "which are above," is good sense, and carries its own reasonableness in it. But if you put any other sense on the expression being "risen with Christ," the exhortation that follows is either an insipid tautology, or impertinent. I affirm that the being "risen with Christ," can imply nothing less than the being "born again." But if the new birth is to be explained away, to mean no more than good resolutions, or reformation of life, or any thing short of a new state, then the passage is unintelligible. Take your own sense of it, and be it what it will, if it does not mean that actual change of state and heart, by the power of God, necessary to be experienced by every soul that would see God, you can make no rational meaning of the exhortation that follows. But now let the being risen with Christ imply the being grafted into Christ, and put into a new state, and the exhortation follows with all possible propriety; it is as if he had said, "If ye be made new creatures with heavenly natures, act suitably to your state, by seeking heavenly things."

How necessary then is it, in order to love God, and obey his laws, that men should first be taken out of the corrupt state in which they naturally are, and have new hearts given them, wherewith to love God, and obey his commands. The first member of this verse supposes the new state that gives power to obey the precepts of God, "if ye be risen with Christ." The second delivers one of those precepts, grounded upon it, "seek those things which are above." What a christianity then is that which reverses this gospel order of things; which addresses men who are fallen, dead to God, and corrupt, as if sound and alive to God, and bids them to be good and holy, in order to obtain that very salvation which must first be obtained in order to make men good and holy. I would desire the attention of men of sense and cultivated understandings to what has been said, and beg them to consider whether I have strained the Apostle's meaning or not. Doctrines ought to be founded on a rational interpretation of the real mind of God in his book. And when we say the Spirit of God enlightens men's minds to understand the Scriptures, it is meant to understand the real meaning of them. The fashionable religion of this age says, "Be good and virtuous, and God will receive you." The religion of my text says, " Come to Christ, that you may be united unto him, in order to be made really good and virtuous."

What it is to " seek those things which are above," I shall have occasion to show in considering the next verse : for the same precept follows in different words, "set your affection on things above, not on things on the earth." To believers God speaks thus : " O my children ! rescued by my grace from destruction, at the expense of the blood of my Son, and delivered from this present evil world through the influence of my Spirit, see that you walk worthy of your high calling. Let not your ambition stop short of any object less than me. Let it soar above the objects of sense, and press forward to your Head, who is at my right hand, in whom I behold you righteous, and who has blessings without end in reserve for you. View yourselves as strangers and pilgrims on earth. Be not entangled in its lusts. Set your hearts on the pleasures of the heavenly country you seek." Such is the spirit of this precept, such its reasonableness and connection with that union with a risen and glorified Saviour, of which the believer is made a partaker. Surely, O real Christians, you are called on to love God, and in loving him to desire communion with him. If God take from you a created comfort, or blessing, while he is your God, you cannot mourn, as they that have no hope. The children of this world may mourn, under poverty and affliction: Earthly blessings are their very heaven: Gold is the god they worship, and therefore when deprived of what constitutes all their desire, and all their felicity, they must be unhappy. But your riches are laid up in heaven. There is your treasure, and there should be your heart. Be diligent, then, in the due use of all means of grace, to preserve intercourse with your God. Walk as men whose affections are dead to earth. Let it appear by your conduct that you are really risen with Christ above all those low considerations which influence the men of the world.

Let us here make use of our Saviour's rule, to try men by their fruits, whether they have faith in him. Certain it is, by this rule, that all those whose affections are set upon the earth are not christians. How many such there are in this congregation, judge ye. What! be christians, that is, be "risen with Christ" from the death of sin to the life of righteousness, and yet be employed in thought, word, and deed, from morning till night, in nothing but earthly concerns! The stale, hypocritical way of evading conviction on this head, by saying, " we must be industrious and take care of our families," will not avail. Spirit of God! do thou show the guilty that it is the work of their heart chiefly, not of their hands, that renders them obnoxious to the Divine wrath. You ought indeed to take care of your families. But where are your hearts? Do they not rove entirely after the world? Your sins cost you not so much grief as your losses in trade. Many are such slaves to money, that they cannot keep out the ideas of business on the Lord's day. Are you as earnest and laborious to have your children lovers of God, as you are to have them rich and affluent? Is the voice of prayer heard in your families? When do you converse with your acquaintance about heavenly things? But I am labouring to prove what is self-evident. Speak, conscience, to every individual concerned. Are not their passions quite still on the affairs of the soul? Are they not all alive for this earth? Will conscience allow *these* to be christians, though they may attend christian ordinances, or even have just christian notions? Intend they not, as soon as they leave this place, to shake off any convictions of guilt that may have fastened on them here? May the Spirit of God prevent their foolish designs, and grant that some souls that are here may be caught in the gospel-net. They will then see they need something more than moral lectures on generosity and avarice, to make them christians; that they are dead in sins, and need to rise with Christ to a new state, that their affections may be changed also. May this point be infixed on their souls, as the one necessary object of their pursuit, to become ONE WITH CHRIST by a living faith! And may those who know they believe in Christ, as above described, prove the reality of their union with him by their heavenly-mindedness.

"For ye are dead, and your life is hid with Christ in God." This is one of those bold metaphors that abound in the writings of St. Paul. There are several others of the same kind interspersed in his epistles, to the understanding and due use of which is required the teaching of God's Holy Spirit, and a mind really humbled with a sense of sin, and looking up to Jesus for wisdom. If they be viewed without these requisites, the spirit of them is lost; it evades the force of the most penetrating genius. Proud scholars are too wise in their own eyes to receive them; and the profane and ungodly will not understand them. To them we may say, as the Herald did in the solemnities of ancient heathen mysteries, " Begone, ye profane."

The verse I have just now read, is one of those passages that enters deeply into the mysteries of the gospel, and lays open its precious peculiarities. Perhaps the full sense of it may be thus expressed: " Ye who are real Christians, are indeed by nature the same as other men; but by believing in Christ ye have received another nature from heaven." Ye are *dead* then to that state of sin and condemnation in which you were born, and in which you lived before your conversion. Ye are " crucified" to it " with Christ, yet ye live, but not you," no power of yours, " but Christ," the new principle of life, " liveth in you." In him you are risen to a state of holiness; and the life you live in the flesh, you live by the faith of the Son of God, who loved you and gave himself for you. You live then to God, and the new nature in you has dominion over the old. It surely must, so sure as Christ is stronger than the devil. Yet have you no independent stock of goodness in you. That righteousness, peace with God, and strength by which you now live the sons of God, is all deposited in Christ your head. Your title to it at first, and your enjoyment of it, and your continuance in it, are all made good to you in the way of believing in him for it. He is your life, your happiness, your holiness, your all. This life of yours is *hid*; it is utterly unknown to the world that lies in wickedness. They have no idea of it; they despise it, and call it folly and madness. It is hid, too, in part, even from yourselves, at times. When your evidences are clouded, it may seem quite hid from you. Nevertheless, this life of yours really exists; it "is with Christ," in his safe hands, deposited for your continual use. It is "hid with Christ in God." For if it be with Christ, it is with God, since "Christ is God." How happy, then, your state; yet what room for humility! Act suitably to this your high calling; and since your life is already in heaven, how properly did I exhort you to seek and love heavenly things.

Such I take to be the full import of the passage, "ye are dead, and your life is hid with Christ in God." The Apostle goes on, "when Christ who is our life shall appear, then shall ye also appear with him in glory." He is your life now, though ye see him not, and know him only in part. But be encouraged to die, in your daily practice, to sin, since a time will come when He who is your life shall appear and own your relation to him, and take you up to reign, in the fulness of glory, in heaven, that where he is, there ye may be also.

Since, then, ye look for such unspeakable mercies, and since the happiness you seek has holiness in its very nature, and is in reserve for you in heaven, not on earth, it follows, " mortify therefore your members which are on the earth." In Christ you have already a sure victory over sin, and the members of the old man; show, then, the power of this victory, in your constant practice; by daily overcoming, and gaining ground more and more over your natural lusts, even to their utter destruction. You are saved "by grace, through faith," and because you are saved, therefore be holy in your lives. Salvation, by faith, and the renewal of the man in inward practical holiness, have both, you see, a necessary place in the gospel scheme. No man can ever see God without both.

He, then, who quarrels with the gospel as if it were an enemy to holiness, and an encourager of sin, quarrels with a shadow, fights without an adversary, and triumphs without victory. But what we must maintain, and what the whole scope of exhortation I have considered requires me to maintain, is, that a free salvation of the soul, by faith in Christ, must be first in order. Holiness, and real good works, as the proper fruits of salvation, may come next in order, as they certainly will do in that heart, where real faith in Christ has taken place. But he that should bid us be good and holy first, in order to obtain, in consequence, the salvation of the soul, would discover his total ignorance of the gospel, militate against the Apostle in direct terms, and show a way that leads neither to holiness, nor heaven. Only consider this plain Scripture truth; "man is dead in sin by nature." What real good works can be expected from him in this state? How can he even be saved by his deeds, who is incapable of good? Common sense requires that there be first a root, a stock of a tree, before there can be fruit from it. Thus the gospel requires that men be first pardoned, and risen with Christ, and have a new heart and principle wherewith to love God, before they can keep his commandments.

The whole that I mean on this all-important affair, is thus expressed by the author of the Epistle to the Ephesians. "For by grace are ye saved, through faith; and that not of yourselves, it is the gift of God: not of works, lest any man should boast. For we are his workmanship, created in Christ Jesus unto good works, which God hath before ordained that we should walk in them." Ye, then, that are "risen with Christ," practise what the Apostle exhorts you to. Desire heavenly things. Show by your charity and liberality that earthly things engage not your affections. Humble yourselves, and be ever looking up to Jesus, your life, for strength, and expect with patience and joy his last appearance, that will crown your felicity.

To those who know not, nor seek to know, what union with Christ is, I would say with the Apostle, "awake thou that sleepest, and arise from the dead, and Christ shall give thee light." Let the time past suffice to have lived in gross wickedness, or unavailing formality. Depend on no moral good qualities, be they never so many, to gain heaven. Christ is the door, and the life. Begin, at length, to seek an experimental union with him, and to be invested with his righteousness. The curse of a broken law hangs over you. This curse attends all you do. Seek for a new state and heart; nothing you do is accepted of God in your present state. It is an awful state you are in. Life is uncertain. If death find you out of Christ, you are lost for ever. Seek him, nor rest till you have brought your soul's concerns to this issue, " Christ is my life, and I am in Christ." See, he stands ready with open arms to receive you, whenever you turn to him, notwithstanding all that is past. " He that is athirst, let him come to me and drink." This is his own invitation. By refusing it you perish in your sins. By complying with it your souls shall live and be happy. " He that cometh to me shall never hunger, and he that believeth on me shall never thirst[*]."

---

[*] John vi. 35.

SERMON XXVII.

THE NATURE AND NECESSITY OF CHRISTIAN HUMILITY.

1 Peter v. 5, 6.

Likewise, ye younger, submit yourselves unto the elder: Yea, all of you be subject one to another, and be cloathed with humility: for God resisteth the proud, and giveth grace to the humble. Humble yourselves therefore under the mighty hand of God, that he may exalt you in due time.

The chapter begins with an exhortation to the Pastors of the Church, which it highly concerns us to consider, who are called to minister in holy things. But this application of the text I shall omit, because I preach to the Laity, not to the Clergy. Were I called on to address an assembly of the latter, nothing could, indeed, be more weighty and pertinent. I have only to beseech you, brethren, to pray for us seriously and charitably, that we may be found faithful in the very arduous office to which we are called, and may both save our own souls and those who hear us. St. Peter exhorts to humility in the text, a virtue peculiarly christian. Let us briefly illustrate his meaning, and then apply it, in some observations, to our consciences.

Young persons are directed to submit themselves

to the elder: The benefit of society in general, and of the church of God in particular, requires it: And so useful a thing is humility, that he recommends a mutual submission to all. It is the true way to preserve peace and unity in the Church of Christ, and to prevent those confusions which pride is ever apt to produce. Indeed the nature of man is so weak and fallible, and we have all so much need to humble ourselves for various evils, that it becomes us to be " clothed with humility." It should cover and involve us in every thing, and from a principle of the fear of God, who " resisteth the proud, and giveth grace to the humble." He who is higher than the highest, regards not any of those distinctions by which men are so apt to value themselves one above another. Before him all are equal; because none have any thing superior to others, but what is his gift, and all are before him " less than nothing and vanity." They are " nothing," if considered as creatures who owe their all to him, and " less than nothing," considered as sinful creatures who deserve to be reduced to a state worse than nothing for their iniquities.

What then is the frame of heart which becomes such a creature towards his Maker? Evidently to be lowly before him, ever sensible of infinite distance from him, obligations to him, and unworthiness of the least of his mercies. To swell with pride, to depend on himself, to boast of his excellencies, to take to himself any part of the honour which belongs to his Maker, is to fight against God, and to affront him in the most provoking manner that he is capable of. It is therefore a maxim of the divine government, which he pursues in all his dealings, to abase the haughty and exalt the lowly. If there is one thing more generally taught through the Bible than another, it is this, being indeed the great practical lesson of the gospel of Jesus Christ, that "God resisteth the proud, and giveth grace to the humble." If men are lifted up, he brings them down, he opposes, baffles, confounds, and crosses them: He makes them feel that he is stronger than they, and that they shall not prevail in their schemes of self-exaltation. But where men lie low before him; yield to his power, wisdom, and authority; give place to him in all things, and cease from all self-dependance, such souls he delights in; on such he loves to bestow the riches of his grace, and he comforts and exalts them as his children and favourites; so that the sentiment is the same, which the Psalmist thus expresses, "Though the Lord be high, yet hath he respect to the lowly; as for the proud he beholdeth them afar off."

How weighty, how seasonable then the exhortation in the text, "Humble yourselves under the mighty hand of God." You are poor, sinful, miserable creatures: Know and feel yourselves such; put your mouths in the dust; conform yourselves to your situation; entertain not a proud thought; cherish every view that makes you mean in your own eyes before your Maker. As you lie under his "mighty hand," who can do with you what he pleases; and as He only can make you happy, wise, and holy, be perfectly convinced that you depend on him only for all these things, and give over all hope, all striving in your own strength. Having a promise of grace, through Jesus Christ by his word, from him who willeth not the death of a sinner, and invites you to come to him by Jesus Christ, and put your trust in him, wait in this hope, bearing your miseries till the fit time come for your exaltation. This time he knows. Leave it with all circumstances in his hands, and be patient till he exalt you.

This is the subject, vast and weighty. If any thing concerns the whole race of men, one as well as another, it is, that all learn to be humble. I believe no man will dispute that we ought to be humble. Such is the effect of the light of the Scripture among us, that it is allowed even by those who are neither humble, nor desirous of being so. But that we may see how much even those who are the least disposed to make a good use of it are indebted to Scripture, it is proper to observe, that before humility was set forth as a virtue there, it was not known to be such in the world. So dark is man by nature, and so unable by his natural reason to enlighten himself, that there was not a Philosopher among all the ancient Greeks and Romans, that knew humility to be a virtue acceptable to God. Had the wisest and most learned of them, Aristotle among the Greeks, and Cicero among the Latins, for instance, been told that men ought to be humble, they would have denied it. Humility appeared to them a mean, contemptible thing, unworthy of what they called the dignity of human nature. They knew neither God nor themselves; they were as unacquainted with the real doctrine of man's corruption, as they were with that of the grace of God in Jesus Christ. Are there not numbers, far more inexcusably, as practically ignorant of these things as they? Is not this the reason that so many live and die without any true relish or delight in the gospel of Jesus Christ? They have just learnt so much by the light of Scripture as to confess they ought to be humble, but are as far from it as the wisest heathens, who knew it not. They are slaves to pride without seeing it; willingly deceiving themselves, and dread to admit that light, which would save their souls.

First, then, I observe, that the cause why so many remain strangers to the blessings of redemption all their days, is because they remain without humility. When in visiting the sick, or conversing with souls to guide them into the way of salvation, we lay open to them the wrath of God against sin, which indeed is needful to make men feel their need of Jesus Christ, how common is it for them to suppose that this alarming representation of things can only be true of some gross and scandalous sinners. They cannot but own, they do wrong things, at times, but their hearts, they think, are always good, nor do they feel the burden of any sin rooted in their nature. Show them the necessity of loving God, they think they always have loved him; and though the carnal mind, which is " enmity against God," is continually proving itself in them, by its exertions against the will and mind of God, they will not allow they have any such evil nature in them. Show them the law of God, how strict, and pure, and spiritual it is, and requiring the obedience of the heart, and branch it out into some instances, as that a lustful look is adultery, as our Saviour teaches, they are disposed to quarrel with the law as too strict, rather than to admit the conviction of their own sinfulness. So true is that saying of our Lord, " no man knoweth the Father, save the Son, and he to whomsoever the Son will reveal him." There is, there is a special illumination of grace necessary, from age to age, to open the blind eyes, and enable them to see their sin in its deformity, and the grace of Christ in its beauty. But though the right way for a poor sinful creature would be to obey simply, and without delay, the divine direction of earnestly seeking it, by prayer in the name of Christ, yet men are not naturally disposed to use this method at all, but to argue and dispute with great confidence, and without the least idea of their own ignorance. And the more learned men are, or the more advantages in point of quality, riches, politeness, or whatever else they possess above their fellow creatures, the more obstinate they are in opposing the Holy Ghost, and the duller they are to understand divine things. I have seen again and again some poor unlettered creatures understand more of themselves, and of the law, and of the gospel, in a few weeks, than many scholars and genteel people do in many years. The reason is, in the latter there is more pride, and " God resists the proud." Assuredly, the mind which most humbly yields to the influences of the Spirit, shall most speedily know them. I would therefore say to you, who for years have had some thought of religion, and yet can get no satisfaction, " ye are proud, not willing to humble yourselves under the hand of God, that he may exalt you in due time." See, then, what you have to guard against, and what your real impediment is.

See, hence also, the necessity of conversion for one sort of men as much as for another. A decent person needs the new birth as much as a scandalous one. Admission to heaven there can be to neither, while unconverted. "Except ye be converted and become as little children, ye cannot enter into the kingdom of heaven." So HE speaks who will judge us at the last day. While you lean to your own understanding, have no more religion than what natural reason admits, and feel not yourselves to be miserable sinners, you are only Pharisees, and are more fitted to admire yourselves than the Son of God; you are enemies to the whole design of Christ's coming into the world, by not submitting yourselves to the righteousness of God, but going about to establish your own. Plato and Cicero were as good, probably better christians than you. In truth, neither you nor they can be called christians, in the proper sense of the word. You must have done with that satisfaction which arises from your superiority over gross sinners. Till then you are like the Pharisee, who said, "God, I thank thee that I am not as other men are." None are farther from heaven than such characters. Neither gross nor decent sinners can be saved without conversion. The reward of your decent morals you have in this life. The pride which you mix with it, is as provoking to God as the grossest sins in the world can be. See here again the necessity of being humble. That is our subject. I would keep it in view throughout, and God grant you to feel the need of learning true humility. If you once learnt it, all the prejudice that you have against the doctrines of the gospel would vanish.

This leads me to observe in what lies the true stress of Scripture doctrines. It is not, as we are continually misrepresented, that we make a certain speculative set of opinions the thing on which salvation turns. No: it would not be worth while for zealous Ministers, in all ages, to labour and suffer reproach for any mere opinions. But the doctrines of the gospel are of a humiliating nature, and till they are understood, men remain proud. The stress lies here. Thus when St. Paul vehemently contends for the all-important doctrine of justification by faith only in the Lord Jesus Christ, he says, " where is boasting? it is excluded. By what law, of works? Nay, but by the law of faith." While men trust in their own righteousness, they are, though they will not own it, proud boasters, and are of all others the most offensive to God, and unfit for his kingdom. You see that I have not been zealous without cause for this doctrine of justification by Christ Jesus only, which for so many years I have inculcated. The cause is, that God may be honoured; that the name of his Son, and the wisdom, and grace of God in him may be glorified; and that men being made truly humble, may admire him, and boast no more of themselves.

So likewise, the conviction of sin, and the knowledge of our depravity, and corruption, and ruined state by nature, is necessary, not for its own sake, merely as an opinion, but because without it men cannot be humble. Conversion, as a doctrine, is for the same reason necessary; for what is conversion without humility? The influences of the Holy Ghost are equally necessary to be known, because men, naturally seek them not, but trust in their own powers, and think not of aid from above, to make them wise unto salvation, and enable them to perform the common offices of life. I desire those who have not attended to this, to consider, why we press the necessity and importance of these doctrines.

Indeed, there have been, and there are, those who assent to them, and yet are no better than others; but they have no spiritual understanding of them, as appears from hence, that they make no use of them. They have not learnt them from the Holy Ghost. His lessons are all practical. Let men who profess these things without feeling their influence, seek to know them in a better manner by the teaching of the Spirit of God, that they deceive not themselves to their ruin.

But mark, on the other hand: The advantage of knowing these doctrines lies here. He who truly knows them, can learn humility by their means; and blessed is that man who has learnt to be humble before God. Angels shall, one day, own him publicly as a brother. However mean a thing humility may seem now, heaven and hell turn on this point: " Are you humble, or are you proud before God?" All Scripture agrees with the declaration of the text, " God resisteth the proud, but giveth grace to the humble."

If I have not said enough to show the importance of gospel doctrines, as the only guides to humility, I know nothing stronger that can be said. What are real good men in all ages? Many are acute and sensible, many brave and generous, many good-natured and gentle. These qualities are not to be despised, far from it; yet if such persons continue in pride, they are odious before God, and must be so. If this, then, be the real importance of the doctrines of the gospel, with what care should we attend to them! How much is it to be lamented, that many hear so little, and so seldom, the word of God, and search the Scriptures scarcely at all. For, surely, the better a man knows these doctrines, the better is he fitted to learn humility.

There is one Scripture doctrine which I do not so commonly bring into view as some others, because it is not so essentially necessary to be known, I mean what St. Paul calls " the election of grace." But I mention it now as highly useful, and an excellent means of teaching a man to be humble. It is what souls, who know divine truth, should seek to understand, for particular purposes, so far as it is revealed. " It is not of him that willeth, nor of him that runneth, but of God that showeth mercy." How humbling a thought is this! How does it cause the soul to be low before God, and lose itself in wonder, love, and praise!

Before I proceed to another observation, let me for a moment mourn over the desolations of the times. You may see, however, that they teach us something on our subject. The excellency of the doctrines of the gospel, I repeat it again, lies in this, that they every one of them teach humility, which is the happiness of a creature. But what is taught by the principles of those who are Socinians and Freethinkers? Do not all these characters wear pride on their very foreheads? Have they not learnt to despise the Scriptures, to decide by the light of their own reason, with the most confident presumption, on subjects vastly above their reach? And what has this light done for them? How has it promoted social peace and happiness? I am astonished that they learn not the least wisdom by all they suffer. But to keep to our subject. Whether you look at the pretended Philosophers on the Continent, or at their Disciples in England, will not every man confess, that great pride is their besetting evil? Do not you see, that a little sprinkling of humility among these, would be the very best thing they could have every way? When we pray, "abate their pride," charity itself could not dictate a kinder prayer for our enemies. But the Scripture doctrines of the new birth, original sin, and justification by faith in Christ, we all know, are not their doctrines: nothing can be farther from their hearts than such sentiments. Learn hence, then, that these doctrines teach humility. This is their rise and glory. But modern Philosophy is sure to be attended with a pride of heart, which, though it may utter many things soothing to flesh and blood, is sure to fill nations with misery, and hell with inhabitants.

Another objection here comes in our way, by which many deceive themselves. I shall state it, and answer it as I can. "I hope I am not self-righteous, I own myself a sinner, I hope for pardon from God's mercy through Christ; I am weak, but I strive to do my best, and I do not think I can do all things by myself; I do not deny the need of help from above." Thus it is that many think and speak, and so avoid conviction; and though their fruits be evidently those of pride, all their days, they deceive themselves with false hope. It is hard work, I confess, to speak to men for their good here, who are determined to oppose every thing, and not to part with the good opinion they have of themselves. I shall dwell only on one point, at present. I shall beseech them to read over carefully, with prayer, our Lord's parable of the vine in the 15th chapter of St. John. Brethren, all men must own, more or less that they are weak and sinful, and need both help from above and pardon of sin. Every man by natural light must know thus much. But this does not come up to the point. " Abide in me. Without me you can do nothing. The branch, separate from the vine, cannot bear fruit, no more can ye, except ye abide in me." Ye may be as proud as the proudest all your days, and yet own yourselves to be weak and not without sin. But do you know that you are not only sinners, but helpless, lost sinners; dead in sin as a branch out of its vine? " Men gather them," says Christ, and " cast them into the fire." Know you this, that you are naturally of no more value in God's sight than such a dead branch, and deserve to be cast into hell fire? For so our Lord, by the allusion, teaches us. And do you feel daily this evil nature, and your perfect helplessness as to all real love of God, that is, to all true holiness? You need the influence of the Holy Spirit, not now and then only; you need every day of your life, nay every moment, a continued derivation of virtue from him through union with Jesus. Here is true conviction of sin, justification by faith, union with Christ, and communion with him. I know these things are the most precious views of real humble men that can be.

Would to God we had more of this union with Christ, this going out of self into him by faith, and living out of his fulness continually! Would to God we were more humble, and brought more simply to it!

This is the breathing of a saint. But it is not yours, who made the objection. See you not that you are not at all in the way which our Lord describes in the parable? Why will you continue to defend your state, as good, when it is bad, and pretend to humility, while you are proud? Take care. Pride will ruin you as much as any other sin. Oh, that you would give over arguing and cavilling, and learn to pray seriously for divine instruction. There is a voice of wisdom in the words, "humble yourselves under the mighty hand of God," which contains far more than I can express. Seek to be taught it of God, that you may be made wise unto salvation.

I turn now to you who are in the school of Christ, humbled under the mighty hand of God, though imperfectly and needing more humbling, that you may be exalted in due time. There is a point in the christian life, better felt and conceived than described in words. Sooner or later all true christians know it, and go through the mortifying but wholesome experience of it. It is an emptying of the soul, a thorough despairing of a man's own righteousness and strength; not only a ceasing from self in the point of justification before God, but in all things, from a conviction which a man finds and feels, that he is nothing but a heap of sin and misery, darkness and confusion. Such a conviction may seem to destroy his faith, and comfort, and holiness, yet in reality, so different are God's ways and thoughts from ours, it confirms them all. For thus he is brought to abide in Christ alone humbly and sincerely, and thus he passes from death unto life, and knows it by experience. The Lord will exalt him when the fit time is come, in this life, by his grace, in the earnests of the Spirit, as well as completely and everlastingly hereafter. In this school, when certain critical hours of distress and relief are both felt in the soul, more is learnt in a little time than before for many years.

This should teach serious minds, exercised with temptations, to trust in God quietly, and bear the yoke, appointed for them to bear, in patience, till he appear for their deliverance. The prouder men are, the more difficulty there is, and the more slowly are they brought to the point. They are apt to be impatient and quarrelsome, even with God himself, and to think it hard that their most earnest attempts to save and sanctify themselves do not succeed. But God is resisting their pride, and crossing their self-righteous attempts after holiness, that they may be made holy in his way and time. "The help that is done upon earth he doeth it himself," and the point of true humility lies in being brought to know inwardly that there is no good in them, that they lie at mercy, and must wait till the Lord do for them what they need. When they give over seeking help in themselves, and leave that to him in faith and patience, he will do it, effectually, and be found their true and complete Saviour. In true humility the soul is brought to know its own ill deserts, that it is a mercy if it be saved from ruin at all, in any way; that it is not for any worthiness of its own, but for his name's sake, and to honour his blessed Son, that he bestows grace and glory.

How divinely suitable then is it, my Christian brethren, to learn that " by grace ye are saved through faith, and that not of yourselves, it is the gift of God; not of works, lest any one should boast; for we are his workmanship created in Christ Jesus to good works, which God hath before ordained that we should walk in them." Thus shall you learn to be truly humble, and when you find that he accepts you freely in Christ, and gives you leave and strength to hope in him, and to glory and rejoice in him: When you find nothing but ruin in yourselves, you will remember and be confounded, and never open your mouths to boast any more, because of your shame when he is pacified toward you for all that you have done. In this way learn humility, and you will learn what will give you the true wisdom.

And now, when the Lord has brought you down, and made you low in your own eyes, and lifted you up in Christ, in the confidence of his righteousness, and taught you to lean on him for his sanctifying Spirit to work in you to will and to do, you should learn to "walk humbly with your God" all your days. Glorify him by humility before men, after having learnt the inward lesson of it in your own souls. Be subject to your elders, your governors in society, your superiors in your family. Be peaceable and lowly; give honour where honour is due; be subject to one another, in love, and prevent quarrels and contentions, by studying to bear and forbear, to submit and to yield. While you take care not to grieve the Spirit of God, by acting against conscience, be careful also that you do not gratify pride and ill humour, under pretence of conscience, as many have done. It is but seldom that you can be vindicated in any contention with your fellow-creatures. Be firm for the faith of the gospel, and contend for its fundamental doctrines, in meekness, zeal, and love. But where your honour and profit, that is, where self is concerned, let all men see how humble, how yielding you are.

Lastly, having glorified God by a life of humility, which indeed, rightly considered, is a life of charity, for these two graces are so interwoven that they cannot thrive asunder, you shall, when the Chief Shepherd appears, receive a crown of glory that fadeth not away. So much evil is in the best, that it is generally necessary for them to be kept low, all their days here, by some cross, some humbling conflict, or other. Your expectations in the world will often be disappointed. Even the fairest and most pleasing expectations of the glory and prosperity of the Church of Christ here on earth will often be crossed. In your families, and in your own persons, many things you must bear contrary to flesh and blood. Learn, however, this virtue of humility, and exercise it more and more all your days, and you will find rest to your souls.

An humble Saint shall be too hard for Satan, with all his pride, and shall triumph over him gloriously at last, as Christ himself did. And when you are brought to see HIM whom you trusted, and hoped in, and patiently expected, and loved, while on earth, you shall say, in the fulness of joy and love, (nor will your bliss be at all hindered by the humility of the confession) " thou wast slain, and hast redeemed us to God by thy blood." A proud man, certainly, cannot heartily make such a confession. In heaven all see and admire Christ and his grace; condemn themselves, and glory in his salvation. It is not possible, therefore, for any who does not really trust in the atoning blood, to arrive at heaven, because he cannot sing that song. None but the humble have any thankful remembrance of the death of Christ, and consequently none but the humble are qualified for the society of the blessed in heaven. Hence you see that this must be the unalterable rule of the divine government—" every one that exalteth himself shall be abased, and he that humbleth himself shall be exalted."

SERMON XXVIII.

ST. PETER'S TESTIMONY OF THE EPISTLES OF ST. PAUL.

2 Peter, iii. 15, 16.

And account that the long-suffering of our Lord is salvation; even as our beloved brother Paul also, according to the wisdom given unto him, hath written unto you; as also in all his epistles, speaking in them of these things: in which are some things hard to be understood, which they that are unlearned and unstable wrest, as they do also the other scriptures, unto their own destruction.

A REMARKABLE testimony is here given by St. Peter of his brother the Apostle Paul. The authority of his writings as divinely inspired is plainly set forth. They are put on the same footing as the other Scriptures. The wisdom given unto him is plainly the wisdom of divine inspiration. Were the writings of St. Paul merely those of a good man, under the influence of the Spirit of God, in the same sense as all good men are, it would be too much to speak of men's " wresting them to their own destruction." Of the divine books alone it can be said, that by the right use of them men are guided into the way of salvation, as by the abuse of them they are led into the paths of destruction.

In the Epistles of St. Paul, we are here told, are some particular parts " hard to be understood."

These passages are not to be passed by as of no value, but to be studied the more carefully, and to be prayed over the more reverently, that by the influence of the Divine Spirit we may take them in their true sense and import, and make the right practical use of them; that they may be for salvation, and not for destruction. The wresting of St. Paul to a bad sense and purpose, here spoken of, is not peculiar to his writings: the other Scriptures are treated in the same dangerous manner by men not well acquainted with their import, and despising the illumination of the Spirit, which alone can make them effectual to our benefit. Men thus "unlearned" are also "unstable." They see not the great and simple point, the knowledge of Christ, which St. Paul has always in view. No wonder that the heart, being not stayed on Christ, runs curiously from one notion to another, and fluctuates in miserable uncertainty.

Such is the testimony given by St. Peter of St. Paul's writings, in general, and such the guard which he sets over us in perusing them, to prevent abuse, and to secure a saving use of them to our souls. All this is occasionally introduced by an observation, that St. Paul had written the same truths to the converted Jews, which St. Peter is here enforcing.

Now the truths illustrated in this chapter are, that the long-suffering of God leadeth to repentance; that because the judgment-day is delayed, wicked men are apt to scoff, and even true believers to lose patience, and be discouraged; but that there are divine reasons for the delay, and that though it tarry it will come. And if we read from the latter end of the 10th quite through the 11th and 12th chapters of that Epistle, we shall see that St. Paul largely inculcates on christians a patient expectation of Christ's second coming, as Peter does, and shows, as he does, that the Lord is not slack concerning his promise, " for yet a little while, and he that shall come will come, and will not tarry*."

I have described as I can the thoughts of the text, and must now proceed to branch out its use into several particulars. Oh, may the Spirit of the Lord shine on the subject, and teach us to understand, and to feed on divine truth, and keep us from abusing it to our ruin!

We have here a solemn call from the Holy Ghost to reverence and attend, with all our might, to the writings of St. Paul in general. Great pains have been taken to discredit them. There are those who profess to regard the four Gospels, and to make light of the Epistles. Unseemly comparisons have been made between them, in this view, as if what Christ spake in person, deserved to be much more regarded than what was written by the Apostles. St. Paul is so full and explicit, so direct and explanatory on the great doctrinal truths of christianity, and strikes so keenly at the root of false religion, that all pretended christians have ever shown themselves very uneasy on account of his writings, and anxious to discredit their authority. They vainly fancy that they can reconcile their false notions with the other parts of the New Testament. St. Paul, they see,

* The Epistle to the Hebrews is the only one we have of St. Paul's which was written to the Jews; and as St. Peter in writing to the Jews allows, in the words of my text, that St. Paul had also written to them, this circumstance seems to confirm the common account, that St Paul was the author of the Epistle to the Hebrews.

is perfectly contrary to them. But this is not to receive christianity itself, but to follow a plan of our own. He who would understand the Scriptures, must first set out with a determination to receive them as the word of God; the whole of them in general, as they have been delivered to us. Of St. Paul's right to the character of divine inspiration, there can be no more doubt than there is of any of the rest. In them all equally Christ speaks. He who believes Christ to be, indeed, what he is, will not doubt but that his Spirit could as infallibly dictate to Peter or Paul writing Epistles, as to Matthew and the other Evangelists writing the four Gospels. It is, then, a groundless distinction which they attempt to make between Christ himself and his Apostles, in this point, for it is well known that our Lord himself committed nothing to writing. You hear Christ speaking, in one part, as much as in another, by the medium of divine inspiration. The only difference is, that in the four Gospels Christ speaks to us while on earth; in the Epistles he speaks to us after his ascension to heaven.

Observe, I beseech you, with what fulness Peter speaks: " Paul writes according to the wisdom given him " from above. " All his Epistles " he calls SCRIPTURES, the usual name given to inspired writings. And of such divine authority they are, that if men *wrest them*, they do it to " their own destruction." It ill, then, becomes a man professing to be a christian to treat St. Paul's writings in that contemptuous manner in which many do. Men who act thus should not call themselves christians. Christians have, in all ages, received St. Paul's writings as inspired. And, in truth, the divinity of the doctrine, the attestation of miracles, the fulfilment of prophecies, and the divine energy attending the preaching of all the Apostles, leave no room to reasonable men to doubt the justice of their claim to inspiration. The witness of the Spirit to them in every age, by the power which has attended these writings on the hearts of men, is a constant, decisive testimony in their favour.

On the whole, if you like not St. Paul, you will not like Peter, nor John, nor James, nor any of the rest. It were easy to show, that they all agree in doctrine; and at the same time it must be observed, that our Saviour himself has taught us (particularly in his last discourse with his disciples before his suffering) that the doctrines of his religion were to be more clearly and fully taught after his ascension than while he was on earth. Even the nature of things shows it must be so. The doctrine of his atonement, and of reconciliation through his blood, and other precious mysteries of his religion, so largely set forth by St. Paul, could not so properly have been laid open, or in so full a manner, before he suffered, as afterwards. This very circumstance may teach us to expect, though the Gospels hold the same truths in effect, that the latter part of the New Testament should be the most clear and explicit. The infancy of christianity is in the four Gospels, the fulness of it in the Epistles. A great part of the four Gospels is meant to prove the divine mission of Christ, and to state the facts of his life. These things are not controverted now so much as the doctrines are. If therefore we be even more frequent in speaking from the Epistles than the Gospels, this circumstance will justify the practice.

But no part of divine Revelation can be dispensed with. All should be reverenced. One part of it is more useful for one purpose, others of it for others. Would you know our Saviour's birth, life, character, miracles, proofs of his mission, death, resurrection and ascension, study well the four Gospels. He who would become a christian indeed has need to know them. And if in our country these things were opposed as much as by the Jews of old, I hope you would hear us continually preaching from the Evangelists, to establish these facts, because they are the ground-work of christianity. But great as the opposition to real christianity is, there is less of it employed in this way than against its peculiar doctrines. Numbers who hate the whole nature of christianity, are yet pretty well versed in the life and death of Jesus Christ, and believe him to be sent of God. Not but that there are many parts of the four Gospels relating to christian doctrine, particularly in that of St. John, which unconverted men cannot endure. But there are, certainly, other parts of the New Testament more applicable to the state of things at this day. The book of the Acts of the Apostles, as it gives so copious an account of the nature of genuine christianity, in the conversions of numbers, and in the work of the Holy Ghost, affords a stronger light into the nature of christianity than the Gospels. Stronger still is the light afforded by the Epistles. For it is plain, that treatises written under divine inspiration, on purpose to explain the whole of Christ's religion, both in doctrine and practice, must give the clearest light of all.

If many, who profess to regard Christ and to

believe the facts concerning him, will yet not receive his real religion, is not instruction on this head very necessary? Now this is the fact. There are very many nominal christians, who will scarcely receive one single doctrine that is peculiarly christian. They go little farther in religion than a moral heathen would carry them. Surely such are not real christians. The Holy Spirit has provided for their correction and instruction. The Epistles are particularly calculated for this. St. Paul was directed in a clear, full, comprehensive manner to lay open the whole. He does it in all his Epistles, and most of all in his epistle to the Romans. He conceals nothing. Those who call him confused, should say he speaks too plain. They like not what he writes: it thwarts their pride and their lusts. It makes'christianity to be a different thing from what they would have it. Hence the quarrel against it.

You now see why there is a particular reason for our making great use of this much-despised Apostle for the good of souls. You see with what care he ought to be read; what danger there is of despising or wresting his meaning, and that you cannot be a christian indeed, unless you consider his Epistles as inspired. Oh! let me beseech those who have been guilty of this contemptuous mode of treating St. Paul, to look unto God for pardon, and to study and pray over his writings with a seriousness they have not been used to; bringing to them no prejudices, but desirous to learn real christianity, as there largely and fully stated. Less than this men should not do, unless they mean to hazard their souls. For if they will not do this, it is plain they do not desire to know or to practise the real will of God. They would be thought to be christians, without being really so in heart and life.

2. I have now to consider a little that learning and stability which the text implies to be necessary for those who would profit by St. Paul's writings. If there be "some things in them hard to be understood, which the unlearned and unstable wrest to their own destruction," we are plainly given to understand that there is a learning and stability necessary, by which a man shall be enabled to enter into their true and genuine import, and feed on them to the real health of his soul. Is there, in truth, a danger of perverting and abusing the Apostle to men's ruin? Yes; if men be "unlearned and unstable," this practical inference follows. You must learn them well, and be stable and firm in the use of what you do learn from them.

There are not wanting persons who would strengthen their disgust and contempt of this Apostle, from the circumstance, that there are in his Epistles "some things hard to be understood." Hence they would conclude them impossible to be understood. This, however, must not be allowed for a moment. They were "given by inspiration of God," and as "all Scripture is profitable for doctrine," we may certainly conclude they were meant to be understood by us, and may be so, if we seek in the right way. There is a possibility of wresting them to our own destruction, which shows what care is needful in the perusal of them. Indeed the meaning, in general, is plain enough, for it is only of some things, in St. Paul, that it is asserted that they "are hard to be understood."

The use, which careless and profane persons very

injuriously make of this assertion is, that it is best to let the Apostle's writings alone; that it is not needful for us to exercise our understandings on them; and that those who study them are self-conceited fanciful persons, who do themselves more harm than good by it. Such language is common enough, among persons who have no care for their own souls, or the souls of others. A general sentence or two, " be honest in your dealings, do the best you can," or the like, serves them for the whole of their creed and doctrine. This, however, is not knowledge, but ignorance; not searching the Scriptures, as our Lord recommends to the Jews, but a neglect of them, little better than downright contempt.

Men may take pains, indeed, in a wrong way with Paul, and so they may, as Peter tells us, with "the other Scriptures, to their own destruction;" but to neglect them altogether, is surely ruinous. For are we so ignorant of ourselves, as not to know that if we be not guided by Scripture light, we really have no light to guide us at all? Lives there a sinner among us who has any certain plan which he knows will hold good to procure his soul's salvation by? The Scripture teaches us a certain way on the authority of God our Maker; we may, if we understand and embrace it, walk comfortably and surely. But let any man who neglects the Scriptures, propose, if he can, a way to heaven which he can be assured is safe. He may fancy a thousand things; but he has no sure ground to tread on. The fact is, he is a sinner, and God is his judge, and HE has revealed from heaven a way of salvation, well attested, and confirmed by all sorts of proofs of which the thing is capable. If we neglect this light, and refuse to be guided by the rules of that one BOOK, which teaches us the way, we shall in vain think to escape by self-deceiving methods. I apprehend that the sin of men in neglecting to be guided by the Scriptures, argues more contempt of God, more affront done to his righteous government and authority, and is more inexcusable than all our other sins. For *them* a remedy might be provided; for neglect of the gospel, there is no remedy.

Let me beseech you, brethren, to take heed that none of you harden yourselves against the Scriptures on account of "some things hard to be understood." The views which naturally offer themselves to your minds may be more pleasing, and may be more easily understood. It was to be expected, that there would be some difficulties in Revelation, because of the infinite greatness of God, and because of the darkness and perverseness which sin hath brought upon us. But, truly, you and I have no business of any consequence, compared with the care of our souls. Life is short; death will soon remove us from this transitory scene; nature is content with few things; "having food and raiment, let us be therewith content." This sentence at least of St. Paul, is not hard to be understood. Indeed difficulties, are only, as St. Peter says, in some things of his writing. Nor will I say that it is absolutely necessary to understand them all; but it is very dangerous to neglect them, and the fundamentals of godliness must be understood, or we perish.

This is an age, remarkable for the pursuit of

knowledge; it is a shame that Scripture knowledge alone should be neglected. For I would ask many of those who represent the Scriptures as too hard to be understood, whether they say so from their own experience? How often have you carefully read over St. Paul's Epistles with a view to understand them? It surely belongs to the Laity as well as the Clergy to attend to them, otherwise they might as well be locked up in Latin, as in the Popish times. Alas! what will you say before the Judge of quick and dead, when it shall appear that for years you never read the Scriptures at all; that the Bible was one of the last books you thought of reading.

Oh! brethren, what is the world worth, which we are so fond of? Its riches soon make themselves wings and flee away. It is, therefore, one of the worst excuses for a man to say that he had no time to search the Scriptures. A little of the world will serve for the body; though of covetousness and luxury the wants are endless. Contract your wishes, your ambition, your desires, into a narrow compass, and take time to search the Scriptures. There the true riches are to be found. You who profess to be really religious, of all men, ought not to neglect this divine study. To profess the gospel, and yet know it not inwardly for ourselves, is sad indeed.

I must guard you against a common mistake. The *unlearned*, who are said to wrest the Scriptures, do not mean, of necessity, those who are unacquainted with languages, arts, and sciences. A man may be learned in these things, and yet be quite unlearned in the Scriptures. On the other hand, a man may have but a moderate knowledge of them, and yet be very learned in the Scriptures; while a man of learning, puffed up with pride, and determined to admit nothing in religion but what he likes, may study all his days in the Scriptures, and only study himself deeper and deeper in error. Such learned men, for want of a right discernment of the great end and design of Scripture, may be "unstable as water;" tossed about with endless diversity of opinions; ever learning, and never coming to the knowledge of the truth; the convert of the last book they read, and knowing nothing at last.

Endeavour to learn the real scope of Scripture, and having attained it, be firm in it. And here "if any man lack wisdom, let him ask of God." The teaching of God's Spirit is necessary. Those who make light of it, are sure to know nothing aright. A dark cloud rests on all your understandings, which Sin and the Fall have introduced. Did you ever feel it? It is not quite done away in the most intelligent and upright saints, while here on earth. With reading we should join prayer for divine illumination. If you never heartily thus prayed from a sense of your blindness, you have not begun right as yet in religion. Those who would know how to pray aright, let them make all the petitions in the 119th Psalm their own. Guard, I beseech you, against the self-conceit so common in this age, as well as against the spirit of sloth, and total carelessness in religion no less common. Be serious. Here is a book of God's own inditing for our use. He promises, if we search it carefully, depend on him truly for instruction from it, and pray to him without ceasing, we shall understand it and find life from it.

Every part of Scripture is profitable; but the writings of St. Paul, have a particular use in this respect, that they lay open the whole system of Scripture, and give us in one comprehensive view the whole mind of God. Some things, indeed, both in them and in the other Scriptures, are "hard to be understood," but not impossible. Seek therefore the more carefully to understand them, that you may be grounded in the great things of salvation, always looking up for that spiritual illumination so often promised in Scripture. Thus you shall find, as thousands have, satisfying knowledge, attended with real holy and comfortable fruits, which men careless of all Scripture, or leaning to their own understanding, while they peruse it, can never find.

SERMON XXIX.

THE SPIRITUAL MARRIAGE AND UNITY BETWIXT CHRIST AND HIS CHURCH.

Psalm, xlv. 10, 11.

Hearken, O daughter and consider, and incline thine ear; forget also thine own people, and thy father's house. So shall the king greatly desire thy beauty: for he is thy Lord; and worship thou him.

THAT the subject of this Psalm, in its ultimate sense, at least, that is, in its most important sense, and that in which we are chiefly concerned, is to be understood of Jesus Christ and his church, none but a prejudiced sceptic, or a person quite ignorant of Scripture, would deny. Indeed besides other strong arguments that might be brought to prove it, we have the express testimony of St. Paul in the first chapter of his Epistle to the Hebrews[*]. The quotation from the Psalm which may be found there, saves all labour of reasoning with those who admit the divine authority of that Epistle. Taking it, then, for granted that we have here represented "the spiritual marriage betwixt Christ and his Church," let the inspired writer's own commendation of the subject, speak for its importance, and produce your attention to it.

"My heart is inditing a good matter: I speak of the things which I have made touching the King. My tongue is the pen of a ready writer." Christ

[*] Heb. i. 8, 9.

the King of the Church is glorious and beautiful, you see, in his eyes. It is "a good matter" that is before him: His heart is in it. Hence his language is warm, affectionate, and copious. And if it be so with the speaker, should it not be so with the hearer? To fix the attention to the real character of Christ, and to let the heart run out into love and the kindest regard toward HIM—this is evidently the meaning of the Psalmist's words, if words are to have any meaning. And thence I infer that a valuable part of the Christian religion consists in the special love of the soul to Christ. It is indeed true, that the highest professions of love to Christ are nothing worth, without a life of obedience, and a regular series of virtuous and upright behaviour; "If ye love me, keep my commandments:" Yet it is equally true that the very best outward actions, if not principled with an inward affection of the soul toward Christ, are of no value before God; "though I give all my goods to feed the poor and have not love, it profiteth me nothing." Brethren, let us weigh both these truths, and not deceive ourselves either with a wordy profession on the one hand, or with external decency of conduct on the other. Thy love, O Christ, must constrain us; it should be in the heart, and there burn, and rule, and sway us! May something of the precious influence which dictated the Psalm be with us in considering it!

"Thou art fairer than the children of men; grace is poured into thy lips, therefore God hath blessed thee for ever." Here the sacred writer expresses love to Christ flowing from an admiration of his wonderful virtues and perfections. It is a sign of the mean taste of the age we live in, that so much praise should be lavished upon the imposing eloquence of men destitute of all honesty, of all principle, while HE who spake as never man spake, who was and is all truth, all goodness, and possessed of every excellence to be found in God and man united in one person, even Jesus Christ should be lightly regarded. But he is "fairer than the children of men," and those who are of his true Church know how to prize him. His Father hath blessed him for ever, and "grace is poured into his lips," to render him most delightful to his people. Nor should they be ashamed of expressing their delight in him. I have no notion of paying so much compliment to a profane world, as to abstain from touching on these Scriptural subjects of that divine love which is between Christ and his Church, because some have abused it to low and unworthy purposes. If we are to avoid every subject that may be abused, we are to meddle with few indeed, or none at all. Who knows not that human friendships and social affections may be and often are much abused, and yet they are good things in themselves, and ought to be encouraged in their place and degree. With God's help, then, I shall not be shy of recommending the love of Christ as really to be felt in the soul, and wish every one of you to seek for it till you know it, and are united to him as the husband and wife are; but in a spiritual, reverent, and holy union; but with a love of the purest and noblest kind, controlling all other inferior affections; moderating and regulating, not extinguishing, those of them that are right, and subduing those that are wrong. Oh! seek this love of Christ, that you may join in the spirit of this Psalm,

"Gird thy sword upon thy thigh, O Most Mighty, with thy glory and thy majesty, and in thy majesty ride prosperously, because of truth, and meekness, and righteousness, and thy right hand shall teach thee terrible things." This is a prayer to the Lamb of God, that he would be pleased to exert himself as a Prince, to destroy the powers of Sin and Satan, and spread his glorious gospel in the world. I am persuaded all that love him feel their hearts joining in this petition. Exercise your thoughts, brethren, on it. It is an interest infinitely more valuable than all other interests in the world. Who that knows this amiable and majestic Prince, the only begotten Son of God, the conqueror of Satan, and the true benefactor, as well as maker of the human race, who governs the world in righteousness, would not wish to see his authority extended, and behold him ruling in the hearts of a willing people through the whole earth. Man's true interest is connected with the prosperity of Christ's kingdom; for truth and righteousness are the very nature of this Prince and his government: and though he be terrible to Satan and the cause of sin, yet meekness is essential to him, and it is not by temporal weapons, (as, alas! how many who call themselves christians have thought and acted) not by force, not by persecution, but by the meekness of suffering, by the power of the word of truth, and by the Holy Ghost, that his kingdom is exalted.

"Thine arrows are sharp in the heart of the King's enemies, whereby the people fall under thee." This is the way. By spiritual conviction he can and does, from age to age, bring down proud sinners at his feet. Those who are now the stoutest and the most prejudiced against his authority, little think how soon and how easily he can humble them and make them submit to his government. May we find it so to our benefit in this life, lest we find it to our ruin in the next.

"Thy throne, O God, is for ever and ever. The sceptre of thy kingdom is a right sceptre. Thou lovest righteousness and hatest wickedness; therefore God, thy God, hath anointed thee with the oil of gladness above thy fellows." Here is a man, you see, exalted above his fellow-men in heavenly power and glory, as the reward of his obedience and sufferings. It is astonishing that any person who pretends to believe the Scriptures, and sees these views of Christ, should deny his person to be what those very Scriptures set it forth to be. He is, brethren, both God and man, as much and as properly one as the other. The evidence is as clear for one as the other. It is in this conjunction that his glorious person should be viewed, and oh! that we knew how to improve the view aright, to humble, to comfort, to sanctify us.

"All thy garments smell of myrrh, aloes, and cassia out of the ivory palaces whereby they have made thee glad." The beauty of perfect holiness, and the sweet odour of sanctity in the person and character of Jesus Christ, are thus described, according to the Eastern taste. For these moral excellencies he is beloved by all minds that are renewed to delight in that which is good, and for these, as well as for his loving-kindness to them, the upright love him. This is an essential circumstance in the experience of every real christian, even of "all them that love the Lord Jesus Christ in sincerity." As it is natural for the worst and most selfish men to love those that love them, a hypocrite may feel a grateful sense of his obligation to Christ, if he suppose himself an object of his special favour; but to delight in him for his moral beauty is peculiar to a renewed mind. In the Song of Solomon, which enlarges upon the subject of the forty-fifth Psalm, this circumstance is mentioned. " Because of the savour of thy good ointments, thy name is as ointment poured forth, therefore do the virgins love thee."

" Kings' daughters were among thy honourable women."—This predicts the subjection of all nations under the dominion of the Messiah, and however unlikely it may seem at present, all the great and the mighty of the earth will, one day, do him service. His dominion shall be from sea to sea, even to the uttermost part of the globe.

" Upon thy right hand did stand the Queen in gold of Ophir." Such is the royal dress, such will be the exalted dignity of all them " that are Christ's at his coming." Mean as the appearance of his people may be upon earth, and contemptible as they seem at present among the splendid characters and men of renown, they will shine "in gold of Ophir," as the sun in the kingdom of God, when " the marriage of the Lamb is come, and his wife hath made herself ready*." To them who are thus united unto Christ by faith and love, make Him

* Rev. xix. 7.

all their salvation and all their desire, cleave to him with purpose of heart, and depend upon him for every blessing—to them the important advice in the text is addressed, which I shall, in a subsequent part of this discourse, distinctly consider.

"And the daughter of Tyre shall be there with a gift; even the rich among the people shall entreat thy favour." This describes the honour which, sooner or later, shall be put upon the Church, by the proud and the wealthy, by whom she has been despised.

"The King's daughter is all glorious within; her clothing is of wrought gold."—Her beauty, like that of her heavenly Bridegroom, is not of outward show. There is no comeliness in either that strikes the carnal mind. The beauty of holiness which she derives from him is inward. Her moral excellence is deep and solid, and the real splendor of her character shall one day shine forth in the sight of an assembled universe. Let all true christians think of this, and rejoice in the hope set before them.

"She shall be brought unto the King in raiment of needle work: the virgins her companions that follow her shall be brought unto thee: With gladness and rejoicing shall they be brought. They shall enter into the King's Palace." No doubt here is a literal description of Eastern magnificence and ceremony in marriage, and Solomon's marriage with Pharaoh's daughter seems really to be the type and shadow in which the first sense of these things is to be understood. But they have mean thoughts of Scripture who can stop there. Nor will Scripture testimony allow us so to do. Oh! how happy will the Church find herself, when in heaven all these things shall be fulfilled. But the earnest of them is even here to be attained.

"Instead of thy Fathers shall be thy children, whom thou mayest make princes in all the earth." Every believer gives up something for Christ. Indeed we must gladly endure to suffer the loss of all things to win him. But the favour and peace of God, and the eternal enjoyment of Christ, is surely infinitely more valuable than these earthly gratifications which we give up for him. In comparison of him, these deserve not to be named.

"I will make thy name to be remembered in all generations; therefore shall the people praise thee for ever and ever." Christ is honoured by means of this delightful Psalm, and will be so for ever by those who know him.

And now that we have seen the spirit and plan of the Psalm, in setting forth the union of Christ and his Church, I shall in the sequel dwell upon the advice given to every member of the Church in the text. It will naturally divide itself into three parts.—1. "Hearken, O daughter, and consider, and incline thine ear; he is thy Lord, and worship thou him." 2. "Forget also thine own people and thy father's house." 3. The blessing attending this advice when closely followed. "So shall the King greatly desire thy beauty."

1. "Hearken, O daughter, and consider, and incline thine ear; for he is thy Lord, and worship thou him." The words are addressed to all those who have fled for refuge to Christ Jesus, and who are making him all their salvation and all their desire. Being convinced that they are "wretched,

and miserable, and poor, and blind, and naked," they have a longing, a passionate desire after acquaintance with him as their true supreme good, and the only worthy and suitable object of their dependence and affections. Some of them may be but babes in Christ, others young men, others fathers. Some may proceed in the divine life, with comfort and serenity, others may be called to conflict with much darkness and temptation. But they have all one hope and one desire, and in their judgment, and from the bottom of their heart, Christ is the happiness they delight in. They have a taste formed for him. Offer them whatever else you please, riches, honours, pleasures, you tempt them in vain to sell their portion in Him; these things satisfy not, are not their element, they would not, if they might, have their happiness to consist in any thing else but Christ.

All these, then, are united, (or to speak agreeably to the ideas of the Psalmist) are married to Christ, for nothing else is requisite to constitute this holy union, but mutual consent. On Christ's side there is no doubt: "He that cometh to me, I will in no wise cast out." The union, therefore, is real and substantial. But never was an union of such infinite disparity entered into. On one side, all is poverty, misery, baseness, and unworthiness. On the other side all is wealth, felicity, dignity, and every possible perfection. "He became," (as Irenæus, a very ancient christian writer, says) "he became what we are, to make us what he is." The spouse of Christ has nothing to bring him but rags, and debt, and distress. Yet in his incomparable condescension and goodness he invests her with the gift of his righteousness and heavenly kingdom, paying her debts, and lifting her up from the dunghill to the throne of princes.

Such are the general outlines of the circumstances of this union, which I would wish you to think of and receive, with that sober reverence and decency of consideration which becomes so sacred a subject. And now the persons being pointed out who are concerned in this exhortation, hear, christians, hear his voice: He calls on you to hearken, to consider, to incline your ears; for he is your Lord, and worship ye him. Is it possible for you to conceive any union in the world, in which you could have the advantage on your side to so great degree? Consider what you are by nature, a slave of sin and defilement, and an heir of eternal torments: (for so all men naturally are, and those who have not learnt this have learnt nothing to the purpose) and here is the only-begotten Son of God your bridegroom. You are members of his body, of his flesh, and of his bones. Or to suit a little the spirit of doubting, too common with very sincere christians, you either are in that happy state, or may by consenting come into it at this moment. What joy, what love, what peace, what humble thoughts of self, what elevated views of God, does this consideration inspire! That your "Maker should be your husband!" That he should bleed on a cross for you! That he should call you to the nearest bonds of friendship and familiarity; to a heavenly eternal kingdom! Oh, what things are these! Meditate on them often and daily. The Scriptures, those delightful fields of instruction appointed for you to range in, abound so much in discoveries of your heavenly friend, describe so particularly and distinctly his character and excellencies, and the great things he has done for you, and the offices he sustains for you as KING, PRIEST, PROPHET, HUSBAND, BROTHER, SHEPHERD, SURETY, that by diligent reading, with prayer, you will find him again and again, and he will be pleasant to your souls. For you should by no means content yourselves with having gained once for all some clear ideas of the excellencies of Christ, and the blessings of redemption. You must meditate on them, that they may interest your affections. You must indeed be looking to yourselves, in order to see matter of humiliation; but you must not look *only* at self, nor too long at one time, nor in a way merely to distress you, and cause despondence. You must also look at HIM who gives "the garment of praise for the spirit of heaviness, and the oil of joy for mourning." Real intercourse with Christ is necessary to be kept up in your consciences continually. His blood which cleanseth from all sin must be applied constantly by faith to keep out guilt, and to maintain friendship with your God.

And that you who know these things, as well as those who do not, may see the excellent consequences resulting from Christian principles practically applied, consider what effects must result from this union. Here is a man conscious of Christ living in him, by his Spirit, renewing his nature, forgiving his sins, opening to him the kingdom of heaven, and bringing him into a state of friendship with himself and his Father, and making him to partake of his Spirit. What a serenity and peace of mind must this produce! And when he reflects on himself also, as most unworthy, what gratitude, what thankfulness, what love! How can he ever feel himself obstinately unwilling to forgive, to whom so much has been forgiven? And with what dignity of sentiment must he rise in his affections above the world and its most tempting delights! How must he pity those who place happiness in courting the creature, when he finds it substantially existing in the friendship of the Creator! This man, it is plain, is and must be the only man in the world for real virtue. Others may talk of it; he only will practise it indeed.

Let me recommend, then, to my audience in general, the study of Christ. May they meditate on the Scripture account of him, and of all his characters and doings. There never appeared any thing like him on earth. It was not possible such a view of things as his religion gives, could ever have been forged by man. Once understand it aright; what it is; and you will be sure of its divinity. Seek to be acquainted with him, till you have in your own soul the real union that has been described.

Let those who have tasted of his grace be faithful to their engagements. " He is your Lord, worship ye him." Give up yourselves to him simply; renew the surrender of yourselves to him from time to time. We are apt to forget him and think little of him. You are called, you see, in the text, to incline your ear: you must endeavour to do this continually; even though you walk in darkness and heaviness. Hear him speak to you in the word, and speak to him again by prayer. You will find that though you may have caused his absence from yourself by sin, he will visit you again. Do not be tempted to think he will not regard your prayers, because they are so poor and imperfect. His heart is gracious, only go on seeking after him.

2. " Forget also thine own people and thy father's house." This was the original duty of husbands and wives, from the beginning of the world. " Therefore," says Moses, " shall a man leave his father and mother, and shall cleave unto his wife, and they shall be one flesh." The allusion is obvious enough; and serious Christians who mean to walk with God in the gospel of his Son, know how to draw honey from those things, whence profane men collect poison. If you would have much converse with Christ, clear discoveries of his infinite goodness and tenderness, and much delightful communion with him, you must forget other things to which you naturally cleave. You cannot serve God and mammon. It was a gross mistake among the ancients to retire from society altogether, and live unprofitable lives in hermitages. Business must be done, and the affairs of human life must be carried on. But who does not see that the world is continually claiming and engrossing a far greater part of our time and thoughts than it is entitled to. If you would indeed enjoy Christ, let him reign in you without a rival. Reckon it as certain, that whatever practice prevents you from enjoying intercourse with him in your soul, is an idol, and must be given up. The love of the world is the grand cause that many who yet have a root of godliness in them, walk so heavily, move

so faintly, know so little of Christ, and bring forth so little fruit. Often then be recollecting yourselves, and saying, " I must forget these worldly things; my spiritual husband claims my heart, and my thoughts and wishes ought to go out after him." If they wander, and you find it difficult to fix them, call them back again and again, till he turn again and revive you, and cause you to rejoice in him. When he makes his goodness to pass before you, you cannot but love him in return, and feel that though you love as you ought parents, children, country, and all other relatives, yet that you love Christ supremely, and would not hesitate one moment when called to it, to part with every thing for him.

Many things must be forgotten or neglected, as it were, by him who means to enjoy the love of Christ. He stands knocking, indeed, at the door of our hearts; but we cannot hear his voice, while we are hearkening to a thousand deceivers. Self is one of these. Reckon it for certain, that if you take much pains in religion, in any way whatever, and yet Christ is not your capital object and the great mover of your heart; if his priesthood, atonement, and intercession are not kept vigorously in sight, then that religion is useless, or worse than useless, be it ever so pompously recommended by any fashionable names in the world. " Whatsoever ye do in word or deed, do all in the name of Jesus." He must be looked to. Through him what you do is accepted. Your business with God must be carried on through his mediation, every moment. This is the religion of a sinner. The religion of

Adam before he sinned might be different. But if you attempt any thing in religion without Christ, you affront both him and his Father exceedingly, and a day is coming that will show you all such religion to be only spiritual fornication.

3. " So shall the king greatly desire thy beauty." So gracious is Christ, that when once he sees you walking close with him and forgetting other things, he will not be shy of you; he will show you his love. You shall have sweet communion with him. You view yourselves indeed as loathsome and vile, and can scarcely conceive how he should deem you beautiful, but when most humbled you are most lovely in his eyes. What he requires in his people is a willing mind, and a sincere love to his person and cause. When he sees this, every duty and service will be accepted. A soul that cleaves to him for righteousness and strength cannot be finally unhappy. For grace, mercy, and peace, is upon all them that love the Lord Jesus Christ in sincerity.

SERMON XXX.

CONFIDENCE IN PRAYER.

1 John, v. 14, 15.

And this is the confidence that we have in him, That, if we ask any thing according to his will, he heareth us: And if we know that he hear us, whatsoever we ask, we know that we have the petitions, that we desired of him.

BEFORE I proceed to state the subject of these verses, I would call your attention to what has been laid down in the foregoing part of this chapter. The Apostle began with asserting, that " whosoever believeth that Jesus is the Christ, is born of God." Whence we may discover something of the nature of divine faith wrought by the Holy Ghost in the heart, which gives a powerful apprehension of Jesus Christ, and disposes the soul to trust to him indeed, and makes man a new creature.

How entirely different is this from that mere human, or historical faith, with which the generality of Christians content themselves to the ruin of their souls; a faith in which the Holy Ghost has no share; which never brings a man to Christ at all; and which leaves its professor under the power of Satan, the world, and his own evil nature. According to the Apostle, the real believer overcomes the world, and is no more enslaved by its vices and customs. If not a single person on earth but himself were disposed to serve God, there is in him a divine spring which would not suffer him to follow a multitude to do evil. With Noah, he would walk with God, while the earth was corrupt all around him, and the nature of that obedience which his faith, which worketh by love, leads him to, makes the divine precepts not grievous, but most pleasant to his soul, and he rests in God through Christ as his centre of bliss, and has the earnests of heaven in his soul, while yet upon earth.

But the principle, or instrument by which these mighty effects are wrought, deserves to be well explained, strongly guarded, and solidly supported. And in no part of the word of God, perhaps, is this more clearly and plainly done than from the 6th to the 14th verse of this chapter. That a guilty, corrupt soul, like that of man, may be encouraged to trust in Christ indeed, may venture to call him his own, and may know that he has eternal life through his name, oh, what a freedom and boldness is this! But in order to this he had need to have a good foundation for his confidence: Nor is it a little matter that can embolden a soul that is truly awakened thus to trust in Jesus Christ. Thoughtless people, who feel not what sin is, and who care not for God and his glory, find it easy enough to believe in their way. They can presume on the mercy of God, and even make so free with him as to sin the more, because he is merciful. It is not so with humble souls, who feel their wretchedness and pollution. Ah! how shall they dare to receive pardon and salvation as a free gift by Jesus Christ!

How can they acquire so much confidence as to do this, who know they deserve only the wrath of God, and who feel themselves tied and bound with the chain of their sins! To encourage them, however, we have no less than six evidences produced by the Apostle, that God really does give them eternal life in his son Jesus, so that they may freely receive it, and make it their own by receiving it. Three of these evidences are in heaven, the " Father, the Word, and the Holy Ghost," the three persons of the blessed Trinity, who unite in their testimony to the truth of this blessed proposition. The other three witnesses are with us on earth, "the Spirit, the water, and the blood, which, in my judgment, mean the written word of God, and the two Sacraments, that of baptism and the Lord's supper. This seems to me to be the only clear and solid interpretation of the passage that I know of. And does not the Spirit in the Word testify all over to us concerning Jesus Christ, and eternal life, as a free gift to us in him? And what is the meaning of baptism and the Lord's supper? Do not they both in emblem and in signification convey eternal life to us by Jesus Christ. We have only to answer their meaning by heartily receiving what they speak to us, and we have eternal life.

Thus St. John brings the matter on the ground of these six witnesses to a simple issue. If we can believe the testimony of a man, much more may we believe that of God himself, and we cannot affront him more than by making him a liar and disputing his veracity. Here is then the proposal. God in his infinite goodness offers to you, to me, to all of us, eternal life by Jesus. Is he worthy of being beloved, or is he not? If he is, there is an end of all dispute.

God *gives* this eternal life; he does not sell it for our works or deservings. Indeed we must know, that we are dead in sin, and have and can have no good works, or it will be impossible for us so much as to understand aright the proposition before us. If eternal life were suspended on our works, we might well pause all our lives long, before we claim this prize as our own. For who can be sure that he has performed what is sufficient? But it is our mercy in Jesus. O! that we understood it aright, and thankfully received this unspeakable gift!—Awakened and distressed soul! come then to God by Christ, and reject not his testimony. For "these things are written, that ye may know that ye have eternal life, and that ye may believe on the name of the Son of God."

In this way a foundation is laid for peace of conscience and a truly holy life. And this is that doctrine of justification by faith in Jesus only, which it is our wisdom and duty to understand and receive, as we value our souls, however all the powers of hell may set themselves against it, backed by human pride. For the glory of Christ is in it, and without it his character of Saviour is but a name.

I would now proceed to explain the meaning of these verses which I have chosen for my text, and then apply them. "This is the confidence that we have in him." *We*, that is, we *believers*; we who come to God by Christ, renouncing our own righteousness; we who prize Jesus indeed, and have been made willing, by the blessed God, to accept that eternal life which he bestows on us, though we know in ourselves that we are guilty, undone sinners. But being made the children of God, and new creatures in Christ, we have a confidence in God as our dear Father, that he will treat us as his children. We are subject indeed to many temptations and afflictions in this life; oft are we ready to faint; and it is with extreme difficulty, indeed, that we can keep up any thing of that repentance toward God, that faith toward our Lord Jesus Christ, and that divine love, by which we walk in the way to heaven. We know our rest is not here, but above. Support, however, and comfort we may expect from him here. "Call upon me in the time of trouble, so will I hear thee, and thou shalt praise me."

This is the appointed way of relief. We must ask of him as a child does of his father, and ask in confidence, for this is the well-grounded "confidence we have in him, that if we ask any thing according to his will, he heareth us; and if we know that he heareth us, whatsoever we ask we know that we have the petitions we desired of him." What encouragement for believers to pray! They are here assured that their Father will hear and grant their requests. In this confidence how safely may they rest in the midst of all trials, waiting till he deliver them! And by proof they find, again and again, that he does deliver them, as it is written, "so will I hear thee, and thou shalt praise me." Hence they are led to thank and praise him, and by experience are encouraged to repeat their supplications as he tries them with fresh crosses;

crosses meant for their good. This is to have real intercourse with God, as a Father, while they are on earth. This adds fervor to their prayer and their religion, and makes their expectation of eternal felicity stronger and stronger. Holding fast their confidence in Christ, they go on in the spirit of prayer, more and more, till they arrive at heaven. Blessed state! Can that man who lives in this way with God be miserable? See what a blessed thing it is to live a christian life. But are there no temptations? May a christian ask whatever he pleases, and meet with no denial? A limitation there is which must be attended to; and it is the only thing remaining now to complete the exposition of the text.

"If we ask any thing according to his will." Let the prayers of believers be regulated by this, and they have an undoubted warrant to expect that they shall be answered, whatsoever they ask. In this point St. Paul's question conveys a clear case of instruction, " how shall they call on him in whom they have not believed," and also the words of our Lord, " all things whatsoever ye ask in prayer, believing, ye shall receive them." It is doubtless implied here, that we ask in faith, nothing wavering; that when we set ourselves to petition the Lord in his Son's name, we make no doubt in our minds but that he will bestow on us the blessings we ask. This is a very necessary point in all true praying.

It must be observed further, that by asking, is not, cannot be meant merely uttering requests with our lips; a man may do that (I fear many do it,) while his heart breathes not in the least after God, nay while he is quite engaged in other thoughts and desires all the time. The asking must be sincere and earnest, for God is a spirit, and requires to be worshipped in spirit and in truth. He values not the service of the lip and knee while the heart is far from him.

But this asking must not only be from the heart, but must be according to the will of God. We must not expect that he will grant us things disagreeable to his own holy will, with whatever earnestness we may desire them. And if we wish to know what is agreeable to his will, and what is not, the Scriptures give us very sufficient instruction herein. But they instruct not those who take no pains in them; who may have a Bible in their houses for years, and scarce ever dip into it with any serious desire to obtain light from thence. How should they know the mind and will of God, who never consult his statutes? What sort of christians can they be, who let weeks, and months, and years roll over their heads, without ever seriously consulting the word of God? Certain it is, that as the word of God is the food of the soul, their souls must be starving in sin, and if they go on thus regardless of his word, (I wish them well to weigh it for their good) their souls will starve in misery for ever.

But, believers, you see, are called on to study the word of God, and to let their meditation be in it by night and by day. From thence they are to learn what to pray for, and how to regulate their prayers. In general, they will learn from thence, that pardon of sin, peace of conscience, the comfort of the Holy Ghost, and whatever is needful for their growth in all real holiness of heart and life, as well as victory over sin and temptation, are, all, things agreeable to the divine will. These may and should be prayed for confidently. We must not, indeed, prescribe to the Lord the way and manner of his granting our requests, nor the time, nor any of the circumstances; nor must we say what degrees of grace and comfort he shall bestow upon us. But the *substance* of the blessings themselves we may and ought to ask positively, in the name of Jesus, and they shall be given.

In asking for temporal things, there is still greater room for limitation and reserve. For the Lord has not promised much of them to his people. "Seek ye first the kingdom of God and his righteousness, and all these things shall be added unto you." Sufficient food and raiment for the body are promised, indeed, in the Sermon on the Mount, and it is therefore agreeable to the will of God that we should pray for them, but no more. Temporal things we should pray for with that modest reserve, upon our minds, expressed in our church service, "as may be most expedient for us;" but earnestly we should pray, in the same collect, that HE would grant us in this world knowledge of his truth, and in the world to come life everlasting. Thus if we pray in faith, and in good earnest, and for things agreeable to the divine will, we have seen how the Lord has graciously been pleased to bind himself, that whatsoever we ask, we shall have the petitions that we desire of him.

It now only remains that this most weighty subject be applied to our consciences. O! christian souls, who seek the Lord, see what great privileges are before you! Look steadily to the connection of things laid down in this chapter. You have no bar to your happiness, but what you choose to make to yourselves. You are assured, over and over, in this chapter, that eternal life is given you in Jesus Christ. Six witnesses, all indisputably strong, evince it. You are encouraged to rest on the divine veracity, and you are certain not to be disappointed. Oh! how could the Lord stoop lower, to do away our doubts and fears, and to invite our confidence in his grace. " For these things were written, that ye might know that ye have eternal life."

Yet though this inestimable blessing be thus most graciously ensured to us, you are, in the course of your pilgrimage, liable to many evils and miseries, sore temptations and afflictions, both of an inward and outward nature. How shall you be carried comfortably and safely through them all? " He that spared not his own Son, but delivered him up for us all, how shall he not with him also freely give us all things?" This is a very comfortable and solid argument. But besides this, you have express promises in the text, and in many other parts of Scripture, of help in every time of need, if you ask for it. Consider how firm and sure these promises are, and make use of them by prayer. Trust in your God and Father in every trial, for HE is your God and Father, who by his own covenant in Jesus, to which you have fled for refuge, stands engaged to hear your prayers. He would have you know, that you " have the petitions you desired of him." A tradesman cannot surely be much distressed, who knows, whenever he shall have an urgent call for money, that he has a friend who will supply his need. This is your very case. It is your wisdom and your duty to cultivate this gracious intercourse with heaven, thus bountifully afforded to you. Be much in prayer continually, and let every disagreeable thing you meet with, call forth your dependance on the divine promises. Thus shall you know for yourselves, that the Lord is faithful to his word, and the repeated experience of it will strengthen your faith. This must, indeed, originally be grounded on the word alone, but yet experience of success will strengthen it. While you go on in this way, how light will crosses sit on you! how pleasant will wisdom's ways be made to your souls! and how will you be stirred up to thanksgiving and praise to your God. This is to live like a christian; a life of prayer and of praise. And your conduct and walk will adorn the gospel, when your heart and conscience are thus regulated by christian principles. But watch and pray, keep up the precious intercourse with your God, and grieve not his Spirit. Always retain exalted and honourable thoughts of your God. For sure there is " none like the God of Jeshurun, who rideth on the heaven for your help, and in his excellency on the sky. The eternal God is your refuge, and underneath are the everlasting arms. Happy, indeed art thou, O Israel, a people saved by the Lord, who is the shield of your help, and the sword of your excellency*." These grand expressions of Moses, a little before his death, have their *glory*, when applied to Israel of old, just going to march, in the fullness of Jehovah's protection, to take possession of the earthly Canaan. But to those who are walking to

† Deut. xxxiii. 26—29.

heaven, in the strength of God, they " abound in glory."

Certainly the sun shines not on any object, in the world, so valuable, so precious, and on the whole so happy, as a true believer in Christ. He lives in heaven while yet on earth. Trouble cannot seize him, but it gives him an opportunity of getting aid from his God, and receiving some fresh token of his loving-kindness. He has a God to go to, in all distresses. The rest of the world tread on the water. Their comforts are as unstable as a shadow. But *he* treads on solid ground. He knows whom he has believed. Others may speculate on religion at a distance. He feels it. He has tasted that the Lord is gracious, and is sure of that which fills his heart with divine love, makes him a new creature, opens his eyes to see the beauty of God, ravishes his soul with the prospect of eternal felicity, and disposes him, day by day, to live above the world, and cultivate every disposition of meekness, patience, charity, and whatever may render him more and more like his Saviour.

Ye are not far from this blessed state, who feel yourselves ruined by sin, and would gladly be saved by Christ, and made like unto him. Come near to him. Stand not aloof. He is no such dreadful object, that poor souls, who feel their own wretchedness, and how suitable he is to them, should keep at a distance from him. He is more merciful and compassionate than you can conceive, or surely he had not left the unspeakable bliss of heaven to undergo for you on earth and on the cross what he did. Come to him, and he will, in due time, comfort and bless you.

I have only a word to say to those whose hearts are set on this world altogether. What can it do for you? You seek above all things the favour of men, of the great and the rich; what can they do for you? Even in life you must feel many evils which they can never redress, and in death they will be sure, one and all, to forsake you. You that are yet young and in good health and spirits, fancy that pleasures and amusements will do much for you. Assure yourselves they are all vanity and vexation of spirit. A little time and experience will make you feel the emptiness of these things. The love of money, by which some of you are governed, is, perhaps, the meanest of all passions. Had you the riches of both the Indies, could they avert the stroke of death, or the anger of God for sin? No. Turn your eyes to HIM who alone can do it. Behold the views laid open in this rich chapter of St. John. See the precious offers of eternal life made to your souls, through Jesus. Place all expectation of bliss on this foundation.

But begin, here, to seek your comfort in Christ's true religion, if ever you expect it hereafter. Heaven and hell are both begun upon earth. Our present life is a preparation either for a happy or a miserable eternity. Our ruling taste and character here is fitting us for the society of the blessed in heaven, or of the miserable in hell. "Whatsoever a man soweth, that shall he also reap. He that soweth unto the flesh, shall of the flesh reap corruption; and he that soweth to the Spirit, shall of the Spirit reap life everlasting."

SERMON XXXI.

IMPORTUNITY IN PRAYER.

Luke, xviii. 1.

And he spake a parable unto them, to this end, that men ought always to pray, and not to faint.

This parable is perfectly similar, in its drift and use, to another recorded in the 11th chapter, where we are given to understand, that importunity will effect what even friendship itself cannot do. "Friend, lend me three loaves.—I say unto you, though he will not rise and give him, because he is his friend, yet because of his importunity, he will rise and give him as many as he needeth." If importunity be so prevalent among men, who are often hard-hearted, how much more with God, who is perfect goodness itself. "If ye being evil know how to give good gifts unto your children, how much more shall your heavenly Father give the Holy Spirit to them that ask him."

Nevertheless, the Lord often delays to answer the warmest and the purest prayers of his dearest servants; and though delaying is not denying, men are apt to think so; and while we measure God's ways by our own, we find ourselves tempted to distrust God, and through distrust to cease waiting upon him; not considering that God waits for the fittest season of answering the requests of those that seek him. Of that season he only must be the judge. But as " hope deferred maketh the heart sick," our Lord gives us another parable, to encourage men to pray always, and not to faint; assuring them of success in the end.

"There was in a city a judge which feared not God, neither regarded man:" a person destitute of any principles of conscience or of honour to move him to the equitable discharge of his office. " And there was a widow in that city, and she came unto him, saying, avenge me of mine adversary. And he would not for a while; but afterward he said within himself, though I fear not God, nor regard man, yet because this widow troubleth me, I will avenge her, lest by her continual coming she weary me." Thus the motives by which profane and wicked men are often influenced to do the thing that is right, are set forth. These motives are not fear of God, not sense of justice, not even regard to character, but desire to avoid trouble, to rid themselves of importunity. Now let us attend to our Lord's application. " And the Lord said, hear what the unjust judge saith, and shall not God avenge his own elect, which cry day and night unto him, though he bear long with them? I tell you, that he will avenge them speedily. Nevertheless, when the Son of man cometh, shall he find faith on the earth?" God's own elect, his dear servants whom he loves with fatherly love, and who are related to him by ties of the nearest kind, will surely be more acceptable to God, and their prayers in all distress and trouble more likely to dispose their heavenly Father to answer and relieve, than the cries of the importunate widow were to dispose the judge, who had no relation to her, no sympathy with her; especially when it is considered that the judge was hard-hearted and unjust, and that God Almighty is the source of all goodness and equity.

What encouragement is this for persevering, ardent prayer! How unworthy of God is it for his people in distress to distrust him, because he does not answer them immediately! If it was for their good, he would; his love being no less to them, notwithstanding all their sufferings. Strange, indeed, if importunity of address will not in the end prevail in the sight of God, as plainly as it will with an unjust judge. Besides, this importunate prayer is needful for us in the way of means, though not needful to God at all. " For your heavenly Father knoweth what you have need of, before you ask him."—Doubtless " he will avenge them speedily." Our natural impatience may tempt us to think he is slow in answering, yet all time, in God's account, is short, compared with the happy eternity reserved for those who love him.

" Nevertheless, when the Son of man cometh, shall he find faith on the earth?" Whether this be understood of God's dealings with the Jews in particular, or with the world at large, it is equally true. I shall not undertake to determine of which it was originally spoken; nor is it, perhaps, of much importance; because God's dealings with the Jews are quite analogous to his dealing with the world at large. Whatever happened to them has happened in type, and the divine character and dispensations, as they will affect all the world, may be seen in the Jewish History throughout. If we understand this last verse of the parable with reference to the Jews, we are informed, that God would speedily avenge his people, his elect, the real christians, of their persecuting enemies the Jews. And remarkable it is, that about forty years after our Saviour's passion, Jerusalem was taken by the Romans, amidst all the horrors of war and famine, while the christians all made their escape from the city, according to the warning which our Lord had given them to flee, when they should see Jerusalem encompassed with armies. When the Lord came to destroy it, he found few indeed believing in him of that nation, in consequence, few praying, few waiting ardently and patiently for him.

It would make a man's heart bleed to think of the dreadful sufferings of the Jews in that siege, as they are recorded by their own historian Josephus. And when we see that nothing happened but what was foretold by our Lord in most exact circumstances, here is indeed a strong proof of his divine mission, and the truth of the Scripture. At the same time we see men take too much upon them, when they undertake to say, that God will not be angry with men for disbelieving the Gospel. It is extreme arrogance, and absurd folly for men to think themselves fit judges of what is fit for God to do. If Christ our Saviour and our God was indeed manifest in human flesh, and if we have proofs upon proofs that God would have us to receive him in that character, there is no saying how infinitely tremendous the consequences of rejecting him may be. It is certainly much safer to argue from matters of fact than from self-conceited conjectures of our own. God has told us already, in the case of the terrible sufferings of the Jews from that time to this day, that to reject Christ, as they did, is infinitely provoking to him. Let men who think it of small consequence whether they receive Christ or not, feel the force of matters of fact at least, and let the sight of vagabond Jews teach them that God's word is true; that not a threat has been denounced but has been accomplished; that those who despise his Son, he will treat as despising himself.

If we understand the last verse of God's dealing with the world at large, we find, indeed, that but a few at the end of the world, when Christ shall come to judgment, will be found believing on him unto life eternal, and by consequence looking for him with delight. To the generality he will come unawares, as the flood did in the days of Noah, while they are employed only in the cares and pleasures of life. His own loving people, though few, shall then be honoured and owned for ever as his; and their enemies and his shall be destroyed with everlasting destruction.

This is the parable. Methinks the view it gives us of God, and the character of his government, is sublime, comfortable, and instructive to all that fear him, and should be terrible to men (if they can be terrified) who live without the fear of him, and expect not to feel that he will punish them at length for all their sins. The present times resemble the state of the world at the second coming of Christ, as it may be well inferred from this parable. Mankind are evidently in a fallen state. The world we live in is evil, and the wrath of a holy God against it is as apparent as the iniquity and contempt of God which is spread through the earth.—Nevertheless, some souls there are, who love God; who mourn over the iniquity of their fellow creatures; who are grieved to see their folly and pride; and who themselves being but partly recovered as yet from their moral evils, groan, being burdened with their own body of sin. They are also vexed, insulted and despised by the wicked world, and evil spirits who rule it for the present.

These persons become reconciled to God, and have attained what they have attained, entirely through a Mediator and Surety, Christ Jesus, God manifest in the flesh, through whom alone all who are restored to God can be restored, and by whom we are all invited to come to God, that we perish not. The sense of evil in themselves and others makes them cry to God day and night, and pray without ceasing; not always in words, but with habitual intention of heart. It is the peculiar character of God's elect to desire perfect restoration in soul and body, to the fellowship and enjoyment of God, with deliverance from all the evils of this present evil world. The little real happiness that is on earth is confined to them; for the wicked are all miserable, and must be so, unless they will be persuaded to receive this Saviour.

Now God's people are apt to be impatient. They want their perfect rest and happiness here, and it must not be. Jesus has bought it for them in another life; and they must wait till he come again and visit this earth. He will then deliver them from all their enemies, drive away the wicked into everlasting punishment, and take them up to his everlasting kingdom, to enjoy it with him and his Father. God is bringing about this grand, final event from day to day; but it is his character to proceed by slow degrees. Men want to have every thing done at once; a sign of their weakness. The real people of God must learn from him that strength of mind, which will make them bear long with his dealings. They may be certain that the time will come, though God suffer them to endure much, and all for their good, till it arrives. They may see that this slow and patient way is characteristic of the blessed God. In the revolution of the seasons, in the growth of plants, in all the kingdom of nature, it is observable. Still the effects, though slow, are sure, and so they will be in the kingdom of grace. If wicked men, to the end, continue careless of God, making free with his goodness, and never heartily returning to him by that only way of faith in Christ in which his immense goodness and mercy will be shown, they will find that vengeance without remedy, and judgment without mercy, will overtake them at last.

In the mean time, let those who love God, learn to bear and wait. After learning to believe in Christ and to love him, there is nothing, perhaps, they need to learn more. They have God's free leave to expect the eternal life, one day to be revealed to their unspeakable joy, which they now look for as given them in his Son. But while they are here they must pray without ceasing, and not faint under the darkest dispensations of God. God has many lessons for them to learn, much for them to do, for his glory and their good. They have many corruptions to be purged; and a thousand things which they meet with they must expect not to see fully explained in this life. They have far greater reason. to expect that God will hear their prayers, give them enduring strength, carry them through every trouble, and at last bring them safe home, than the widow had to expect any thing from the unjust judge. Much will importunate prayer avail with God. Prayer is the mean of constant support and deliverance, and all blessings are received this way. Let them not faint, but expect to suffer much, looking to the next world for happiness, and checking their continual aptitude, in weak impatience, to expect it in this. Let them hold fast confidence in God through their Saviour's merits, and the joyful view of his final appearing. Let them keep on praying now, watching, standing fast in the faith, quitting themselves like men, and being strong.

I believe I have given in words (oh! God of Israel, give us it in heart and spirit) the true christian temper, whence the spirit of patient constant prayer is to be drawn; and if I mistake not, here is matter of instruction in duty, and of powerful comfort in spirit held forth to God's believing people. Here is, also, terror and confusion indeed to his enemies; nothing but woe is by them to be expected. In this fearless age, I wish they may learn to fear God and an hereafter, while it is not too late: and may good be done by God this day both to the righteous and the wicked.—I have set forth the general use of the parable; but it may not to be amiss to branch it out into a few distinct heads.

1. There is great room for encouragement to go on praying, and to expect a happy issue out of all troubles to the people of God; because the Lord

calls them his own elect. "Shall not God avenge his own elect?" The relation between God and them is more intimate than any other whatever. That between the head and its members, the vine and its branches, the husband and the wife, are Scripture-comparisons of the matter. But the relation between Christ and his elect, that is, real believers and godly men, is nearer than all this; for " he that is joined to the Lord is one spirit," and the " love of Christ passeth knowledge." To perceive, then, aright the force of this, suppose a husband was to see his beloved wife oppressed and insulted, how would he feel! how ready would he be to defend and deliver her! The Lord Jesus regards thus, but with far greater tenderness, and unmixed with any malicious or bad motives, (for the revenge spoken of in the parable is only in condescension to human modes of speech) the Lord Jesus, I say, regards thus his poor suffering members here on earth with the keenest compassion. " In all their affliction he is afflicted." " Thy Maker is thine husband*, the Lord of Hosts is his name." " The Lord hath called thee as a woman forsaken and grieved in spirit," distressed with cruel enemies like the widow of the parable, "and a wife of youth, when thou wast refused, saith thy God." " For a small moment have I forsaken thee, but with great mercies will I gather thee. In a little wrath I hid my face from thee, for a moment, but with everlasting kindness will I have mercy on thee, saith the Lord thy Redeemer." This is the kindness of the Lord toward his people. How much more certainly will their cries be heard by such a God, than

* Isaiah liv. 5.

the widow's by the judge! His they are already: If He has pardoned all their sins, and has loved them freely, even when "dead in trespasses and sins, much more being reconciled, they shall be saved," by him. "He that spared not his own Son, but delivered him up for us all, how shall he not with him also freely give us all things?" But who are God's elect? A character of them follows, "which cry day and night unto him." It contains too much instruction to be lightly passed by, and therefore this forms a particular head of instruction.

2. Alas! none know but God's elect themselves, what trouble they often undergo. Yet they are the only happy people after all. What occasion, say many, for so much praying? You who despise praying and praying people, give sad marks that as yet at least, whatever may be the case with you before you die, you are not to be ranked among the Lord's elect. You feel no spiritual want and trouble, because you are spiritually dead. You never knew what a broken contrite heart was: Slight views of sin, and therefore slight views of the Saviour, you have always had. Praying is with you a formal thing; as a duty to be discharged, and then all is done. But God's elect know, that though the Lord has shown them mercy, and promised them eternal life, they are still encompassed with such constant troubles, that they are obliged to "cry day and night to God," What troubles? Let every believing soul declare. They are often assaulted with temptations, sore and strong, to unbelief and to despair from the devil, who since they fled from him to Jesus, has gone "about like a roaring lion," raging against them. They have to fight, also, against the

evil world in which they live; and, what is worst of all, against themselves, the flesh. All their strength is in Jesus. They groan and cry to him night and day because of oppression. He hears them, and gives them continued victory, on the whole; but they are obliged to pray still. None but themselves know what conflicts they have in private, by night and by day. They could as soon live naturally without meat and drink, as live spiritually without prayer. It is not to be conceived, as we learn from our Lord in this passage, that God should turn away his ear from their cries, which often ascend in " groanings," saith Paul, " which cannot be uttered." They groan for the peace of God; and after that is obtained, for skill to preserve and maintain it. They groan for the comforts and joys of the Holy Ghost, for divine light and communion, for victory over self, the world, and the devil, the three enemies against which, in baptism, they are engaged to fight, as Christ's faithful soldiers and servants, unto their lives' end.

These are not mere metaphors and comparisons: They have a deep and a strong meaning to those who are in earnest, and God's elect will not rest till they are filled with all the fullness of God, according to the mighty working whereby our Saviour is able to subdue all things to himself. They press forward " to the mark for the prize of their high calling," labouring to attain the happy resurrection of the dead, which St. Paul speaks of as the end he aimed at. And they are assured they shall attain it; for all their enemies shall be subdued: the mystery of God will be finished; and their Lord and they with him shall reign for ever and ever. This is their happiness. They are engaged on that side which will finally prevail, and prayer is their weapon.

Let me exhort you, then, who know the Lord, to "pray without ceasing," and to prove yourselves indeed " God's elect,". by praying night and day. Oh! if there was more of this, there would not be so many languid, drooping christians as there are. On this occasion let me call on masters of families to pray with their housholds morning and night, as well as alone to wrestle with God. Let me call on all God's people to pray earnestly in this trying situation of national affairs*. God only can give wisdom and healing counsels; God only can give humility and peaceable dispositions; God only can heal all our divisions; and may we be cemented indeed to himself and one another by the healing blood of his love.

As to you who know you are so far from crying day and night to God, that you despise or neglect prayer; in whose closets and families God never hears the voice of supplication, you may be as certain by your prayerless character that you are dead in sins, destitute of God's love, and out of Christ, as of any religious truth whatever. Oh! begin now and lament before God your hard, dead state, Surely, since praying has been so much despised, the souls of men in our church have grown worse and worse. We have lost not the *power* only, but even the *form* of Godliness, more and more. Consider ye who despise praying; God is of another mind. He takes notice, to the honour of his servants, whom he calls his elect, that they " cry day and night to him." He does not call this enthusiasm or hypocrisy. There is all reason to believe, from the representation in the parable, that their praying is highly acceptable to him. He encourages them in it. He assures them, by this parable, that not a petition shall be lost. Follow ye their example. Begin to pray, and beg of God to let you know for what you should pray, lest ye perish. You are on praying ground; and if this be the burden of your cry, " Son of David have mercy on me! Lamb of God, that takest away the sin of the world, grant me thy peace," the Lord will hear, and do, and save you. Yet neither you nor any of us know what we should pray for as we ought; but the "Spirit helpeth your infirmities, and maketh intercession for us with groanings which cannot be uttered."

3. "Though he bear long with them." The people of God may have prayed again and again for particular blessings, and yet the Lord grants them not yet. He exercises their faith and patience. Hence their sanctification grows, and hence their eternal happiness also. In particular things, as well as in the whole of his dealings, this is the Lord's way. Therefore, next after establishment in the faith and love of the gospel, to have a contented, resigned, patient frame of soul, should be the great object of the believer's prayer. " Ye have need of patience," says the word of God, and his grace only can give it. The husbandman waiteth for the precious fruit of the earth, and hath long patience for it—be ye also patient; stablish your hearts; for the coming of the Lord draweth nigh*.

4. But to talk of patience without faith, would be to build castles in the air. Our Lord complains, " when the Son of man cometh, shall he find faith

on the earth?" intimating that but few believers will then be found. What is the christian's ground of patience? What is to encourage him to wait patiently in all trials, both with respect to particular difficulties, and the whole of his probation, but this? "Verily there is an end, and thine expectation shall not be cut off." What is the expectation? Life eternal, the fullness of joy, and at God's right-hand pleasures for evermore.

But what right has he, a sinner, to these? The inheritance is of faith, that it might be by grace, and so become sure. God gives it of promise, and not by the works of the law. The christian's forerunner is already entered, who has bought him a seat in heaven, and given him the title free and full, and who bids him be confident that he who began a good work in him will perform it till the day of his appearing. So that in this view patience has a firm foundation. Every believer may say, "my troubles will soon be all over. My Saviour will take me to joy eternal, unspeakable. In my present trials he will be with me, and give me a happy issue out of them all."

5. "I tell you that he will avenge them speedily." Take a short view with me of the end of all things. A day is coming when we expect Jesus Christ to appear in the air, before whose face the heavens and the earth shall flee, and all the works thereof be burnt up. Before him shall be gathered the whole race of men then living, and all the dead. I speak simple facts. Affected ornaments of speech are never, perhaps, more improper than here. Let the greatness of the facts speak for themselves. Among the rest we of this place must appear; some on

who have here believed the testimony of Jesus. Others on the left, when HE shall be "revealed from heaven with his mighty angels, in flaming fire, taking vengeance on them that know not God, and obey not the gospel of our Lord Jesus Christ, who shall be punished with everlasting destruction from the presence of the Lord, and from the glory of his power. When he shall come to be glorified in his saints, and to be admired in all them that believe, in that day."

Those among us who have now believed in Christ, for all their comfort, joy, and salvation, oh! how will they admire him when they see him—Him whom they so long panted after, and on whom as their unseen friend they depended in sore trials. Their joy and triumph, their endless bliss in his smiles, how great it will be, you will not expect that I should say. But what a call is here for God's people, to live above the world, and its cares and pleasures, and press forward for the attainment of the resurrection of the dead. Let not our ambition stop short of this. Oh! let us be more heavenly-minded; more detached from the world, than ever we have been yet.

But why should not the Lord's people be more numerous than they are? Awake, awake ye whom the sleep of sin is carrying to hell: ye who know that the mark of God's elect, " crying day and night," belongs not to you. Awake, then; for there is but a breath between you and perdition. Behold the crucified Saviour. You and he may be one, and he will plead your cause, if you will seek him now above all things. If not, you must meet him as your avenging Judge.

SERMON XXXII.

CHRISTIANS IN DANGER OF LOSING THOSE THINGS WHICH THEY HAVE WROUGHT, AND NOT RECEIVING A FULL REWARD.

John, Epistle 2d, ver. 8.

Look to yourselves, that we lose not those things which we have wrought, but that we receive a full reward.

St. John is exhorting christians to abide in Christ, to adhere to his doctrine, to preserve their fellowship with the Father and the Son, to love one another, to walk in the truth, to beware of seducers, and to see that they be not weary of the commandment of faith and love in Christ Jesus, but to keep constantly what they had been taught from the beginning.

How it may be with others, each must judge for himself; but I find the necessity of pressing on my own heart repeated admonitions, warnings and rebukes, that I be not weary, but patiently persevere in the ways of God. After a length of time we are all apt to faint, to grow languid, to lose christian simplicity. What need have we to feel the force of the exhortation in the text, "Look to yourselves, that we lose not those things which we have wrought, but that we receive a full reward." There is not only danger of losing the means of growing in grace and of making farther advances in the divine life, but, what should greatly alarm us, even of losing the soul itself by losing what has before been gained, if we slacken diligence, and give way to temptations. And this has often been done. Many begin in the spirit and end in the flesh. The Apostle asks the Galatians, "have ye suffered so many things in vain, if it be yet in vain?" And he tells the Corinthians, that they are saved by the gospel which he preached to them, if they keep it in memory, "unless they have believed in vain."

I have chosen, then, a subject very suitable to the state and circumstances of those of you, who for years have attended to the preaching of the gospel, and have known, or seemed to know, something of its power. I would speak after the Apostle John to the aged, or to christians of a long standing.— As it was then, so it is now, many things in a course of time intervene that were little thought of, to stop the growth of christians, and to cause them to decline from the faith and love of the gospel. Therefore there is the more need to "take heed to the things that we have heard, lest at any time we let them slip." And while I am speaking to those who have long known divine truth, may the Lord Jesus himself speak to them; for he can speak to the heart, and with power.

We shall more distinctly conceive the subject, if we consider, 1st, what those things were which we wrought in the beginning of the gospel—2d, wherein lies the danger of losing them—and, 3d, the means to be used in order to preserve them. For though wherever the Lord has begun a good work, he will carry it on to the day of Christ, there are many awakenings and strivings in religion, which come to nothing, and the Lord's own people are preserved by his fear put into their hearts, through which they are kept from departing from him.

1st. Let us consider "what those things were, which we wrought formerly." I shall in few words endeavour to bring them into your recollection. We are apt to forget them; and those who are sinking into a coldness and deadness of spirit, usually entertain only faint conceptions even of those things which once they received with joy, even as life from the dead. When the gospel came to you, brethren, it found you, like other men, dead in sins, and, it may be, very much offended with its plain truths, unwilling to be disturbed in the good opinion which you had of yourselves, and to be brought out of the course of sin and vanity in which you lived. But I speak of what was *really* the case with the sounder part of you who profess the gospel truth. You were awakened and enlightened. You began to repent, to pray, to turn from the vain pleasures you followed, and to feel the necessity of purity of heart. As you were led on, you found your inward corruptions strong and stubborn, and began by degrees to know the total fall and ruin of your nature. When the cause of God's law threatened you with destruction, and your own sinful nature and habits seemed to hold you tied and bound as with a strong chain, was it not pleasant to you to hear the refreshing sound of the gospel of peace? For it is not understood properly, nor felt powerfully, nor embraced thankfully, but by sinners sensible of their wretchedness. Did you, then, receive it as an ordinary and unaffecting message, or did you hear with joy, as worthy of all acceptation, that "Christ Jesus came into the world to save sinners?" And this view of the doctrine of justification by Jesus Christ, free, full, everlasting, and without any conditions of worthiness on your part, you embraced from a necessity that you found of being saved in that way, if ever you were saved at all, from a conviction that you had no good thing in you, and from a pleasure which you found in its suitableness to your own case. It was delightful to you to be humbled, and to see God glorified in his Son Jesus. The ways of sin were made bitter to you, and your pleasures you now sought, not in the world, but in Christ Jesus, and the way of holiness in him. And does not this house in which we are now assembled, and your closet, and many particular spots of ground, put you in mind, that there you have poured out your heart in prayer, felt and bewailed your wretchedness, made your complaint to God, and showed him of your trouble? Having found communion with God, as a reconciled Father through Jesus the Mediator, you were encouraged by small tastes of his love to go on and seek for more. And did not you confess that you now found a peace to which before you were strangers, a pleasantness quite distinct from any thing you ever before were acquainted with?— This increased as you became more acquainted with Jesus, and you found it no deception but a reality, that he manifests himself to his people, and fills them with peace and joy in believing. For as you grew more established in the faith of the gospel, you found more peace and refreshment from him, and dared to trust him more freely with your cares and burdens, and ceased more from useless and hurtful strivings

These are some of the things which you have wrought, which you were taught to connect with the hope of glory. These, though very delightful for the present, were not, however, meant to be transient pleasures, like those of the world, but rather to be encouragements to you, to look to those which are eternal. You expected with joy the second coming of Jesus, and you loved his appearing. When you could meditate on the Son of God, and view him sometimes in one and sometimes in another of his characters, as Shepherd, Husband, Prophet, Priest, and King, did not your heart exult within you, and did you not long to be with him? When you beheld heavenly glory to be real, and yourselves interested therein, through grace, did you not feel and find the world with all its profits and cares to be nothing to you? Look now at the influence of all this on the life and conversation. Were not you then made low in your own eyes, and so humbled for your sins, and earnest for salvation, that you were willing to be despised and to bear your cross for Christ's sake? You thought a little of the world sufficient; and having food and raiment, were content. You had meat to eat that the world knew not of. Your heart being cheered with heavenly pleasure, was brought off from the lust of the world and the pride of life, and being softened and enlarged with divine love, you could now forgive injuries, and love the brethren of Christ as your dearest friends. The stubbornness of nature being subdued, you learnt a measure of resignation to the divine will. Yet these things were not learnt without labour, nor acquired without conflict. Watching, prayer, and close attention were necessary, and Satan's snares, and your own deceitful heart, and the suggestions of an evil world, cost you many a pang. Yet though sometimes foiled, you were enabled to rise again, and to bring forth fruit with patience. So much experimental godliness, as you have thus gained, though but little in quantity, is yet so precious in its nature, and so infinitely valuable, that surely you ought not to lose it for the sake of what you blush to own—the trifles of the world. And yet many do put themselves into great danger of losing this treasure, through various causes which I am now to consider.

2. The causes are various, through the various circumstances, tempers, and situations of different persons; but indwelling sin, aided by the crafts of Satan, operates upon all. Is it not so, brethren, that some of you who once were thriving in God's ways are now grown sickly? That you have lost, in a great measure, your zeal, your love, your desire to promote the cause of Christ in the world, and have not now either that communion with Christ in your souls which you once had, or that desire for it? You are conscious that your relish for godly discourse is abated, and if through the week you are full of the world, it can scarcely be kept out of your hearts and heads on the Lord's day. You have not now that earnest and steady spirit of prayer you once had. Your love of the brethren is grown cold; and the breaches and declensions in the church of Christ afflict you not, as in times past. You are more retired into self, or, at least, carry your affections very little beyond your own family. These are all symptoms of a declining state in religion; where they are habitual. And if you have had them for years, and do not set yourselves earnestly

to cure them, it is a sign they are very strong upon you. The case is worse when you can even vindicate them, or encourage yourselves under them from a notion of God's grace in Christ. You are then far advanced in the evil indeed, and are sunk very dangerously. It was never meant that God's everlasting love to his church, and his care of his elect, should lessen their diligence in striving against sin, but increase it.

Some, indeed, have so completely lost the little religion they once professed, by a plainly lewd, or drunken, or worldly conduct, that there needs no proof of it, but what they give from their own daily conduct. With others, though the decline is not so visible, yet any one may see it who considers what they once were. They themselves, though sensible of it, are not so careful nor so vigorous in their endeavours for a recovery as they ought.

Among the causes of such declensions, the love of ease and a slothful temper is a principal one. A christian life, whatever some may think, requires the labour of the whole man. He that would serve God, indeed, must not think of serving him without labour and pains. If men are not on their guard, they are apt, through the impatience of constant work, to give way to the love of ease, and then sin and Satan get an unhappy advantage over them. Pride and self-conceit lead others astray. They grow too wise for their teachers. They dispute and argue, little sensible of their own ignorance, and often land in some soul-destroying heresy. Unsound views of the doctrines of grace cause them to live presumptuously, and hide from their own eyes both the evil and danger of sin. With others a rugged, bitter, or impatient temper is indulged and encouraged. Such characters are exposed to the suggestions of Satan, who will fill them with prejudices against even the best men, and narrow their minds so completely, that they shall lose the best advantages for growth in grace. With others the child-like simplicity of taste, in divine things, is gradually lost, and their soul contracts a leanness from the want of it. But the most common cause is the love of this present world, which eats out the love of God, and makes dreadful ravages on many souls.

Having thus spoken to your cases, so far as I could, from observation and experience, let me desire your attention to what should be most important to us, the means of curing these evils. And here I must repeat our Saviour's words, "What I say unto you, I say unto all, Watch." Consider, brethren, what great things God has done for you in bringing you to know yourselves and the way of salvation by Jesus Christ, and what an endless, inexhaustible fund of bliss he has prepared for you. If a merchant, who has with much care, diligence, and frugality amassed a considerable fortune, considers what care is requisite, not only to improve it and transmit it to his children after him, but also to preserve it, that he may not by foolish extravagance and imprudent thoughtlessness lose what he has gained, much more should you be zealous to preserve and augment the heavenly treasure already acquired. Shall peace and communion with God, the fruit of so much self-denial and diligence, be lost? Shall Satan triumph over you at last, and say, "there, there, so would I have it?" And shall all this be lost for want of that care and diligence which are necessary to preserve it? Have you any thing else to gain that can be equivalent to so vast a loss? Is real happiness to be attained in any other way? Having the light shining upon your path, and the experience of so much goodness of God already, will you faint by the way, and slacken your pursuit of godliness on account of the difficulties which you have to encounter? In all these difficulties you have the promise of the divine aid, step by step.

Consider these things often, and be stirred up to vigilant attention. Watch over your besetting sins and peculiar temptations. You should know what these things are by experience. Avoid them; guard carefully against those things which you know by experience impede your progress, and pray daily and constantly in secret. Let no business, however urgent and importunate, prevail with you to neglect this. If you do not cultivate an intercourse with God through Christ, in this his appointed way, you must wither, and all your graces must pine and languish. Repent and do the first works. What were those works in which you were diligently employed, when the Lord was with you, and caused his face to shine on you? You were "fervent in spirit, serving the Lord," distributed to the necessities of the saints, opened your heart and hand for the relief of the needy, attended the means of grace carefully, promoted brotherly love among the people of God, mortified your corrupt affections, and forgetting things behind, were always reaching forward to things before.

It was in this way, striving to "give all diligence to make your calling and election sure," that you once laboured. In this way you must go on; and that you may find food and strength to carry you forward, let no day pass without some diligent searching of the word of God. Stir up in your minds the exceeding great and precious promises of the gospel. You will find the need of them, when your mind is dulled by temptations, your conscience oppressed with guilt, and your understandings darkened by the sloth, stupidity, and blindness of corrupted nature. Times will occur when it will seem impossible for you to overcome the difficulties that stand in your way. Your own strength and resolution will fail, and all the resources of natural reason will be found far too weak to fight against sin, the world, and the devil. Labour, again, to obtain from the effectual grace of God an enlivening sense of the precious doctrines of salvation. You still have need to learn, that justification before God is by faith, and not by works; through the righteousness that is in Jesus, and not through your own. This great truth you still have to learn afresh, and as it were for the first time; and that the things which are impossible with men are possible with God. When you are enabled to lay hold on God's covenant through Jesus afresh, and to rejoice in hope of the glory of God, it will be your wisdom to learn, by a diligent perusal of the word of God, and as an antidote against your doubts, and fears, that " the Lord knoweth them that are his," that he has chosen you in Christ, and will be with you even to the end; that he has not left you to stand or fall by your own management, but that you are kept by the power of God through faith unto salvation, to the praise of the glory of his grace. For though you must carefully use all the means I mention, you must not think that your salvation rests on them, nor strive in that spirit, which can only produce bondage, anxiety, and distress to persons sensible, as I suppose you to be, of your own great weakness. You must lay the foundation deeper, and go quite out of yourselves, to rest on the Lord Jesus, and the covenant of grace in him, ordered in all things and sure, and labour to attain a principle of steady and simple faith, grounded only on the divine promises. When you see how freely Jesus is yours, and you are enabled to receive him by faith alone, meditate much on his excellencies, and upon the wonderful union of all that is lovely in him, as a full portion of bliss to rest your souls upon. And, then, when your heart is a little warmed with his love, and sensible of the vast importance of his grace, can you bear to think of quitting your hold on Jesus, of losing him, and that full reward, the " rest which remains to the people of God," when you shall awake up after his likeness, and be satisfied with it? When he shall say to others, "come ye blessed children of my Father," can you bear to think of his saying to you, " depart, ye cursed?" What! have you a spark of love to Jesus, a lively idea of the bliss of being owned by him and enjoying him without a cloud for ever, and yet bear to part with him? No: Do not your hearts rather say, " Lord, try me, correct me, lead me by whatever painful experience thou pleasest, only let me not miss of thy salvation."

It is in this frame that you are to be stirred up,

brethren, to seek him diligently, and walk with him closely, and thus would I stir up your souls and my own, that I " may rejoice in the day of Christ that I have not run in vain, nor laboured in vain," and that you and I may rejoice together. We shall not then think it hard that God has scourged us, and by losses in temporal things, disappointments in trade, or public calamities, diminished our temporal wealth, if by these and other chastisements he has brought us nearer to himself, and has at length enabled us to receive the full reward, without " losing any thing that we have wrought."

Often think of that time, and to represent it more strongly to your minds, embrace the opportunities he affords you of showing forth the Lord's death till he come. At his table give him your heart: commune with him as he invites you to do; look for a sight of his beauty, a glance of that eye of kindness and tenderness, which is worth more than millions of worlds; a draught of that living water which satisfies the soul, and a taste of that meat which whosoever eateth shall live for ever. Wash away your guilt in his atoning blood, and take up your pardon, and fresh strength from above to serve God. If he meets those that rejoice and work righteousness, in all his ways, peculiarly so may you expect it in this commemoration of his death.

But there are many, I fear, who have yet wrought nothing good, and are so far from being in a way to receive a full reward, that they have wrought only the works of the flesh, and have served Satan instead of God. I have been exhorting Christians to take heed not to lose what they have wrought, and not to be deprived of their full reward. I can only exhort you to begin the work of salvation while it is yet day, " the night cometh when no man can work." Soon will your day of grace be over. Will you still flatter yourselves, that you have time enough yet; or will you, after all the warning given you from the word of God, presume on his mercy to save you, though you know not how, nor why, though you never be converted all your days? What shall I say but warn you still by repeating the same thing, that " except ye repent ye shall surely perish." As the godly by a patient continuance in well doing shall not lose the things which they have wrought, but receive a full reward, so neither shall you lose the things that you have wrought, if you go on in impenitence and unbelief, but receive a full reward, for the wicked " shall go away into everlasting punishment, and the righteous into life eternal."

SERMON XXXIII.

TO BE HEAVENLY-MINDED, A NECESSARY PREPARATION FOR FUTURE HAPPINESS[*].

2 Cor. iv. 16, 17, 18.

For which cause we faint not; but though our outward man perish, yet the inward man is renewed day by day. For our light affliction, which is but for a moment, worketh for us a far more exceeding and eternal weight of glory; while we look not at the things which are seen, but at the things which are not seen: for the things which are seen are temporal; but the things which are not seen are eternal.

The Apostle is describing the comfort and support of his mind amidst the afflictions to which he was exposed in the discharge of the Ministry of the Gospel. Very grievous indeed were those afflictions; and no situation in life could be conceived so calamitous as a state of constant danger and persecution, of contempt and reproach, of poverty and distress; but though troubled on every side, he was not distressed; though perplexed, he was not in despair; though cast down, he was not destroyed. He tells us in the Text, that he fainted not; and why? He repeats it again and again, that for this cause he fainted not, because he had

---

[*] This Sermon, one of the last of Mr. Milner's compositions for the Pulpit, was preached August 6th, 1797, in the Church of Holy Trinity, Hull, on occasion of the death of the Rev. Dr. Clarke, his predecessor, whom he survived only a few months.

received mercy; he believed and therefore spake, "knowing that He which raised up the Lord Jesus, shall raise up us also by Jesus, and shall present us with you." Though his outward man perished, his inward man was renewed day by day.

This is the peculiar secret of christian happiness, that even while in all outward things the believer is a constant sufferer, and his prospects in the world are decaying more and more, and death appears likely soon to close the whole of his visible life, yet he has an inward life nourished by the bread of God which giveth life to the world, even Jesus Christ the Son of God, which life waxes stronger and stronger, and tends to a perfection of a blessed immortality. While the Apostle thinks of this, he calls his present scene of affliction LIGHT; it is also BUT FOR A MOMENT: but the glory to which he is reserved he calls a WEIGHT, it is solid and substantial, and it is ETERNAL. Even his present afflictions are blessings in disguise; they are preparing and fitting him through grace for the glory that shall be revealed, and this they do, not merely because they are afflictions; for then they would have the same effect on all men; for all men are exposed to afflictions; but they have this blessed tendency on the minds of real christians, because they look not at visible, but invisible objects; and they alone of all men are true arithmeticians in divinity; they calculate the value of time and eternity, and are in some degree affected as they ought, in consequence of the calculation.

The Apostle goes on in the next chapter to express the confidence with which he expected to enjoy this heavenly kingdom; even now he speaks of a house, the building of God, as his own, and confesses that God, who had given him the earnest of the Spirit, had wrought him for the self-same thing. But I must not enlarge upon the Apostle's general argument, which runs through the fourth and fifth chapters of this Epistle. Blessed is that man who, in any degree of real experience, can go on with the Apostle, and make his feelings to be his own. How light to him will be the evils which flesh is heir to! (for besides the sufferings to which every real christian, as such, is exposed, I need not say that man, as man, is born to trouble as the sparks fly upward:) Such a one can realize christianity, and find in his own soul, according to the measure of his faith, hope and love, though he may not attain the Apostle's degree of those precious graces, the consolation and support which are here described. But let no man think himself a real christian, whose heart is set upon worldly things, I mean who makes them his great object, the main-spring and guide of his desires and pursuits. There are many infirmities which attend the most genuine christian: But worldly-mindedness is not a ruling principle in his character. A covetous christian is as great a contradiction in terms as a sensual or intemperate christian.

Having several observations to lay before you from the subject of the Text, my first (and it is a very obvious one) is this, that if ever we mean to enter into the kingdom of God, we must be heavenly-minded. The thing speaks for itself. How shall that man arrive at the end of a proposed journey, who moves not a step on the road? How shall he reach an object which lies due North, who directs all his motions to another object which lies due South? "Ye cannot serve God and Mammon. If a man love the world, the love of the Father is not in him. The friendship of the world is enmity with God." The force of these passages, and numberless such passages as these in Scripture, is not to be evaded by saying that we must be diligent in business, and attend to the duties of our station. We ought so to do, and this world's process involves even true christians in many things, which, however, by no means seize their affections. God looketh at the heart! Can we say with the Psalmist, "whom have I in heaven but thee, and there is none upon earth that I desire in comparison of thee." This single mark of heavenly-mindedness is decisive of the character. As our desires are, so are we. He who supremely desires to be with Christ; who prefers that enjoyment which the gospel offers of heavenly things to every thing earthly; who is a stranger upon earth, sensible of his natural guilt, receives God's chief mercy in Christ Jesus with all thankfulness, and waits for the coming of his Saviour to complete that felicity of which he has here the earnest by the Holy Spirit, he is the christian. Hence alone St. Paul could rejoice and patiently endure, and be faithful unto death. If in this life only he had hope in Christ, he would have been, as he says elsewhere, most miserable.

Those whose affections are earthly, will either faint or despair under sufferings, or will walk in forbidden ways to relieve themselves. How can such expect to be owned by Christ at the last day? Indeed, how perfectly unsuited are their notions and taste to the kingdom of heaven! It is impossible that they should be admitted there, or even be happy if they could be admitted. "These shall go away into everlasting punishment." They are Scripture words, brethren. If you would escape the wrath to come, you must firmly believe that you are in real danger, and that there is no hope while you remain unconverted. For " except a man be born again, he cannot see the kingdom of God."

To be heavenly-minded, then, is absolutely necessary: No man ought to allow himself in the hope of salvation, till he is. How to become so is the great lesson of the christian religion. It is not learnt by any doctrines but those of the Scripture, and I would to God this congregation were earnestly engaged in the search of this "death unto sin and new birth unto righteousness." Whoever has at all reflected how naturally we all cleave to the world, how exrremely unapt we are to desire or to seek things which are above, will confess that we need a marvellous energy from God to make such a change in our affections and dispositions. St. Paul confesses that this change was of God. " He that hath wrought us for the self-same thing is God, who also hath given unto us the earnest of the Spirit." And the grand engine by which the Spirit of God inspires the heavenly-mindedness, which is our present subject, is faith. Not that poor, barren, dead faith, undeserving the name, with which so many content themselves. Such a powerless principle can never be sufficient to render a person heavenly-minded. For will any man say, that his general assent to christianity, in the lump, has made him set his affection on things above? The practice of numbers who are called christians, and who call themselves believers without a serious inquiry, without examination, without attention to any one capital truth of christianity, shows that they have no taste for spiritual treasures. Their faith has nothing in it of the nature of trust, reliance, or confidence in Christ; brings them not into any state of communion with God, or any grateful exercises of mind toward Jesus Christ as a Saviour. Their own consciences bear witness, that their faith does nothing for them in cheering, comforting, and composing their minds in affliction, or in animating them to obedience. If we only look at the general outlines of those great objects which christianity sets before us, we may see that such persons can hardly be said duly and properly to believe any one of those objects to be real. Heaven, hell, the resurrection of the just and the unjust, the sinfulness of sin, the all-sufficient merit of Christ to redeem souls from it—— do such nominal christians really and duly believe these things to be true? If they did, is it possible that there should be no practical influence on their tempers and dispositions, on their lives and conversations? Could St. Paul with this nominal faith, think you, have been so supported in affliction, and so joyful in tribulation, as he describes himself to have been?

Let me entreat you, brethren, to apply these considerations to yourselves, as you see cause; and if many have reason to conclude that they never yet have duly believed christianity, let them give up their ruinous false confidence, and learn divine wisdom before it be too late. In the mean time let the grand motive, christian faith, be distinctly understood, and have its due weight on your minds. Much instruction concerning it is afforded from the chapter before us, and the next. They teach us, that faith is a realizing principle. The christian looks at things invisible, and not at things visible. He walks by faith, not by sight. While he feels the miseries of this short life, he faints not, because of the prospect of an exceeding and eternal weight of glory; knowing that He who raised up the Lord Jesus, shall raise up him also by Jesus, and present him with all genuine believers. Such a christian has a divine light shining in his heart, by which he sees the glory of God in the face of Jesus Christ, and while he knows and confesses his total unworthiness, he yet can rejoice in God's mercy through Christ forgiving all his sins, and imputing righteousness to him. Whoever is thus influenced by the spirit of christian faith, will find old things passing away, and every thing made new. Like the sun illuminating a dark place, every object receives a new tincture from the light of faith, and is gilded with a pleasing brightness. The gloom of distress and the melancholy of woe are dispersed, and "the path of the just becomes a shining light, that shineth more and more unto the perfect day."

Such is the instrument and agent, by which a real christian becomes heavenly-minded, and it is our wisdom to be looking to God through Christ for divine instruction herein all our days: but afflictions must be expected. Sin hath made this world miserable. Nothing is more foolish than to expect that to be made straight which God hath made crooked. "The creature is subject to vanity." This was not our original state. It is the consequence of the fall of man. He that would seek for happiness, should be sensible that this is the case, and be humbled before God from a consciousness of his own guilt and depravity. It is foolish to dispute against facts. The grave reasonings of some, who would labour to represent human nature as in a good state, and by no means so wretched and evil as the Scriptures represent it, seem to me as childish as the gay dreams of felicity with which thoughtless youth is apt to be pleased, and which soon vanish before a little experience of the world.

Afflictions therefore should be expected; and here we may say, if the righteous scarcely be saved, where shall the ungodly and the sinner appear?" Believe it, brethren, nothing can be farther from true wisdom and the way of peace and safety, than a life of levity, mirth, and pleasure, such as that which the worldly mind indulges. It is unsuited to our condition, as frail, sinful, wretched mortals, and must be highly offensive to the Almighty. Humble yourselves, ye sinners, " and purify your hearts, ye double-minded." Let your laughter be turned into mourning, and your joy to heaviness. Those whom God will really exalt, he will previously humble and lay low, and it behoveth careless sinners the more to attend to this, because, as St. Peter says, even the righteous are " scarcely saved." They need affliction to try, to purify, to humble them; to wean them from every idol, to bring them to a greater degree of conformity to the Captain of their salvation, who was himself " made perfect through sufferings."

Let men who follow Christ, and who are seeking " through faith and patience to inherit the promises," while they expect affliction, doubt not, but in the way of heavenly-mindedness, to find its salutary effects. Let them not look at things temporal, but at things eternal. I own it is hard, nay impossible, to do this in the strength of nature. Under present disagreeable pressures, how apt are all christians to be swallowed up with present cares and anxieties, and to forget that the end will be speedy, and that their Redeemer is keeping them by his power through faith unto salvation. But those things which are impossible with men are possible with God. Without Christ we can do nothing; but abiding in him by faith, christians! you may do all things. While in faith you look at things eternal and invisible, and derive strength from his mighty aid, you shall be defended and comforted in all dangers and adversities. And though the outward man decay, and you feel the infirmities of the flesh, how pleasant to know, to find " the inward man renewed day by day," the mind more stayed on God in Christ, the affections more steadily fixed where true joys are to be found! How cheering to behold your salvation growing nearer and nearer, and the time hastening apace when you shall " be absent from the body and present with the Lord," removed from a world of vanity, to a scene of unfading bliss, of uninterrupted enjoyment, where you shall realize those objects of desire which you now discern at a distance, and see face to face the Lord of glory, who with aid unseen supported you through life, and will be your portion for ever. In this view the glory before you will appear weighty, the present affliction light, and even the most grievous things you ever met with, will promote your heavenly-mindedness, and prepare you more and more for the enjoyment of everlasting rest. All this, and far more than I can describe, you will feel to be the happy effect of looking "not at the things which are seen, but at the things which are not seen."

Those who have attained a measure of this grace will, I am sure, be striving for more, and will be sensible how little they have attained. Those who know and practise nothing of this christian art of turning miseries into blessings, should at length learn that they need conversion. To what purpose do they call themselves believers, if their belief realizes nothing invisible; if they be enslaved to present objects; if Christ and the medicine of his grace be to them altogether unknown, in point of power and efficacy? For till they be in Christ, and become new creatures, they cannot make this happy use of afflictions. They cannot be heavenly-minded, while their souls cleave to the dust of the earth. They need to be quickened, for they are "dead in trespasses and sins;" and if they ask what they must do to be saved, I can give no other answer but this, "believe on the Lord Jesus Christ, and thou shall be saved." Let them, by prayer and supplication, by careful attention to the word of God and the means of grace, seek till they find, as other souls have done, that there is a God in Israel that hears the cry of the humble, and who is "rich in mercy to all who call upon him." Blessed be God! "His hand is not shortened that it cannot save, neither his ear heavy that it cannot hear." Men need to feel their poverty and guilt, else their very prayers are mockery: but while Jesus lives to intercede, those who in the deepest manner are conscious of their vileness, may cheerfully expect to receive even abundantly above all that they can ask

I have now finished the general illustration of this practical subject of heavenly-mindedness. I own I chose it with a special reference to the mournful event which is fresh upon all our minds. Even without that reference, I could wish you to retain the ideas of St. Paul; for they are most weighty and most instructive. But as referred to the sudden departure of our late worthy Pastor*, they, to my mind at least, give a more powerful impression: for his character and spirit, and the providences of God which attended him, do much illustrate every one of the particulars to which I have spoken, as I shall now endeavour to show.

He was, brethren, heavenly-minded. He was not so naturally. No man ever was heavenly-minded by nature since sin entered into the world, except the Lord from heaven, who came to take away our sins, and in whom was no sin. But your lamented Pastor was made so through divine grace; and the grand spring which produced this change was faith in Jesus Christ: Not that poor, barren, counterfeit of nominal profession, which is the great disgrace of the christian name, but a lively dependance on God's free unmerited mercy through Christ. You knew his activity, meekness, compassion, and

* The Rev. Thomas Clarke, D. D. was only 45 years of age at the time of his decease. He was a native of Hull, and admitted a Student of Trinity College, Cambridge, about the year 1769, from whence he removed to Clare Hall, in order to enjoy the benefit of a Scholarship given him by the Mayor and Corporation of Hull. He took the degree of B. A. in the year 1773, and became a Fellow and Tutor of his College. In the year 1783 he was presented by the Mayor and Aldermen to the Vicarage of the Holy Trinity Church, in Hull, where he resided till his death in the summer of 1797. He married the only sister of W. Wilberforce, Esq. M, P. for the County of York, but left no issue.

unwearied efforts to do good, and to promote every liberal and beneficent plan for the relief of misery, and to check the torrent of vice and impiety; in which last endeavour he was content to suffer reproach, and to bear the calumnies of the wicked and profane. This, however, is a species of persecution which, in every age, all faithful followers of Christ must expect. But amidst all these his good works, he viewed himself as an unprofitable servant, and in one of the last conversations I had with him, I well remember what a deep and strong sense he expressed of the preciousness of Christ and his salvation. His confidential friends know how much he felt the sinfulness of nature, how thankful he was for the grace of the gospel, and how perfectly convinced of the emptiness of that nominal religion, with which it has been but too fashionable for men to content themselves.

But affliction was his lot, and his peculiar affliction consisted in extreme debility of body. Serious and conscientious as he certainly was, decidedly on the side of godliness, and opposite to that of profaneness, I do not hesitate to say that his light affliction, wrought for him an "exceeding and eternal weight of glory," through the sanctification of the Holy Spirit which accompanied it. For of him it was eminently true, that though his "outward man" was perishing, yet his "inward man" was "renewed day by day." He felt in his own experience the uncertainty of all worldly things, and the suddenness of his departure reads a lecture to us all on the vanity of this life, with a louder sound than I can give it.

Notwithstanding the extreme debility of his

frame, divine strength was made perfect in his weakness, and he could with the Apostle glory in his infirmities, that the power of Christ might rest upon him. Through affliction, by the divine blessing, he remarkably grew in grace, attained that strength and firmness of christian faith and love, which he evidently displayed among us. Though happily for himself, he was removed from us at a time when we had reason to hope that his remaining in the flesh might have been more profitable than ever. But God's ways are not as man's. It behoves us reverently to acquiesce in the divine disposals.

While I thus speak of your late worthy Pastor as a serious, genuine Christian, and as a pattern for our imitation, let me beseech you to remember that he faithfully delivered to you the pure doctrine of salvation by Jesus Christ, and very affectionately exhorted you to receive it in your hearts, and to adorn it in your lives. And I have the strongest reasons to believe, though you saw and knew his active exertions, that he would have laboured much more abundantly among you in the best of causes, if he had been able. The spirit was willing, but the flesh was weak. You, however, who heard from him the way of salvation, should remember that you will have an account to give at the day of Judgment, how far you have profited thereby.

This place, indeed, cannot be said to be at all wanting in christian instruction. Let us take heed, brethren, that we provoke not God to leave us to darkness. If sermons after sermons on the truth of the gospel affect not our hearts in a holy and heavenly manner; if under a multitude of means of grace, we can remain lukewarm and earthly-minded, we turn that which should have been a blessing to us into a curse. Be not deceived: God will not be mocked, and He who has suddenly quenched one Light, can quench also all the Lights which he has been pleased to raise up among us, and leave us to follow our own imaginations—the greatest curse that can befal a sinful people. God may well say of this place, " what could have been done more for my vineyard, that I have not done in it." The alarming progress of lewdness and profaneness of late years, is not what should be expected from such a place as this; and the many who decently hear and assent to divine truths without practical influence, have deep reason to examine themselves and to consider their ways.

From you, who have long followed the ways of God, a greater measure of Christian fruitfulness is reasonably to be expected, and I thank God there are those among us who do thus bring forth fruit. To them and to all others who have ears to hear, I would, by way of conclusion, earnestly recommend that heavenly-mindedness with which I began this plain discourse, and which I wished to make the central point of the whole. Let me beseech you to be thoroughly serious, and never to trifle in religion. " If ye be risen with Christ, seek those things which are above, where Christ sitteth on the right hand of God. Set your affection on things above, not on things on the earth."

END OF VOL. II. OF SERMONS.

Luke Hansard & Sons,
near Lincoln's-Inn Fields, London.